MW00439037

THE VIEW
FROM WITHIN

THE VIEW FROM WITHIN

Jazz Writings, 1948–1987

Orrin Keepnews

New York   Oxford
OXFORD UNIVERSITY PRESS
1988

Oxford University Press

Oxford   New York   Toronto
Delhi   Bombay   Calcutta   Madras   Karachi
Petaling Jaya   Singapore   Hong Kong   Tokyo
Nairobi   Dar es Salaam   Cape Town
Melbourne   Auckland
and associated companies in
Berlin   Ibadan

Published by Oxford University Press, Inc.,
200 Madison Avenue, New York, New York 10016

Oxford is a registered trademark of Oxford University Press

Library of Congress Cataloging-in-Publication Data

Keepnews, Orrin.
The view from within.
1. Jazz music—Collected works. I. Title.
ML3507.K43   1988   785.42   87-34971
ISBN 0-19-505284-6

"Jelly Roll Morton," "Art Tatum," and "Charlie Parker" are from *The Jazz Makers,* copyright 1957 by Nat Shapiro and Nat Hentoff. Originally published by Rinehart & Company, Inc.

"A Jazz-Pilgrim's Progress" originally appeared in *Saturday Review.* Copyright 1956, Saturday Review. Reprinted by permission.

"The Existential Jazz Aura of Lenny Bruce" (1966), "Inside the Recording Booth" (1967), and the book review of *Ladies and Gentlemen LENNY BRUCE!* (1974) all appeared in *Down Beat* and are copyrighted in the years indicated by Maher Publications, a division of John Maher Printing Co. Reprinted by permission of *Down Beat* Magazine.

"Cannonball at the Jazz Workshop," © 1986, Landmark Records.

"Producing McCoy Tyner" appeared in *Keyboard,* © 1981 Orrin Keepnews.

The following album notes are all reprinted by permission of Fantasy, Inc.:

"The Bill Evans Sessions" appeared in the booklet accompanying the set *Bill Evans: The Complete Riverside Recordings,* © 1984, Fantasy, Inc.

"Previously Unissued Performances" is adapted from liner notes for *Evidence* (© 1983 Milestone Records) and *Blues Five Spot* (© 1984 Fantasy, Inc.).

"NYC Underground"—© 1981 Galaxy Records.

Wes Montgomery (*While We're Young*)—© 1973 Milestone Records. Johnny Griffin (*Big Soul*)—© 1973 Milestone Records. Cannonball Adderley (*The Japanese Concerts*)—© 1975 Milestone Records. Nat Adderley (*Work Songs*)—© 1978 Milestone Records. Bill Evans (*The Interplay Sessions*)—© 1982 Milestone Records.

2 4 6 8 9 7 5 3 1

Printed in the United States of America
on acid-free paper

This book is for Lucy—who has read every word
(and listened to every sound) for all these years

Acknowledgments

This book could not have come into existence without the direct and indirect cooperation, friendship, and helpfulness of a great many people. In the very beginning there was *The Record Changer,* which in its own stubborn way managed to survive long enough to provide my on-the-job training as a jazz writer; for making that possible, I remain grateful to the late Bill Grauer, to Jane Grauer Cannon, and to Paul Bacon. Over many years my sons, Peter and David Keepnews, have served frequently (and sometimes willingly) as sounding boards for my ideas and opinions. Ralph Kaffel and Saul Zaentz were responsible for my 1970s tenure at Fantasy Records, which put me in position to write most of the album liner and booklet essays included here. The several musicians who are the subjects of a number of these pieces are permanently appreciated by me for a variety of important reasons; above all (as always), the quite literally immortal Thelonious Monk, in so many ways my teacher. Sheldon Meyer is surely the most supportive and patient of editors.

In addition to and quite apart from the copyright and permission notices that are a necessary adjunct to a compilation such as this, I am thankful for the courtesies personally extended by (in no particular order): Nat Hentoff, in connection with the chapters from *The Jazz Makers,* and Nat again, along with Martin Williams, *re* selections from their long-departed magazine, *The Jazz Review;* Dick Hadlock (in his own words, "the final owner" of *The Record Changer*); Al Bendich of Fantasy, Inc.; Jack Maher, publisher of *Down Beat;* Tom Darter, former editor of *Keyboard,* and Jim Crockett, its publisher; Hiroshi Aono of Victor Musical Industries, Inc., of Japan; and Carole Haller at *Saturday Review.*

Contents

THE VIEW
FROM WITHIN

Introduction

Producing jazz records has been my major preoccupation for more than three decades. It's the way I have for the most part earned my living and gained my creative satisfaction since the early 1950s, when I ruined a perfectly good hobby by transforming myself from a jazz fan into a professional.

But for all of that time (and, to be strictly accurate, for several years before) writing about jazz has also been of great importance to me. One way of looking at it, I think, is that I find it necessary to communicate about this music in as many ways as possible. The opportunity to collaborate in the recording process with some over-whelmingly talented jazz artists has of course provided one major form of communication. But I also have a burning desire (as anyone having had even casual contact with me must be aware) to talk at great length about the music to all available listeners and captive audiences; and there is this very comparable urge to write about it in a variety of ways. I have almost always been fortunate enough to have had outlets pretty much at my command: in the very beginning I was an editor of a highly specialized jazz magazine which always had space that needed filling, and for most of my career as a producer it has either been a necessity or an available luxury for me to annotate many of my own albums.

In school I had wanted to be a writer. If World War II hadn't interrupted the flow by briefly turning me into a crew member on a bomber, I undoubtedly would have gone on to journalism school. My only pre-jazz job, which lasted seven years, was as a young very-associate editor at a major New York publishing house. (As several veteran liner-note writers can testify, I have remained an editor, using my frequent position as the final authority to cut and patch and rewrite with a sometimes reckless and not always patient hand.)

When I trace my roots as a music writer as far back as possible, I must admit that I actually began for what can be considered commercial reasons. As a staff member of the Columbia College newspaper, it was possible to pass myself off as a "reviewer." This enabled me to acquire press tickets to Saturday afternoon concerts at Town Hall that featured some of the best Dixieland musicians in New York. Of even more value was my ability to trade the promise of a write-up in the *Daily Spectator* from time to time for a couple of rounds of free drinks at a fairly young downtown club called the Village Vanguard. Since I am recalling the very early '40s, the then-and-now owner of the Vanguard was also quite young, but Max Gordon was surely never so naive as to believe my reviews in that college paper were really helpful to his performers—who ranged from fledgling singers like Pearl Bailey and Carol Channing through the authentically tough Leadbelly to (on occasion) jazz players like Art Hodes and Max Kaminsky. But Gordon was always a gentleman; it pleased him to befriend the teen-age journalist, which helped me to make a big impression on several young women, and probably means that Max has to take a share of the blame for my life-long involvement in hanging out at bars and paying attention to jazz.

Perhaps fortunately, I can find no surviving examples of those earliest efforts. So I can physically trace my origins as a jazz writer only as far back as 1948, when my former college classmate Bill Grauer took over the operation of an esoteric collectors' magazine named *The Record Changer* and asked me, as his only professionally literate friend, to be his managing editor.

This was by no means a gradual introduction to the field. Immediately, and for almost a full decade (until the growth pressures of Riverside Records led Bill to sell the magazine at the end of 1956), it proved to be a very demanding although virtually non-paying sideline. Most of my time in the dingy almost-basement storefront at the lower edge of Harlem which housed the *Changer* was devoted to editing and rewriting the work of jazz enthusiasts who were for the most part less than fully qualified as authors, and to some quite routine journalism of my own. However, I did manage to find a solid handful of occasions on which I could write to my own satisfaction, and about a dozen such pieces—commentaries, interviews, book reviews—strike me as warranting inclusion here.

In retrospect, though, the magazine's greatest significance for me is that, to put it quite simply, it was in two ways directly responsible for altering the entire direction of my life. To begin with, at the very start of Grauer's tenure as publisher, we were invited to the Greenwich Village home of the already awesome Alfred Lion. A large-scale collector, and noted in our world for Blue Note, the staunchly purist label he had founded back in 1939, Lion was about to plunge into the uncharted waters of bebop. That was why we were there; the new and presumably malleable *Changer* editors were to listen to test pressings of the debut recordings of the latest Blue Note artist, Thelonious Monk, and to meet the man himself. Chapter 4 of this book provides a good deal of detail on that evening and its profound impact on my as-yet-unsuspected future as a jazz producer.

Second, at the end of the first chapter you'll find my tale of a bizarre record-bootlegging scandal involving RCA Victor as both manufacturer and victim. As described in my preface to that account, it was this highly atypical *Changer* venture into investigative reporting that shoved me straight into the record business. As one eventual consequence of my altered working environment, album liner notes were to become my principal literary output for a good many years to come.

It wasn't only my activity as a writer that was channeled in new directions by the birth and expansion of Riverside Records. Jazz was to be the way I supported my family, but it also developed into a lot more than that. Dealing with jazz and its people, being involved in the creation of an endless stream of records, writing and talking and thinking about the music on what sometimes seems to be more than a twenty-four-hour-a-day basis—all this has for better or worse become a permanent focal point of my life.

Accordingly, this book is largely made up of very personal writing. There's not much in the way of musical analysis, perhaps because I have always been much more concerned with helping to bring music into existence than with dissecting it. And while there is certainly no shortage of opinion, or of critical judgments, most of it has to do with specific performers and with my working relationships over the years. Although I'm well aware of several people who have at various times both written about jazz and produced it, I really don't think anyone else approaches my length of hands-on studio and record company service combined with a reasonably consistent body of writing. I make this observation neither to brag nor to complain but merely to point out that at least I have for a long time been able to write from a unique perspective.

However, I should also admit that being in this position can create some problems of its own. During the early years of Riverside Records, I wrote all the liner notes (it was one way of holding down costs). In preparing this book, I reread a great many of them, in the belief that I would find there a substantial amount of still-valid contemporary writing. I was, for the most part, wrong. There was far too much biographical data, listings of song titles, and just plain hard-sell advertising; heavy enthusiasm, no matter how well-intentioned or even accurate, doesn't hold up after a couple of decades. The only significant exception appears to have been my annotation of several Monk albums. I would seem to have been more relaxed, perhaps just more seriously proud of these accomplishments, and I have been able to string together some sensible observations from a number of those short essays to make up one element of the segment that is devoted to Thelonious. Otherwise, it was largely a matter of waiting for the second time around. I'm a lot more satisfied with the results of being able to write at length—and with considerably better perspective—for various 1970s reissues and 1980s compilations. These later pieces manage to express a lot of what I wanted to say about friends like Cannonball Adderley and Bill Evans, among others.

It is rather frightening to realize that I have been writing on the subject of jazz for quite so many years. It is also rather surprising to find that I am still entirely willing to stand behind so much of what I've thought and written over that time. Some of it, of course, has to be evaluated within the context of its original setting. Having a great deal of experience in the field of reissues, I am aware of the dangers of trying to update older material. So there has been very little editing or revision by hindsight here. On the other hand, I have felt it important to identify when these various pieces were written and in many cases to explain something about how they came into being.

Finally, I have chosen to conclude this collection with one newly created essay, on a subject that I obviously approach with some very strong opinions. When reading it, I would ask you to remember that it comes after forty years of writing about jazz and thirty-five years (and still counting) of helping to create it.

San Francisco
January 1988

1

The Young Traditionalist

The Record Changer, during virtually all of somewhat more than a decade and a half of existence, was a strange combination of a literary/intellectual "little magazine" and a mail-order auction block for fanatical jazz collectors. It had begun at the very outset of the 1940s as a mimeographed record list (I have a copy dated June 1941, and it clearly is not the earliest), the brainchild of two Washington, D.C., collectors. By March 1942 the sheet had a name, a rather obvious pun. (It was designed for people who wanted to exchange records; and in those pre-LP days a record changer was the mechanical device enabling you to play a stack of discs in sequence.) With the addition of articles of fact and research and strenuous opinion, it gradually became a full-sized monthly featuring authoritative writers like Nesuhi Ertegun, George Avakian, anthropologist Ernest Borneman, and Charles Edward Smith.

When my involvement began, following its purchase at the start of 1948 by Bill Grauer (himself a rabid record auctioneer), the pattern was well established. The magazine stayed afloat because of its complex multi-paged sections of classified record advertising; it also printed just about any manuscript submitted by the scholars and enthusiasts (quite similar in dedication but widely divergent in literary skill) who were part of its small but intense audience. Few were professional writers; none of them expected to be paid, nor were they. Grauer and his wife Jane handled the auctions and all clerical necessities; our friend Paul Bacon was the art director. I satisfied my own compulsions by editing, rewriting, and otherwise pulling into shape for publication the motley contributions— although I doubt if many of our readers would have known or cared if I had left them untouched. I also wrote a wide variety of

7

articles, under more than one name. Much of my work was
routine-or-less hack journalism or dealt with ephemeral issues;
some expressed enthusiasms I definitely did not maintain in later
years. On the other hand, there were more than a few pieces about
which, for one reason or another, I retain positive feelings. As the
work of a young man—this *Changer* period began in my mid-
twenties and lasted about eight years—who was just starting to
have strong and (after a while) increasingly informed opinions
about jazz, they seem to have more than a modest amount of
staying power.

An Interview and an Opinion

Joe Sullivan and Pee Wee Russell were two of the first jazz musicians, heard in person when I was quite young, to make strong
impressions on me. They turned out to have a lot in common:
neither was any kind of showman; neither really belonged in the
Chicago style/Dixieland context where circumstances most often
placed them; both drank more than average even for their world;
both were frequently undervalued by their colleagues as well as by
the jazz public. Eventually I came to recognize that both also
understood the blues better than most of their associates—and to
me that has long been the best rule-of-thumb for evaluating a jazz
musician.

My Sullivan interview was a very early self-assignment, and I
took it most seriously. I didn't know him, but managed to set up a
meeting by phone. I made my wife accompany me to Joe's cluttered Greenwich Village apartment for what turned out to be two
evening-long sessions, and she took copious notes as Sullivan volunteered all sorts of deeply sincere and personal information and
opinions, some of it too much so for the sensitive young interviewer to consider publishable. We were well into the second confessional night when Joe suddenly stopped talking and turned to
me with a confused expression. He had a question: "Exactly what
did you say you were doing this for?"

Perhaps with that scene still in mind, or maybe just because I
had come to know Russell fairly well through observation and
conversation in various New York clubs, I decided to express my
feelings about Pee Wee in a personal-opinion piece, without any

attempt at a face-to-face question-and-answer session. I think it was a wise decision. I also like both pieces; I'm not at all happy with my gratuitous comparison between Sullivan and "any bebop pianist you care to name," but it would be difficult to edit out, and it does serve as a strong reminder that 1949 was a long time ago in my life.

On Piano: Joe Sullivan
1949

Think about piano players—not some local talent you admired last night, some new flash who's sweeping the country, or some obscure primitive available only on a friend's battered collector's item. Think about the men whose skill is unquestionable, whose reputation is solid and long-lived: Jelly Roll, Earl Hines, Fats Waller. And when you turn to the white musicians, you come up, immediately, with the name of Joe Sullivan; it'd be hard to find another that belongs in that company.

It's Joe Sullivan we're concerned with at the moment: the big, bespectacled, mild-looking, fortyish Irishman, born—as you might have suspected—in Chicago. He's played the blues, pops, and Dixieland standards for twenty years or more, always with drive, thoughtfulness, and unwavering affection for the traditional style. In big bands, small combinations, and as a single; in all manner of clubs, bars, speakeasies and the assorted odd spots you find on a one-night stand.

But as a matter of fact you'd find it fairly difficult to hear Joe playing these nights. There being few nightspots left in New York devoted to anything like traditional jazz, and the vagaries of noncommercial music being what they are, it's only at Friday-night gatherings at the Central Plaza or barnlike Stuyvesant Casino, or on Sunday afternoon sessions at Jimmy Ryan's last outpost of jazz on strip-conscious 52nd Street, that you're likely to see this eminent Chicagoan hunched over a keyboard. Otherwise he is more likely to be found in a one-room apartment on Greenwich Village's Christopher Street, a room whose principal item of furniture is—or at any rate seems to be—a battered upright, which is where we went to poke around in Joe's memories of the good old days in Chicago, New York, and way places. The old days of Bix, Tesch, Pee Wee, Davy Tough; of Louis, Jimmie Noone, Johnny Dodds—

it's always a bit startling, we thought and Joe agreed, when you start cataloguing the old names to realize how many of them are no longer around.

Perhaps it's inevitable that memories take on a glamor they may never have had to begin with, that some smoke-filled cellar with bad liquor and worse wages is recalled only as a place you could jam all night with a handful of good men. Or perhaps it's more likely that the earlier, less jittered days of this century actually had relaxation and humor, an atmosphere that produced its own special kind of jazz.

In any case, Joe Sullivan is by no means *that* old; his kind of music is obviously a part of our times. It just *seems* that it must have been another age in which Joe jammed with Bix and Freeman and Tesch until six, seven, eight in the morning at the Three Deuces in Chicago. "It was like playing in a brewery. It was good—a good atmosphere. Bix was himself," Joe remembered, and he recalled one glorious morning at eight, in the Deuces, with everybody drunk, and Bix playing "In a Mist" and "Candlelight" on the piano and then switching to blues on the cornet, with Sullivan taking the piano. "It was wonderful—I felt like a girl must feel with a new coat or dress."

But Joe hadn't come to jazz by way of Beiderbecke. To be strictly biographical, he was introduced to music by a nun at Our Lady of Mount Carmel, who slapped his hands because he didn't hold them correctly on the keyboard. Born on November 5, 1906, on Chicago's North Side, youngest of nine children and the only one interested in music, although his father played the fiddle. Music lessons at home, at Mount Carmel, at the Chicago Conservatory: "twelve years of classical." His first jobs were at dances for the employees at Montgomery Ward's—he played lunchtime music—and for the Chicago Surface Lines. By this time jazz was starting to seep in. He listened to records, and remembers standing outside the Nest (later and better known as the Apex), straining to hear Jimmie Noone, or outside Kelly's Stable, where Baby and Johnny Dodds were playing. By this time Joe was going to Lake View High School, and was playing at summer resorts. He met George Wettling, and remembers clearly the time he went with Wettling to a nearby resort to hear the cornet all the musicians were talking about. Either he was playing alone that night, or else Sullivan's memory has decided that he wants a solo picture: "There was no piano, no drums, just Bix. He was terrific."

But despite that early impression, despite the sessions at the Deuces and a record date organized by the then-embryonic promoter, Eddie Condon ("Nobody's Sweetheart", "Liza," "China Boy," "Sugar")—despite all these white-Chicago ties, Sullivan was strongly aware that there were two roads to take in jazz. "There was Louis and there was Bix, and all that each of them stood for. As far as I'm concerned, Bix was all by himself. To this day I love him like I love my right arm. But I go by way of Louis."

It wasn't a matter of disliking the Chicago style. Although Joe now says, "I made a definite break," he has always done much of his playing with the men he started out with: Condon, Wettling, Freeman, the ones who were "drawn to Bix and had made up their minds to follow him."

"I wasn't letting Bix down," Joe said. "To me that was a pattern of the music that was going to go on." (Here he shook his head, sadly and wistfully. "Whoever thought that we'd end up with that goddam bebop.") It was just that the Negro music, somehow, touched him more closely. "I discovered that my heart was set with the different colored musicians—the fine musicians we look up to to this very day. Sitting in with the Kelly's Stable band—Johnny and Baby Dodds—to me it was such a thrill that I was afraid I'd play something that wasn't good. When I was getting my way around after that classical training, I felt on the defensive, felt I wasn't worthy of playing as they were used to. It was only when they accepted me that I got the confidence I needed. Whatever I owe, I owe to those guys."

Two pianists whose influence on his style Sullivan quickly admits were around Chicago in those days. Jelly Roll was in and out of town in the '20s. Earl Hines was with Armstrong at the Sunset. When Joe, then in his early twenties, decided to go on to New York with a band including Gene Krupa, Tesch, Freeman, and Condon, "Earl told me to be sure to look up Fats Waller. I had already heard him play, liked his playing, and later became very friendly with him. I learned a lot from him—not that he tried to teach me anything, but I listened, and learned."

The trip to New York had been on a false lead. Singer Bea Palmer was supposed to open a night club, but she didn't, and the young musicians were stranded in their hotel room, with the bill piling up. "We were panicky—and I mean panicky." There was an abortive attempt to play behind a vaudeville dance team, but the Palace Theatre didn't take kindly to their jazz. But there were enough places that did take to jazz and, eventually, jobs came: road tours and speakeasy spots with the ever-shifting personnel that made up the nucleus of jazz in the East at the tail-end of the '20s—Red Nichols, Max Kaminsky, Davy Tough, Mezzrow, Pee

Wee, Condon, Freeman. Joe recalled a job at the old Hollywood Restaurant in New York. Nichols fronted a band that included Gene Krupa; "Nobody's Sweetheart" was a big favorite, and they were requested to play it constantly. One night, after the sixth time, Condon had enough. "For God's sake, not again," he said. Nichols fired him on the spot.

Sullivan went into the Stork Club, with Red McKenzie, Jack Bland, Josh Billings, and Condon. He stayed there until one day in 1931, when he and Condon drove up to work in a taxi to find the place full of prohibition agents and police. Someone had put the finger on Mr. Billingsley, after a long spell of immunity, and the job was raided out from under them.

After that, Joe put in a period as a soloist, the first entertainer at the first of the series of clubs on Fifty-second Street to be known as the "Onyx." This one was one flight up, a variation on the usual one-flight-down location of the speakeasies of the era. As a result, Sullivan's habit of beating time for himself led to complaints from the down-stairs neighbors. "I guess my foot was too much like a drum," he comments; the management inserted a rubber pad under the foot, but that was kicked away after one number. Possibly to keep the peace, Joe went down to New Orleans soon thereafter, for his first big-band job. It was with Roger Wolfe Kahn's non-jazz outfit, but the personnel did include Charlie Teagarden and Artie Shaw. As an indication of the penalties of the commercial life, this band once was called upon to play "Stormy Weather," the top favorite of that day, some eighteen times in one evening, but Joe doesn't recall that anybody reacted as strongly as Condon had to "Nobody's Sweetheart." Maybe the musicians expected that sort of thing.

But what they couldn't have expected, and what Joe recalls moist vividly from that tour, were the first of the now-famous intellectual leanings of the many-faceted Artie Shaw. "Whenever it was time for his solo, someone had to poke him. He kept copies of Schopenhauer and Nietzsche on his music stand, and was always reading them, even during numbers."

Then, in the second half of the 1930s, came what is best described as the pianist's "Crosby period." He spent a year and a half on the West Coast, working principally on Bing's radio program and in movies, then on to New York for the first of his two hitches with the Bob Crosby band. He toured with them until the day he fell out of bed in Houston, Texas. He injured his shoulder, not seriously, but X-rays revealed a touch of TB. So back to California for another eighteen months, with Bob Zurke replacing him in the band. Sullivan did more movie work; principally he recalls the Crosby picture *East Side of Heaven,* in which Louis Armstrong made his film debut. Later he went back to Bob Crosby, for a tough grind of road tours and radio work. It was during the prewar big band heyday; the Crosby group would come dashing into town on Mondays to rehearse for a radio show, would broadcast, make their quota of records, and tear out again by 11 o'clock that night for a week of one-nighters and college proms.

Joe had a liking for the Bobcat style, but it was a difficult, unsettled life, and undoubtedly he had a hankering for small-band music. So in 1939 he stayed in New York, going into Cafe Society Downtown with a "not very good" band. It was quickly obvious that a change in personnel was in order, and Sullivan took advantage of the opportunity to bring in a mixed band. It may seem rather startling to realize that having Negroes and whites in the same jazz band was a radical innovation as recently as ten years ago—it startles me, I know. There had been a few cases of interracial sitting in, on a "guest star" basis; Benny Goodman had used Teddy Wilson in his quartet while Jess Stacy played with the full band; but this was the first time a club had hired such an outfit on a full, six-nights-a-week basis.

Sullivan's own tastes in jazz made it fitting enough for him to gather together this group (it had Ed Hall on clarinet; Danny Polo, tenor sax; Benny Morton, trombone; Andy Anderson, trumpet; Billy Taylor, bass; Johnny Wells, drums). Ten years before he had played piano on one of the few early mixed record dates, the celebrated Louis Armstrong *Knockin' a Jug,* with Jack Teagarden, Happy Caldwell, and the late Eddie Lang and Kaiser Marshall. But that had been in the youthful, jam-session spirit of the 1920s: the date was decided on and arranged in less than twenty-four hours. Jack Kapp (then at Okeh, now with Decca) was talked into giving them a studio early in the morning. Joe recalls picking Louis up after work—"He was at the Savoy or the Renaissance then, and we all went to some after-hours joint and drank until 8 a.m. We were all tired; I remember Louis standing backed up against a wall; and he must have been almost out on his feet from exhaustion. But I think he played better horn that morning than he had in a long time."

The goings-on at Cafe Society were a bit more prosaic, but it was Sullivan's first real opportunity to play at length with Negroes since the time he had originally hit his stride with the Chicago Kelly's Stable band. In 1940 he went into the Famous Door with an otherwise all-colored group: Joe Thomas, trumpet; Albert Nicholas, clarinet; Claude Jones, trombone; Manzie Johnson, drums. He moved about on Fifty-second Street during the war years, returned to California for a while and then back to New York for a year and a half of solo work at Eddie Condon's showplace.

Which brings us back to the present, to a Joe Sullivan who is still as firmly rooted as ever in the traditional style he first knew and loved. The future of his kind of jazz doesn't look any too encouraging; there are no "modern" pianists whose work appeals to him, and few among the younger group of traditional-style players who can excite his enthusiasm. He liked what he heard of part of the Lu Watters band on the West Coast during the war years; and has played occasional sessions recently that included good young horns, but it's all too obvious that the emphasis among newcomers is on other things in jazz.

But the picture is not as bleak as that may sound. It is true that there is a much greater gulf, apparently, between the tempo and tastes of the present day and the Chicago-New York jazz circuit of Sullivan's early playing days than there was between that period and the youthful environment of Jelly Roll Morton, Louis, and the others who shaped Joe's style. But it is clearly a pessimistic exaggeration to say that *no one* is carrying on the New Orleans-Chicago traditions. Whether or not the comparatively few younger players of this style will turn out to be musicians of sufficient stature to keep this kind of music alive in the future remains to be seen. But more important, at least for the present, than that unsettled question, is the too-often-neglected fact that the kind of jazz played by Joe Sullivan, and men like him, still retains a tremendous amount of validity and meaning and enjoyment for us. Superficially, 1949 and the 1930s are vastly different times. I have never been inclined to argue with those whose support of bebop is based on the fact that it is "music of our times." To the naked ear it is apparent that bop sounds like the jittered-up world of today, and that a Joe Sullivan chorus on his "Little Rock Getaway" sounds like upstairs at the old Onyx Club, or an 8 a.m. session with Bix in a place that smelled like a brewery. And it is also undeniable that there is an air of nostalgia to any account such as this one, that makes it seem a bit more like ancient history than a story of the very recent past.

But if for no better reason than that Sullivan, and jazzmen of his type, are still with us—comparatively young, still playing heartily—incurable romantics like myself (and, I suspect, most readers of this magazine) will go on enjoying what they play. And as long as such musicians continue to play, they continue to remind us that "yesterday" and "today" are fairly empty relative

terms. A fine musician, steadfastly interpreting jazz in the style
he has selected, and to which he has chosen to remain faithful,
remains a rare treat that the vagaries of current taste cannot
minimize. The very fact that *we'd* a damn sight rather listen to
Joe Sullivan than to any bebop pianist you care to name probably
is—all by itself—a most convincing argument.

Inside Pee Wee
1950

A tall, gaunt, stoop-shouldered fellow, something more than forty
years old, with the face of a sad clown and a general air of vagueness and absent-mindedness about him, Pee Wee Russell hardly
seems likely to fit anyone's conception of what a jazz musician
should look like.

A total stranger to jazz would probably be a bit surprised to see
him pick up a clarinet; after the stranger had heard him play for a
while, the chances are that he would be more, rather than less
baffled. The growl tones, the slurs and blurs of Pee Wee's music,
have been known to provoke bitter arguments. The question
seemed almost invariably to be: does he play the best, or the worst
clarinet in the world?

The unanswerable argument has died down now; not only is
Russell an accepted and almost legendary figure in the Dixieland
world, but it must also be admitted that he is no longer on the top
rung. In the current New York-Chicago pattern, the top rung and
the spotlight belong to a slicker, brasher, brassier type of musician:
Bill Davison blasting from the center of the podium or Eddie
Condon chatting with the customers are the ones more likely to be
either praised or damned these days. And the reason for Pee
Wee's slipping out of the spotlight is not only a change in public
taste or in publicity. Even those who love Russell's work the best
will grant that he is not playing as well as he once played on early
Chicago record dates.

Admitting that the fellow has always been a puzzle, and that he
is not now a center of attraction—although he is still a respected
jazz name, it may seem a bit far-fetched to come right out and
claim that Pee Wee is, in effect, *an object lesson in the nature of
improvised jazz, a living embodiment of the peculiar virtues and
drawbacks of this music.* I won't deny that that statement may
sound like the sort of thing a jazz writer dreams up when he's

desperately searching for "significance." But I won't apologize for
the claim, either. It seems to me that not only can the enigma of
Pee Wee be explained in those terms, but that all of us—or at least
that total stranger to jazz whom I invented a couple of paragraphs
ago—can get some valuable hints about all of jazz by looking at
Pee Wee that way.

Go back to the first time you ever heard Russell on record: for
me I think it may have been on the Summa Cum Laude "Sunday."
Then recall the first time you saw him—I remember early one
evening at Nick's, when the band was sitting at a table near the
stand, and I had never seen any white jazzman in person, and I
knew without hesitation which one was Russell.

It has become quite a cliché in jazz writing to talk about a
musician's style and solos as expressing his "ideas" or his "personality." But notes are not as easily communicative as words, and while
one man's inventiveness or power may please you and stir you, it is
no real indication as to whether he beats his wife, agrees with
Nietzsche, or brushes his teeth regularly. And while I'm not claiming that you can learn these things by listening to his clarinet, it is
nevertheless unquestionable that there is an overwhelming unity
about Pee Wee. Only a man who looks and acts as he does *should*
be able to play exactly as he does. The wry, shy, ironic humor, the
hesitant, almost-humble gestures—these are identical in the appearance of the man and in the sound of the clarinet. Charles
Edward Smith wrote in *Jazzmen* that Pee Wee "looks like the sort
of person about whom anecdotes are told"—and I think you can
hear that in the music, too.

This sort of thing should not be over-generalized; there are
many musicians whose personalities and music are vastly more
difficult to isolate and comprehend. But Pee Wee stands as the
basic minimum, as a kind of proof that jazz is demonstrably a
matter of men creating a music that *is* what they feel and what they
are.

It is also true that Russell is a remarkably unchanging musician.
This is undoubtedly at least part of the reason why he is not today
the influential figure in jazz that he has been. Whether his playing
has declined because of his physical decline, or whether it's the
other way around, I wouldn't know. But I would guess that he was
living at the same pace, or harder, in the golden era when men as
different as Teschmaker and Goodman were clearly being influenced by his playing. It's more likely that the trouble with Pee Wee
today is that his kind of music doesn't really exist any more, except
for his own playing and that of a very few other deep-dyed

Chicagoans. Listen to almost any old White Chicago record, and then listen to a Condon's-type band of today; the difference is immense, but Pee Wee's style is virtually unchanged. If you are as closely tied up with your music as he must be, you either must want to go along with such changes, or else be bewildered and pretty badly hurt by the fact that the world has changed, and the music has changed, and you can't and don't want to change. I don't know *why* Pee Wee's music has remained constant, but it isn't hard to guess. The kind of unity of man and music in Russell that I have been talking about certainly indicates something deeply ingrained and single-minded. Anyway, Pee Wee's style must have been formed back when he was playing weekend dates in Missouri, listening to Fate Marable's riverboat band and to Charlie Creath playing rough blues on the cornet in St. Louis. His style is undoubtedly something quite inevitable—inevitable and doomed, I suppose—but it's a wonderful kind of music and it's an awe-inspiring kind of personal dedication.

A certain trombone player, at the recent height of his popularity, took to making Pee Wee something of the butt of his rough-hewn humor, calling him "Pee Wee the People," a joke I always thought more obscure than it was worth. It may be naive, but I've always thought there was an unconscious embarrassment in the ribbing, a half-realized dealing with someone who had something, as a musician and as a man, that few people ever have—an internal completeness and sense of personal satisfaction. Although Pee Wee himself is undoubtedly quite unaware of all these obscure metaphysical values.

I don't want to get either mystical or maudlin, so I'll stop before I start mumbling about "the peace that passeth understanding" and the like. Instead I'll close with the memory of a night in Boston in 1945. Russell was playing with Max Kaminsky and a loud but uninspired local rhythm section. At the time Pee Wee could rarely be heard over the combined din of band and audience. But for one number everything slipped into place; there was silence and you could hear him playing quite beautiful blues in his accustomed style: growl and blur and more notes hinted at than he or anyone else could ever play.

Some Book Reviews, Mostly Negative

Originally an editor by profession, I took upon myself the bulk of
The Record Changer's book reviewing, although two pieces partially reprinted here actually belong to a slightly later time period.
It has always been easy, even for someone much more tolerant
than I, to be tough on most jazz-related literature: particularly in
the 1950s, a lot of nonsense was being brought out, and I placed
much of the blame on the peculiar naiveté of some of my former
counterparts, the "bright young editors" at various publishing
house. In these examples, I concentrate on two of the most prevalent and aggravating types: autobiography and fiction.

Even though undoubtedly only the Billie Holiday book is still
remembered by anyone, I find that many of my comments retain
considerable relevance—including acid statements about the superficial coyness and deceit of most as-told-to celebrity life stories,
and about pseudo-knowledgeable novels that falsify the jazz life in
purple prose. My critiques of the three autobiographies are reprinted in full. However, in dealing with the three long-forgotten
novels, I have chosen to delete as much as possible of the no longer
particularly meaningful details of plot and background; this properly shifts the emphasis over to my general observations about the
pitfalls and shortcomings of jazz fiction.

Four of these six selections are from the *Changer*, but the reviews of *The Horn* and *Blow Up a Storm* appeared in early issues
of a worthy but short-lived literary successor to that magazine: *The
Jazz Review*, edited by Nat Hentoff and Martin Williams. And the
single most virulent review I ever wrote is not included in this
section because it seems more logically located in a later chapter
dealing with the subject of that book, Lenny Bruce.

Beware of Sparrows
1951

*HIS EYE IS ON THE SPARROW. By Ethel Waters, with Charles Samu-
els. 278 pages. Doubleday and Co. $3.00.*

The first thing to note about a book like *His Eye Is on the Sparrow* is
that it was definitely not written with an eye on the jazz audience.
Even the recent autobiographies of jazz musicians like Condon
and Mezzrow were directed at what is known as "the general pub-

lic"; the intention was to shock or amuse the reader, and to give titillating backstage glimpses by means of lots of anecdotes and the use of a maximum of famous names and odd characters. Ethel Waters, although she first achieved fame as a "blues singer," has had comparatively little to do with jazz. But her book does follow this standard pattern of the entertainer's life-story.

In addition, it employs a device that is standard equipment when a ghost-writer is called upon to translate the words of a Negro into acceptable prose. This device leads to what the book's jacket blurb describes as "rich, colorful idiom": it consists of a liberal sprinkling of self-conscious slang, occasional lapses into literary-ish English, and then redeeming uses of words like "rambunctious" and an ever-present verb like "suspicioned."

This artificial trick, which has always been a pet gripe with this reviewer, may not bother too many readers. Actually, Charles Samuels has done a pretty fair job of using this tar-brush with some restraint. But it is a good tip-off on the extent to which the book may be considered (to quote again from the jacket) "magnificently honest."

The general public has taken to *His Eye Is on the Sparrow* quite avidly. Ethel Waters is known to a far wider audience than most jazzmen happen to be; she is a celebrated actress; she did rise from beginnings of fascinating and almost unbelievable sordidness and poverty; and, as the title stresses, there is here a good deal of that emphasis on faith and religion that seems to fill a large public need these days. The book is well up on the best-seller lists and was a selection of the Book-of-the-Month Club; so this review is apparently a minority report. Its primary purpose, then, should be to discourage those jazz fans who might otherwise think that there was something here for them.

Well, there is *something*—there is a detailed account of the kind of rough, discouraging background from which many a Negro entertainer has come, and of the hard knocks of the T.O.B.A. vaudeville circuit. But it is all served up in a manner that thoroughly dilutes its values. The information offered is somewhat obscured by the irksome "idiom" and by an abrupt and staccato style that leaps about from one subject to another, from one incident to the next, in disjointed and unsettling fashion. And it is distorted by someone's apparent conviction—either Miss Waters's, Mr. Samuels's, or the publisher's—that it was necessary to prove that Ethel has always been The Greatest.

Ego is a natural enough quality in a public performer; and certainly this autobiography is far from the only one to puff its hero or heroine at the expense of almost everyone else. But it is a little less than "completely realistic" (which, again, is what its jacket says) in episodes like the one in which young Ethel, a beginner in vaudeville, is described by Ethel as having cut Bessie Smith all to hell when they sang on the same bill in Atlanta—despite Bessie's paid claque in the audience.

And there is an aggravating slur on the very capable Fletcher Henderson, who was her accompanist for quite some time. She tells a questionable tale about his reluctance to play "that chump-chump stuff that real jazz needs," so that she had to force him to practice with some James P. Johnson piano rolls until he could give letter-perfect imitations of them.

"Naturally, he began to be identified with that kind of music, which isn't his kind at all," says Miss Waters. "The funny part is that . . . from playing the music I made him imitate," Henderson has become "well known for this sort of music instead of his own."

The lack of connection between Henderson's style and Jimmy Johnson's, and the conflict between this little tale and Henderson's achievements as band-leader and as creator of exceedingly un-"chump-chump" arrangements for Benny Goodman, will be painfully obvious to the jazz fan, even though it may all be swallowed whole by most of the book's readers. It was such material that made this reviewer a good deal more sensitive to the fairly subtle back-hand taps administered in passing to such performers as Bill Robinson ("I wasn't knocked over") Florence Mills (" . . .she had a small voice"), and Josephine Baker (who got to France in the first place only because Ethel turned down the job).

This approach isn't just limited to the discussion of personalities. It permeates the whole story. Miss Waters is most candid about the slums and red light districts in which her childhood was spent, but she works to give herself the cleanest possible record. I won't question that, as she says, she doesn't drink (except on doctor's orders) or smoke, but why knock the reader over with repetitions of these virtues? And why a woman who is constantly mentioning her "love affairs" sees fit to insist, in the same book, that she was never "promiscuous," is a bit baffling.

The combination attempt to keep the heroine appealing while simultaneously telling a seamy-side-of-life story runs the authors into a whole host of inconsistencies. Take the extreme emphasis on her deeply religious nature, for example (and God, I'm afraid, often is represented as just short of being Miss Waters's personal manager—"God had helped me in my work" means she had received what she considered individual special attention). This has to be worked in along with the anecdotes about how she "slugged and disabled" numerous rivals for her numerous men. There are also rather too many accounts of continual back-stage argument, back-biting and jealousies to fit with Ethel's picture of herself as *constantly* in the right and misunderstood. And snatches of mock modesty about "what the world has called my artistry" could have been left out of this swaggering story of a woman who in another spot compares her guest appearance in a Negro revue to "a circus with Sarah Bernhardt."

Finally, there are touches of racial stereotype that don't sit well at all. It's not too bad, I guess, for her to make silly generalizations like "Invariably, whites dance in a broken rhythm, don't listen to the music, and count," or "whites . . . seemed to get little fun out of life," or "The master race . . . looked fed up with everything." But it's certainly poor taste to toss in a dialect story about a "stupid Irish bus driver" and a "dumb" cop, "also Irish, of course" (Ethel, who had "never driven a car before," had smashed into the bus).

And worst of all are the frequent hunks of "philosophizing" on the general theme of "my people": the Negro, "gay and game . . . with his music and his laughter, his love of God." If Miss Waters— who does have a lot to say, first-hand, about discrimination and oppression—really believes *that* pap, then it's too bad someone didn't do her the favor of deleting it from her book.

All things considered, it would have been better and more valuable, if less sensational, if some outside party had written a book *about* Ethel Waters.

I may seem unduly harsh on what is clearly a minor, commercially-intended book, but it is exactly the commercial success it is enjoying that makes it seem of some importance to warn off the readers of this magazine. And if any clincher is needed, take note of this comment on why Ethel Waters likes the company of musicians: "Musicians are as daffy and uninhibited as so many jolly little monkeys."

This remark, like the entire book, may have *some* truth in it, but what a hell of a way to put it all!

Satchmo
1955

SATCHMO: My Life in New Orleans. By Louis Armstrong. 240 pages; photographs. Prentice-Hall: New York. $3.50.

I am having a great deal of trouble making up my mind about this book, which is of course no sort of admission for a reviewer to be making. One thing can be stated with certainty: you are not apt to consider the time you spend reading it to have been wasted.

It can also be definitely noted that this is not entirely the book it might have been expected to be—that is, assuming that you have been sharing my perhaps naive hope that the autobiography of Louis Armstrong (even a partial autobiography like this one) would turn out to be something of a jazz classic. This is where my indecision comes in. Granted that this is a disappointing book in some respects, is it bad enough to warrant being attacked; or is it valuable and interesting enough to be granted a *Record Changer* seal of approval (for whatever that's worth)?

Perhaps it's best, under the circumstances, merely to lay the more important cards on the table and let you work it out for yourselves:

First of all, this is an account of early-century Negro life in New Orleans (ending at precisely the time Louis joined King Oliver's band in Chicago, which implies—although no one is promising— further volumes to come). It tells some of the familiar stories, either as told before or with slight twists: the Bunk-*didn't*-teach-me version of the early-influences story; the Waifs' Home; Daisy Parker; no one meeting the train in Chicago (although now it's a policeman who directs him to Lincoln Gardens!). It adds a number of new details, but with the emphasis more on the social environment than on jazz—Louis's tendency is to list a lot of jazzmen, recall a few with admiration, but spend most of his loving care on accounts of saloon life, hard times, and fights. His approach varies strangely: in some instances he seems to be censoring himself a bit, but on page 86, for example, he comes right out and tells about his brief experience at going along with the rest of his gang, all of whom "had prostitutes working for them." The question must be: how accurate and, therefore, how valuable is all this? Is this true source material; is it the honestly-intended rememberings thirty-odd years after the facts (which is more likely than the first alternative, and the next best thing to it); or is it at least partly a matter of distorted emphases and retouching to provide the picture the author thinks is wanted? There are, it must be noted, far too many exact conversations and minor details—since these of course must be "re-created" or invented, how is one to know what to trust?

Another important point to be considered is the way in which this book is written. We Americans have a distressing habit of assuming that a man who is very talented in one field is automatically qualified in other, unrelated fields. Thus an earlier generation, impressed by Henry Ford's mechanical genius, paid attention to his views on peace and on labor relations. A more recent example is the great surprise with which the country watched Herbert Hoover, the "great engineer" and a notable feeder of hungry Europeans after World War I, prove himself an inadequate president from 1929 to 1932. Similarly, there is no reason in the world why Louis Armstrong, a wonderfully talented jazz musician, should be expected to play author. A while back, his writings had a small vogue in magazines: I recall specifically the New York *Times's* bright idea of having him review Alan Lomax's book derived from Jelly Roll Morton's Library of Congress conversations. Louis's "style," which I found (not at all unexpectedly) to be halting and often laboriously cute, was clucked over by that species of cultural dilettante who likes to adopt jazz from time to time. To my mind, the prevalent attitude was lousy with only half-concealed condescension.

Now, the foregoing is admittedly a personal prejudice of mine. There are those who feel that unadulterated prose by Louis is legitimately valid and interesting. Okay; but that is *not* what you get here. Neither do you get smoothly ghost-written Louis, which could have been an improvement (if handled by a sympathetic and skilled and jazz-knowledgeable writer) or an abomination (if done by a hack full of half-knowledge). Instead, you get Louis with a fairly heavy dose of what is known in publishing as "editing." That is, Louis with grammar tidied up a bit, syntax clarified a bit, organization probably smoothed out a bit. As a result, the prose here is pretty sensationally flat, colorless, and awkward. The worst possible choice would seem to have been made.

I am also bothered by a recurring attitude, quite concretely expressed in one sentence as "I have always loved my white folks and they have always proved that they loved me and my music." I suppose one can blame no one so much as Armstrong himself—although it would be comforting to think thoughts about how one can charge our society as a whole with having boxed the Negro into a position where such commentary as that is required. But I suppose the major lesson to be learned is that we should all get to be a little more hard-headed in our attitudes towards Louis. Not

all successful (artistically and/or commercially) American Negroes
find it necessary to go in for this sort of over-affable reverse
racism. Louis, however, apparently sees no reason not to play it
that way. All right, then; this only means that this great musician
is not an absolutely flawless god on all counts (which is only an
extension of what I was saying two paragraphs ago about his
literary efforts). I, for one, do not intend to be shocked or disturbed any more by evidence of this sort of thing. Unhappy, yes;
but that's all.

And that's about the size of it. A book with some interesting-
to-read facts or half-facts about a New Orleans boyhood; not *too*
much about jazz; a rather debilitating literary style. I guess I
don't really like it too much, but mainly it's probably that I'm
disappointed because it doesn't live up to personal expectations
that I undoubtedly had no right to have in the first place!

Lady Sings the Blues
1957

*LADY SINGS THE BLUES. By Billie Holiday with William Dufty. Dou-
bleday, 229 pages. $3.75*

The "celebrity autobiography" is a type of book that undoubtedly
will always be with us. Promising, and sometimes even delivering,
glamor and backstage secrets and lots of casual name-dropping,
such books have a very understandable appeal. But for those readers who consider the person whose life story is involved to be an
"artist" rather than a "celebrity" (and the difference is of course a
vast one), such an autobiography can be a source of squirming
annoyance that is strictly in the fingernail-across-the-blackboard
category.

Applying the above generalization to the book at hand—which
is Billie Holiday's *Lady Sings the Blues*—let me very quickly add
that I'd recommend it to most readers of this magazine. Not that
you're apt to be satisfied with it. But, coming to the book with
the background knowledge and special interest that most *Record
Changer* readers have, you're in a position to find it more valuable and more comprehensible than the non-jazz public will.

The basic trouble with *any* "celebrity autobiography" is that it is
not honestly conceived. (There may be exceptions to this sweeping
statement, but none come to mind as I write this.) When a living,
still-active professional entertainer writes, or causes to be written,

an account of his life and career, it seems inevitable that it turn out to be motivated by press-agentry, ego, or a desire for self-justification. These are simply not good reasons for writing books, even though interesting books may sometimes inadvertently result. (I'm sure the same objections apply to the life stories of politicians and authors, but that's beside the point at the moment.)

Now if the celebrity involved is outside of my field of special interest, I don't care very much. But when it is a jazz personality, I can't keep from feeling . . . well, *embarrassed* is probably the best word to describe it. For in almost every case, and no matter what the writer's motives were, it strikes me as one more case of the exploitation of the jazz artist. I get this feeling whether the person involved is someone I deeply respect as a creative artist (Louis Armstrong, Miss Holiday) or someone I don't (Mezz Mezzrow, Eddie Condon). So I suspect that it is not the specific individual I sympathize with—after all, nobody forced them to do or to permit this. It is, rather, that I feel a sense of betrayal: a betrayal of the whole cause of jazz, and of that constant negative battle that so many of us automatically keep fighting—the battle to keep jazz from being so completely publicly misunderstood. Now I realize that there is probably a good deal of impracticality in what I have just written, but it is something I feel too deeply to keep quiet about. And I suspect that I am not alone in feeling this way.

It is, let me emphasize, somewhat unfair to use *Lady Sings the Blues* as the jumping-off place for this dissertation. It is by no means the worst of its kind. I'm reasonably sure that Doubleday published this book largely because of its sensational aspects—dope, prison, and the rest of Billie's well-headlined troubles, and its view of some of rough behind-the-scenes aspects of the Negro musician's world. But there may also have been some feeling of presenting a social document. And in any event, this book avoids that musical self-righteousness and little-boy preening about being "bad" that was so constantly evident in Mezzrow's book. It also avoids the tasteless egotism and contrived brashness of Eddie Condon's autobiography. *Lady Sings the Blues* is, like most of its kind, a ghost-written book ("by Billie Holiday with William Dufty" is the credit line), and it does have its share of that artfully ungrammatical and doggedly colloquial writing that is supposed to seem "natural" and always sets my teeth on edge. But in this respect it is far less offensive than Ethel Waters's masterpiece of hokum and even less irritating than the recent Louis Armstrong book (which wasn't ghost-written, but merely neatened up a bit). Mr. Duffy, who is an assistant to the editor of the liberal New York newspaper, *The Post,* cannot be accused of over-indulging in dialect jokes. His main defect, actually (apart from the extent to which he can be blamed for the things I complain about in the paragraph that follows), is that he tends to indulge in little moral sermons on occasions. While they are not marked off as his, they are quite plainly not Billie's creations, and at least one (on narcotics and what to do about the problem) struck me as in highly dubious taste.

What is wrong with *Lady Sings the Blues* more than anything else is that people to whom Billie Holiday is only a name, a few records, and some concert and night-club appearances are either going to be woefully misled by it or terribly annoyed by it. For it is not a particularly honest book. It would appear to be frank and accurate up to a point—and it is quite probably a true (and often a very moving) picture of some prisons, of Southern *and* Northern Jim Crow in the music business, of real poverty in Harlem. But there is a pervasive air of self-pity that gets me down, and there is a distressing (and rather transparent) vagueness at key points. We gather, for example, that Billie's first arrest on a narcotics charge came *after* she had gone through a successful cure; but, thereafter, I defy any reader to tell from the text whether she is saying she is "on" or "off" the stuff at any given point. Similarly, the whole previous matter of how she first acquired a habit is glossed over rather bewilderingly. All this seems part of the unfortunate overall "almost everybody done me wrong" spirit that led one jazz magazine to headline its review of the book: "Billie Wails."

In a sense, however, this lack of full candor cannot be called surprising. Not, all least, to those of you who can—as I noted at the start of this piece—bring something more with you to the book than the "average" reader can. You can appreciate, certainly, that an up-from-poverty, kicked-around, jailed Negro singer *has* to hold something back, and *has* to push her side of the story to the fullest. To do otherwise would, under all the circumstances, be superhuman. And *you* can set her words against a context that includes the actual musical product created by Billie and by others whom she deals with here. Keeping these things in mind tends to increase tremendously the meaning of what you read. It's not really fair to a reader, of course, to ask for this sort of extra work. But the point is, if you approach this book forewarned and forearmed and interested in learning from it (and not necessarily in learning precisely what the author herself chooses to emphasize), you'll surely find it worth having read.

(In all such books, the general accuracy of the facts presented is of importance, if only as an indication of how careful and reliable a job has been done. I found very few mistakes: Don Redman's name is given as "Redmond," which perhaps bothered me more than it should, but this is nothing at all in comparison to my favorite boner, found in Mezzrow's book, where the Chicago-born patron of Negro jazz let his ghost writer refer to pianist Lovie Austin as a "blues singer." Miss Holiday's writer is guilty of one importance failure to clarify that did make me quite angry, and I'd like to clear it up right here. In the late '40s, Billie was involved unpleasantly with a promoter-agent type named John Levy, who, she says, tricked her into taking the rap for him on a dope charge, etc. Mr. Levy's present whereabouts are unknown to me. However, on the current scene is a John Levy who is the personal manager for George Shearing and others, and who was Shearing's bass player until about 1951. He is *not* the same man; as far as I can discover, there is no connection whatsoever between the two men. I wish Billie or Bill Dufty had seen fit to make this distinction in the book.)

Portrait of the Young Artist as a Man
1952

MUSIC OUT OF DIXIE. By Harold Sinclair. Rinehart and Company: New York. 306 pages. $3.50.

It has never been easy to write a novel about an "artist," and yet novelists keep trying it all the time. The results are usually pretty bad.

I happen to think it's important that there be good and valuable books written about writers and painters and composers and musicians. (I also think it important that there be good and valuable novels written about farmers, and scientists, and pickpockets—but that is a much larger and somewhat different point and somebody else should write about that for some other magazine.)

Having a special interest in jazz, I consider it very important that there be, from time to time, books that say valid and perceptive things about the art and business of jazz, about the lives and emotions of men who play jazz, and about their relationship to the whole of society. I think that people who know jazz, and people who don't, can get from such novels added insight into one particular segment of our culture, and—if it is a good enough novel—can also get insights into the nature of all mankind. And this, although it may sound a touch stuffy, is after all perhaps the major function of fiction.

There are undoubtedly many reasons why authors who attempt this task usually wind up way off the mark, and I found myself sort of shoved into thinking about some aspects of this when I happened to read a book that doesn't miss the mark by very much at all. Harold Sinclair's *Music Out of Dixie* doesn't ever seem to be trying to be a Great Big Important Novel. It is episodic, it limits itself to a fairly narrow span of time, it has so little formal "plot" that it might not even fit the normal definition of a novel. . . .

Of the novels about jazzmen that I have read and recall with any distinctness, only two had ever seemed to me to have much merit. Dorothy Baker's *Young Man with a Horn* occasionally slipped into over-blown hyper-emotionalism and just plain corn (and was capable of being twisted, with apparent ease, into an abominable movie—which might perhaps be held against it), but it did a remarkable job of capturing the romantic-emotional feel and pull of jazz and something of the way it sounds (although writers might just as well admit that you just can't do much about translating music into descriptive words). An almost unknown book by Henry Steig, *Send Me Down* (published by Knopf in 1941), was sprawling, over-long, rather lopsided and confused, but it nevertheless gave a remarkably vivid picture of the daily grind and everyday attitudes of young white jazzmen of approximately the early Benny Goodman and Dorsey Brothers era.

These two books had formed my personal jazz-fiction library. Now I'm ready to add *Music Out of Dixie,* which (despite its meaningless title) is surely one of the most persuasively authentic books about an artist of any kind that has been written in a long, long time.

It is by no means a flawless book. When Sinclair does work at producing a plot, he runs along pretty routine lines, and he is guilty of some quite arbitrary hauling around of characters and coincidences in order to make sure that his hero gets to sample just about every possible facet of the jazz world of New Orleans and thereabouts during the heyday of Storyville and just after it was shut down. . . .

I think I appreciated this book as much for what it *didn't* do—for the aggravating traps and pitfalls the author managed to avoid—as for anything else. I started this review by noting the difficulty of writing a novel about an artist. *Music Out of Dixie* certainly is a book about an artist, a dedicated man who wouldn't dream of doing anything else but play his music. But it pleases me exceedingly by the way in which it goes about being a comparatively rare example of this very common general type of fiction.

Certainly there have been vast numbers of books published (and even vaster numbers of manuscripts destined to remain unpublished) that seek to tell the story of a sensitive and misunderstood young man, so dedicated to his art that he casts aside all else in the world and doggedly consecrates his life to Being Creative.

The variations on this theme are many, but the general structure is usually as standardized as if it were a religious ritual (and in a sense it almost is). There is likely to be a bull-headed businessman of a father who feels that all art is effeminate and tries to bully his son into being a "man." There is scorn, or at least insufficient appreciation of the artist, from all but a very few of his friends; there is heartbreak when his efforts are sneered at by the public or by the commercially-minded hacks in his field of endeavor. Strangely enough, sex is usually good to the young artist of fiction, but it comes either in the form of mad young wenches who inhabit the Bohemian world he lives in and fling themselves at him for one-night stands, or in the form of Good Girls who want to tie him down to a life of family responsibility. This, of course, never can be, for the essence of the artist-in-fiction is Conflict: he must be in opposition to the crass standard virtues that rule the dull normal man; he must scramble away from love, family, comfort, material success and all the other things that would keep him from following his shining star. Perhaps the truly dedicated and talented artist does behave, in real life, something like this fictional tortured soul. But I wouldn't want to bet much cash on it. . . . Most novels-about-artists lose whatever accuracy they have to begin with by the unfortunate circumstance of being largely written in wild-eyed, shamelessly sentimental, and rather breathless prose. The usual technique of writing about a dedicated man tends to depict "sensitivity" and "talent" solely in terms of overwrought descriptions of constant mental anguish and soul-searching and purification by fire. As a result, the artist-hero usually tends to give the reader a stiff pain in the neck; rather than feel deep sympathy, you're apt to feel an irresistible urge to tell him to go take a cold shower.

Of course, one reason for this may be that the novel is all too often a first novel and little more than an autobiographical exercise in self-pity written by a young man who sees the Misunderstood Young Artist about whom he is writing as a romantic projection of himself.

Harold Sinclair happens to have written five novels. If he ever did suffer from a misunderstood-young-artist complex (I wouldn't know whether he did or not, not having read his previous books), he certainly had worked it out of his system before starting to work on this one. It would be very helpful, I'm sure, if we could get some sort of law passed providing that every young writer would have to get at least two books under his belt before being allowed to be turned loose on themes of this sort. I would certainly assume that Sinclair's being an experienced writer has a lot to do with the calmness and the quiet skill of this book, and also with his never losing sight of the fact that his hero is a man living in and with a real, everyday world: all too frequently the central character of a novel-about-an-artist seems to be spending his time in a vacuum that has just about nothing in common with any facet of the real world.

Fiction about jazz is usually free of the self-pity, if not of the overwrought sentimentality, of the standard novel-about-an-artist. But it has other sins to be chastised for. Particularly if you let the general term "fiction" include the occasional play and the almost-annual movie. Anyone with any familiarity with jazz music, and with the attitudes and way of life of the men who play it, does not need to be reminded of how embarrassing it can be to sit through the results of Hollywood's explorations into the field. There is no point and no pleasure in going into *that:* suffice to say that the heroes of jazz-type movies are usually very dedicated fellows who make very painful faces to express their earnestness; they learn to play trumpet at the knee of an old darkie, and end up winning wild acclaim while blowing high notes and Harry James-ian treacle at that inevitable jam-packed Symphony Hall concert. Any resemblance to reality or to the actual problems of a jazzman's life would be unpardonable accident.

Of course, people who write without any true knowledge or understanding of the facts or background of their subject are doing a very stupid and hopeless thing. But, somehow, people do try to write novels about painters when they (apparently) barely know what a palette knife might be; and people do try to write about jazz musicians while under the impression that Irving Berlin and Paul Whiteman epitomize jazz and without knowing much more about the background of jazz than that Basin Street is in New Orleans and Fifty-second Street isn't. Harold Sinclair—to return again to my shining example of the right way of doing things—happens to know something about jazz. He also happens to know New Orleans well enough to have been chosen in 1941 to write "the New Orleans volume in the American Seaport series" that Rinehart has published. This knowledge, believe me, helps.

The importance of *Music Out of Dixie* to me, then, lies partly in itself: as a highly interesting and convincing portrait of a man, a city, a period of time, and an attitude towards a music; and partly in the use I have tried to make of the book as an object lesson in how a certain important and much-abused type of novel should and should not be attempted. If any dogmatic set of rules can be drawn up from this somewhat rambling essay, they would be something to this effect: to write a book of any value about an art or an artist you have to know what you're talking about, you have to have some perspective, and you also have to be fairly sure you're not really writing a romantic dream about yourself. . . .

If you accept my original premise that this general type of novel is of importance, it follows that jazz, in particular—being a much-maligned and misunderstood art-form for which we all presumably have great affection—is very much in need of books as good as, or even better than, *Music Out of Dixie.* Now I only hope that a few other writers set fit to follow Sinclair's example—but I must admit that I don't really expect it. This book is probably only a glimmer of light in the wilderness. But then you can't have everything, can you?

The Horn
1958

THE HORN. By John Clellon Holmes. Random House, 1958.

One of the most distressing elements of the stereotyped public attitude towards jazz is the feeling that jazz is some sort of dark emotional jungle and that therefore it is properly within the province of what I suppose is still called the *avant-garde* novelist. Jazz, according to this view-point, is all caught up with murky, turgid thoughts (you know: how to hit that big unattainable note, the one that killed Kirk Douglas in the movie) that ordinary people wouldn't understand anyway. Of course jazz, being practically by definition a part of the non-conformist world, is forever being adopted as a sort of tag-along side-issue by one cult or another (from the Jazz Age speakeasy crowd, through the American Communist Party, on down to the Beat Generation). All that can be pretty hard on jazz, but rarely is it any rougher than on those occasions when a youngish novelist stakes out a claim and comes up with another of those "authentic and powerful" books about jazz. Now, when young novelists try to invade other kinds of specialized fields (like Time, Inc., or atomic science, or hoboing, for example), either the publishers' offices are full of people who know all about it (*Time*) or they send the manuscript to an expert or two (atomics) or everyone probably agrees that it really isn't supposed to be taken as reality (On-the-Road-ism) and all is more or less well. But the dark continent of jazz is something else: bright young authors are popularly supposed to know more about the mysterious music than almost anyone, and I daresay that the bright young authors' bright young editors would scarcely admit to being so square as to need help in making a jazz novel authentic. So, the manuscript gets into print unimpeded, and as a result we have books like *The Horn*.

It is bad primarily because Mr. Holmes doesn't know and thinks he does know. Few things are worse than the hipness of the ignorant. In this novel, Mr. Holmes gives us a central character who is closely modelled on Lester Young. On the surface, that is. He wears the sort of clothes Pres does; used to hold his horn at that strange angle; was very tight with the character in the book patterned very closely on Billie Holiday; and is now considered to be over the hill, although still an idol. This sort of thing is known as *roman à clef*—literally a "novel with a key"—the key being that such a book involves real people, more or less disguised, and half or more of the fun is in figuring out who they really are. The purpose is usually satire, mockery or scandal-mongering (it's tough to apply the libel laws to fiction). In the past such books were used for things like poking fun at Disraeli; at present it is well-known that you can increase sales greatly by letting the word get out that the magazine publisher in your novel is really Henry Luce. I am not accusing Mr. Holmes of any low motives: for all I know, in this instance we may have an author who feels that by using fictional counterparts of Pres and Lady he is really helping himself to make his big emotional and aesthetic points. But I very much doubt that there is any value in what he is doing here.

One reason I doubt him is simply that this happens to be the first time I've ever read a *roman à clef* that includes a character based on someone I know well. Pres and Billie, as it happens, I've barely met. But there is one character in these pages who wears dark glasses and lives a pretty secluded life and writes weirdly angular tunes and is named Junius Priest. But it wasn't until I came to the bit about this fellow having Billie's picture on his ceiling (only it isn't Billie here; it's the modelled-after-Billie character, if you follow me) that I remembered this as an anecdote I'd once heard about Thelonious Monk and realized that Priest was supposedly Monk (don't blame me: I'm just reporting the facts). My point here is that I know Thelonious fairly well, and so the surface devices used by Holmes never registered with me, because I never for a moment even suspected any real connection between this character and Monk. There just isn't any. And I feel justified in using this to support my immediate doubts that the Lester and Billie similarities here are anything other than aggravating window-dressing and red herrings (now *there's* a combination for you). . . .

I hope no one thinks I am trying to be personally nasty to Mr Holmes. I am not. . . . My real purpose is to do the cause of jazz a service: I am hoping that readers who have friends or relatives contemplating writing "an authentic and powerful novel about the world of jazz" (to quote the jacket of *The Horn*) will cut out this review and mail it to them, or pin it on their bulletin board, and maybe it will scare them off. If so, it might conceivably scare off a potential good jazz novel, and if that should happen I'd be truly sorry. But I know that if it scares off any, it will surely scare off some bad ones. The odds are with that bet.

Jazz Novel
1959

BLOW UP A STORM. By Garson Kanin. Random House, New York.

Those who note the book reviews I write from time to time may have gathered that one of my dislikes is the "jazz novel." I do like to think that I am not hopelessly prejudiced; that should a really worthy book suitable to being described by those two words come along, I would welcome it loudly and warmly as a long-awaited friend. But the day of its arrival has not yet come, and Garson Kanin, who is a Broadway and Hollywood director, a playwright (most notably the very funny *Born Yesterday*) and inevitably an ex-saxophone player, has not even advanced us a moment closer to that day by writing *Blow Up a Storm*.

The problem is once again, as it so often is, that those who choose to write fiction about jazz don't really know the first thing about the music and those who live with and by it. In formulating (I decline to use the verb *creating*) this novel, Kanin has attempted a job roughly similar to writing a saga of the pharmaceutical business after having spent six weeks as a soda jerk in a drug store. But presumably the potential publisher of such a novel might have someone check to see whether the ingredients in the prescriptions were correct, or at least correctly spelled. Jazz, however, is accepted as a *terra incognita* (if I may allow myself a quick shift in metaphor); let a dusty traveler show up claiming that he has been there and knows all its secrets and he is immediately taken at his word, without even an elementary cross-examination or a glance at his credentials.

Usually, jazz novels are the work of terribly earnest young literary rebels, all full of Art and the Struggle of the Creative Artist and similar turgidity, and charitable folks can excuse them by attributing it all to their being young, or being friends of Jack Kerouac, or things like that. But Mr. Kanin has no such easy way out. He is a pro, a man experienced in the theater and in writing, and it says on the jacket that "for two years he . . . put aside all theatre and film activity in order to write" this book. I find this not only incredible but saddening. The fact is that Mr. Kanin *can* write; he puts together a sentence and a scene adeptly, and he has tried to give this book another plot besides the one about the tortured artist who makes good and/or goes to seed. . . . The disheartening aspect of this "jazz novel" is that it is such a different kind of bad one: not the mystical-corny Portrait of the Artist kind of badness, but the off-handed, superficial, slick-professional kind, and from a man who might have been expected to know better. Who might at least have been expected to be enough of a pro to know the one really relevant fact—that no one is ever going to get anywhere writing a "jazz novel." After all, *Hamlet* isn't a "Danish-royalty play," nor is *Moby-Dick* a "sailor novel." The idea is to start with people, and then when you put them into a particular time and setting and group of circumstances they'll still be people: plausible, real-type people, capable of making you give a damn about what they do and what is done to them. That is what literature is supposed to be about. I know they teach this very early in all the writing courses, and it's quite elementary. So won't someone tell me why it is that when a writer gets onto that fabulous, colorful, riotous, pulsating Thing Called Jazz, he almost always turns out one kind of nonsense or another about a contrived and preposterous collection of non-people? And when is someone who has some knowledge and understanding of jazz—and therefore is qualified to relate properly the specifics of the jazz setting to the universalities of life—going to write a novel you can read without squirming?

Actually, there have been a handful of nearly successful efforts: Henry Steig's 1941 *Send Me Down*—long out of print; Harold Sinclair's *Music Out of Dixie;* and even, to some extent, Dorothy Baker's pioneering but long over-praised 1938 romanticism, *Young Man with a Horn.* But the percentage is woefully tiny.

Anyway, I don't really expect answers to my *why* and *when* questions. I'm only asking, sullenly.

Three Thoughtful Pieces

Undoubtedly the greatest reward for being the copy editor, particularly in so opinionated a field as jazz, was that I had a free hand in revising the work of others, but no one was ever in a position to control or censor my *Record Changer* writing. On the whole, however, I did keep myself fairly well in check—except perhaps for those book reviews.

My editorial complaint about the absence of a sense of humor in jazz fans unfortunately would seem to remain valid. By way of explanation, the movie parody I refer to in "Humor in Jazz Writing" announced in all-white major studio production of the life of Jelly Roll Morton, with Van Johnson in the title role.

The other two are much more in the nature of period pieces. It is surely not a bad idea to be reminded of the now unbelievably fearful atmosphere of the McCarthy-ridden early 1950s, which didn't often impinge as directly on the normally apolitical jazz world as it did in the 1953 firing of our friend and record reviewer Bucklin Moon. If I am now inclined to feel smug about having taken a bold public stand back then, I can easily deflate myself by pointing to my obligatory defensive remark about recognizing "the great menace of Communism"—when a major point about this bizarre period in American life is that matters such as the Moon affair didn't have the slightest connection with that particular "menace."

My detailed 1952 account of "Jazz and America" was written for the *Changer*'s tenth anniversary issue. In reading it now, please recall that this was long before "black" was to replace "Negro" as the descriptive word of choice. (This usage has cropped up in a number of places earlier in this volume without seeming to require any special comment. But the nature of this article called for it so frequently and prominently that I find it impossible to avoid some sociological note about vocabulary.) Otherwise, read the piece verbatim for the rarity it is: a sober evaluation of the '40s, without a trace of self-consciousness, from the advanced viewpoint of the

early '50s. I was not yet thirty years old, and had not yet produced
my first record, but I was very sincere and *very* assured.

Jazz and America
1952

Jazz is basically a Negro music. And jazz (although we insiders like
to think of it as a vital part of American culture) has always had to
struggle under the weight of a social stigma. This stigma derives, of
course, from the highly emphasized fact that jazz supposedly origi-
nated in the whorehouse district of New Orleans. It has developed
into a strange, double-edged scorn. On the one hand there is the
intellectual's scornful dismissal of jazz as low-brow stuff, not worthy of serious artistic or intellectual consideration. On the other
hand there is the attitude of the average citizen, who feels that any
art-form is strange, suspect, and somehow unmanly. And members
of these two very different groups seem to agree that jazz is pretty
dirty stuff, associated with drunkenness, bawdiness, and other
forms of immorality.

These two facts about jazz—that it is Negro and that it is, traditionally, scorned—are of course by no means unrelated. And while
these facts have no real direct relevance to the music and its merits,
it can't be denied that they have been very important influences in
shaping the history of jazz, more important perhaps than we jazz
enthusiasts (who *do* take it quite seriously, do not find it immoral,
and do not see anything automatically wrong about being Negro)
are apt to remember.

At any rate, no summing up of the past decade in jazz, the ten-
year period through which *The Record Changer* has lived, would
be complete without a good hard look at what has happened in this
period with regard to the position of jazz in American society as a
whole. The two aspects of the subject are closely inter-related, but
it seems easier to examine them separately: to look first at the
changes in the status of the Negro in jazz, and then at the status of
jazz as an art-form in our society.

I. The Negro in Jazz
You can't look at jazz at all accurately if you let yourself forget that,
in one very real sense, it owes its very existence to the ugliest blot on
the record of our democracy. If it had not been for Negro slavery,
there would in all probability simply be no such thing as jazz. The

music has undergone vast changes over the years; many influences have been at work on it, and there have been many important infusions of white talent. But despite all this, jazz and jazzmen have been and remain importantly affected by the systematic segregation and official or unofficial denial of full rights to American Negro citizens in just about every part of this country throughout the eighty-nine years since actual slavery was abolished.

Thus there are some things that cannot fully be set down in any factual record of the '40s or of any other period of time. Things that go to make up the attitudes and reactions of Negro jazzmen in a predominately white culture, of white jazzmen playing a predominately Negro-based music, of white audiences (both the "educated" listeners, like readers of this magazine, and the casual entertainment-seekers). But we can at least bear in mind these instincts and intangibles, as we take a look at what the past ten years have meant.

There have been some impressive gains; some earlier victories have been solidified. But there have also been a few grotesque sidelights, some shocking reminders that progress isn't always a straight and easy road. Let's arbitrarily break the subject down into two broad categories for specific examination:

Mixed Bands: Of course, back in early New Orleans, the very idea was unthinkable. And when young white jazzmen in Chicago, in the '20s, begin playing in imitation of Negro music (getting it largely second-hand, from the records of the Negro-inspired N.O.R.K. and O.D.J.B., and occasionally absorbing it at Negro night-clubs), they did not often go so far as to breach the color line and actually play *with* Negroes.

But there were notable exceptions, such as Sidney Arodin with Jones and Collins, and inevitably there eventually were enough men who didn't give a damn about anything but playing with good musicians whose style and ideas they liked. Besides, if you were white and played jazz, the public stamped you as playing "nigger music"; so why not get the benefits of the situation, too. There was the *Knockin' a Jug* session; in the '30s there were thoroughly mixed bands playing behind Billie Holiday and Mildred Bailey recordings. On the whole it came easier on records; not *easy,* but easier than when bookers and club owners and leaders had to consider a band that came face to face with its audience. But by the mid-'30s there was the careful insertion of Negro specialists (notably Teddy Wilson with Benny Goodman) into units of regular commercial swing orchestras. It was in 1939 that a fully mixed outfit, led by Joe Sullivan, opened at New York's Cafe Society, and it was slightly before the start of the 1942–52 decade that Cootie Williams, Charlie Christian, and Lips Page took over full-time jobs right in the middle of the line-ups, the first two with Goodman, the third with Artie Shaw.

So "mixing" cannot be classified as a gain originating in the past ten years. But the solidification of the gain—to the point where, happily enough, not too many people even think to notice it—can definitely be credited to this period. The New York group loosely describable as "the Condon mob" began in about 1942 to employ that now vastly overworked device, the jazz "concert," and you could find Red Allen, J. C. Higginbotham, Benny Morton, Sandy Williams, Ed Hall, and a great many other Negroes on the stage of Town Hall with Eddie Condon and his associates. Mixed record dates have, in the past decade, perhaps become more the rule than the exception (possibly helped along by the growth of numerous independent labels, operated by jazz-lovers who were totally un-bound by the Jim Crow taboos the major companies often re-tained). Even network radio, by and large no friend of the Negro, gave way briefly late in the decade for Rudi Blesh's *This Is Jazz* program (unsponsored).

But the color line has by no means disappeared. The occasional token appearances of single Negroes in white big bands, Billy Eckstine's tour of the country with George Shearing's mixed (three and two) group, even Louis Bellson's appearance in the Ellington band, are advances, but they don't tell the whole story from a general, nationwide angle. That whole story seems to be that rec-ord dates and small clubs are one thing; hotels, one-night stands, and movie theaters often are another. Sure, Jack Teagarden even went South with Louis's band; but at about the same time Charlie Shavers didn't go South with Tommy Dorsey. Sure, you'll find Negro musicians in the pit orchestras at Broadway musicals; but New York's Number One stage-show movie house still segregates its casts (allowing an occasional Negro star to head an otherwise-white bill, but never vice versa; and almost never booking a Negro band or single Negro second-string comics or dance acts in with whites).

There is, of course, another important angle to be emphasized, lest we seem to be saying that all would be perfect if only jazzmen could all be jumbled together regardless of color. Style is a vital limiting factor: for somewhat obvious, fairly complex reasons that go far beyond the scope of this brief report, there are few areas in jazz today where Negro and white styles merge closely enough to make playing together at all sensible. It is surely not Jim Crow that keeps Negroes out of the traditional-minded West Coast bands. It's simply that there are few if any Negroes interested in devoting themselves to that kind of music. In the East, where there is a fair number of old-style Negro players, you had no color line in the bands organized by such as Jimmy Archey, Bob Wilber, Conrad Janis. Similarly, Negroes who can fit into the Condon-Dixieland style (Ed Hall, Vic Dickenson) are accepted. For better or for worse, it must be noted that the greatest limitation on mixing (at the small-club, few-social-pressures level) is simply the immense musical gap that was created during the decade, leaving traditional jazz, strangely enough, primarily the white musicians' field.

Modern Jazz: Here is the other side of the coin. If you can say that Negroes were "permitted" to play with whites in the traditional-type set-up, you must say that the beboppers only "permitted" whites into their school.

Bop was unquestionably the most important and explosive social phenomenon in jazz during the past ten years. It would seem to have embodied many forms of protest, perhaps brought to the surface by the ferment of the war years: protest against the position of the Negro, against the position of the Negro entertainer, against the musical stagnation of big-band swing, against the exaggerated concept of musical illiteracy which was supposedly the trademark of traditional jazz. For some or all of these reasons, and perhaps for additional reasons, bop came forth, and it took shape as a complex, neurotic, strange, undeniably exciting music and as a predominately Negro music, although there were important white contributions.

The subject is too complicated to wrap up in a single paragraph, but it must be noted that "progressive music"—as distinguished from bop—was a white music, that it was played by big bands who played most of the places big bands usually play and who (Kenton, Herman, Raeburn) included no more than a sprinkling of Negroes. Many of Herman's sidemen later went on to play small-band, small-joints jazz in mixed groups. This could possibly be combined with some facts already noted to provide an approximate rule-of-thumb: Mixing is okay these days, provided it takes place on records, where no one can see the color of the performers, or in places where only a limited, "hip" audience can see them (be it Birdland or Stuyvesant Casino); but out in the great big world of hotels, theaters, and the broad American public—watch your step.

Bop also led to one of the most shocking bits of journalistic nonsense of the decade: the ridicule and the sinister implications poured forth by *Time, Life,* and assorted other publications. It must be admitted that there were frightening elements in bop—both in the music itself and in the men associated with it. Excess is always frightening to those of us who lead normally sheltered and sedate lives; and any revolution (both the bloody kind and the artistic kind) almost inevitably contains excesses. So the very sound of the music shocked some people; and the aura of Negro protest, plus the clothing styles, the beards, the rumored and actual narcotic addiction, the conversions to Mohammedanism—these things were pretty weird and frightening to some people, too. Actually, all these manifestations were fairly irrelevant to the music (except as concrete and rather accurate expressions of the protest-attitudes involved in bop), but the press made them seem the only important elements in it.

Of course, the entire situation was greatly complicated by the fact that the weird aspects of bop were not entirely confined to the honest artistic efforts of sincere musicians. The bop movement was certainly saddled with more than its share of exhibitionists and phonies; there were all those characters who dressed and talked that way just because it had become the thing to do; there were all sorts of commercialized "hipsters" who, to the general public, were indistinguishable from the sincere jazzmen. And it is undeniable that dope, marijuana, and extreme psychotic behavior were often enough quite truthfully to be associated with bop.

But these facts do not seem to be nearly as important as the public's *reaction* to the facts and fables circulated about bop. Truth, falsehood, or exaggeration—almost no one appeared willing to bother to find out which it was. The reaction was apt to be simple condemnation. It was a clear underlining of the unpleasant fact that jazz is still very much to be regarded as strange by at least some segments of the public. It is part of that standard American stereotype that insists that all art and artists are strange and make people uncomfortable. And jazz, being a Negro music and a sinful music, stemming from brothels and moving on to drink and marijuana and other unclean things—why, jazz and jazz musicians (particularly Negro jazz musicians) must be about as weird as you can get.

Certainly fewer people must actually feel that way today than before this decade began. The advances to be noted in the second section of this article indicate that we can be hopeful about *that*. But the story of bop, and the all-too-usual reactions to the legends that sprang up around it, must make one wonder just how much of an advance has been made, and just how many fewer people automatically accept the stereotypes.

II. The Status of Jazz

The acceptance of jazz as something fit to be mentioned in the presence of ladies and gentlemen undoubtedly began way back when Paul Whiteman and George Gershwin (whatever you may think of the "Rhapsody in Blue" as "jazz") put white tie and tails on the stuff. The cause was helped along when such diverse writers as Hugues Panassie and Winthrop Sargeant (whatever you may think of the merits of their books) put jazz in print and between hard covers. But unquestionably the past decade has been the one in which the most tremendous strides were made toward actual, meaningful acceptance of the music by thinking Americans, and in this field the picture has been full of hopeful signs and real achievement.

It must be noted, before even beginning to look at the picture of the decade, that there are limits to this progress. All the books, concert-hall appearances, and professors in the world aren't going to influence the people who just *know* that jazz is just a lot of raucous noise, that it is dirty, that it is played by a lot of hopped-up Negroes and white men low enough to associate with them. It's sad but true that a fair number of the people who gaped at the picture-magazine layouts on bop goatees and berets also happen to consider college professors pretty queer animals, too, and aren't going to be impressed if some of them find jazz worthy of serious study. But we might just as well forget about those lost souls, and concentrate on the advances that jazz has made in making itself understood and appreciated by those who were at least somewhat open-minded to begin with. Again, let's devise some broad, arbitrary categories to look at:

The Concerts: Beginning here means taking the least important thing first. For, in retrospect, it must be admitted that the jazz concert idea, as a means of winning general approval and improved cultural status for jazz, was a rather superficial and specious gimmick. We were told, at the start of the '42–'52 period, that one way to clear up the sour public attitude towards jazz was to get very high-toned. Take jazz out of the smoke-filled, liquor-ridden cellars and thus—apparently automatically—give it respectability. Ernie Anderson used language like that in publicizing the first of the Eddie Condon Town Hall concerts in New York, and the promoters who followed took much the same tack.

From the perspective of 1952, it seems obvious that this was, for the most part, pretty meaningless talk. Apparently the key fact was that not enough people had been coming to the night clubs that featured jazz. Maybe they just didn't want to spend all that money for cheap whiskey; maybe they actually didn't like the dingy atmosphere; maybe you actually could attract a different and larger audience with afternoon hours, plush seats, and printed programs. There was also, of course, some talk about this being the making of jazz as "serious" art; apparently it would now seduce critics who wouldn't be caught dead in a bar. But that sort of talk we have always had with us, of course. Sometimes it makes sense; more often it is wishful thinking, or indicates that some highbrow has just "discovered" jazz for himself.

Anyway, the concerts were successful for a while, and until very recently there seemed to be at least one a week in New York, a goodly number in other large cities, many on seemingly perpetual nationwide tours. There were Dixieland concerts and bop concerts and mixtures of all sorts. For a while they were interesting novelties and worth some attention (and when, during the war, they put the Eddie Condon concerts on the radio with some regularity, they certainly reached a very substantial new audience). Eventually there got to be just too damn many of them, and while they still are scheduled here and there, now and then, it seems clear that this over-commercialized idea has just about run itself into the ground.

About all that would seem to remain of the concert idea by now are two set-ups for whom the term "concert" is actually a misnomer. For almost the entire decade, a shrewd promoter named Norman Grantz has sent units of varying personnel back and forth across the country under the general billing of "Jazz at the Philharmonic," and he continues to find substantial audiences for the various melanges of bop and jump served up under that rather meaningless title. And, in recent years, on New York's lower Second Avenue—a thoroughfare uncovered for jazz in 1945 when the sponsors of Bunk Johnson stumbled onto its huge halls and nominal rents—you can find Dixieland of sorts being played every Friday night. Neither type of affair is any sort of concert; and it is interesting and ironical to note that the New York spots are places where the customers sit at tables, drink, and dance, in almost exactly the sort of atmosphere from which the early jazz concerts claimed to be rescuing them.

In short, considered as a social force affecting the status of jazz in America, you can write off the concert era as a dead loss. It didn't change the music; it had only a minimal effect on the size and type of audience. (You can probably sum it all up by using as an example a famous concert held four years before the beginning of the period we're considering, and putting it this way: when they put the Benny Goodman band into Carnegie Hall, it wasn't so that the left-overs from last night's Jascha Heifetz concert could get to hear him; it was primarily just because there were enough Goodman fans to fill Carnegie.)

The Writers: The 1942–52 period has been a busy one for jazz writers, and during this time, they have unquestionably accomplished much. When the decade began, there had been a few jazz books published, and they had created some little stir, but they had not much circulation outside of jazz circles (or, at best, general musical circles); they had really done little to make jazz more understandable or more palatable to either the intellectuals or the "average citizens" who had, for their own separate reasons, united in scorning jazz.

There were perhaps three notable jazz books before the '40s. Hugues Panassie's uneven but pioneering *Le Jazz Hot* rates praise for being the first, if for not much else; Winthrop Sargeant's *Jazz: Hot and Hybrid* did focus some "highbrow" attention on jazz, but it was primarily a rather misguided attempt, by an otherwise erudite outsider, to generalize from insufficient knowledge. Fred Ramsey and Charles Edward Smith's *Jazzmen* succeeded in setting down with remarkable (if not consistent) accuracy the color and the "feel" of jazz; it has lived through this decade and it will probably live through many to come, and it remains a wonderful introduction to jazz as a music produced by human feeling rather than technique (and that is certainly by far the best way to be introduced to jazz).

In contrast to this rather meager output, the 1940s produced a flood of books about jazz and jazzmen. It is always hard to tell, when we are still so close to the situation, which was cause and which effect: did these books create a more favorable climate for jazz among the people who read books, or did the books come into being partly because jazz was gaining a wider acceptance? Probably it's a mixture of both. On the one hand it's certainly true that jazz, just by staying in existence, has made itself known to an ever-increasing public, and has received ever-increasing "serious" attention in the universities and similar places. On the other hand, jazz scholarship was obviously served quite well by the many books published during the period: Rudi Blesh's *Shining Trumpets* and (with Harriet Janis) *They All Played Ragtime;* Sidney Finkelstein's *Jazz: A People's Music;* several discographies; and other works of varying merit from Panassie, Barry Ulanov, Robert Goffin and others—all adding up to an impressive and important body of writing. There has also been a noticeable opening up of the pages of rather highbrow magazines: you can find articles by men like Marshall Stearns and Ernest Borneman in a magazine like *Harper's,* to cite just one example.

There is no denying the importance of these books and articles—some of them were excellent explanatory works; and even the bare fact that so many were written and accepted for publication is of some importance. Unquestionably these works have done much to open the minds of scholars, musicians, and assorted intelligent readers to the merits of jazz. But in one sense these writers were attacking only the easy part of the problem. It must be assumed that their presumably aware and somewhat musically educated audience was more or less ripe to be informed of the significance of jazz. The scholarly writers—although all of them show some partisan blind spots and although the job of education is far from completed—*did* do a big job in reaching this type of audience, so it should not detract from the praise due to them to suggest that just possibly they did not do the *most* important job of the decade.

Perhaps, when we have had enough years pass by to see this decade in some sort of perspective, that most important job will turn out to have been done by a handful of quite different, very unscholarly books. Probably the biggest obstacle jazz must surmount on the road to "respectability" is the prejudice of the average American. It has been mentioned previously in this article that the man in the street often manages to think of jazz almost simultaneously as something immoral and something "arty" (it's no small trick to manage both of these simultaneously, but it seems to be done). One way to fight this attitude must certainly be to convince that hypothetical average man that jazz is a music belonging to, and expressing the thoughts and emotions of, *people.* Not just plain people like the guy next door, of course, but still human beings: with warmth, virtues, sins, families, with a capacity for love and a need to pay the rent that makes them not too unrecognizably removed from other people. All the technical and historical analyses in the world aren't going to do much good along those lines. But another kind of book, one that paints a believable human portrait, can do a lot of good, at least potentially.

There have been some attempts along just those lines in this past decade, perhaps following the trial blazed by the use of the "human approach" in *Jazzmen.* It isn't easy to evaluate books like Eddie Condon's *We Called It Music,* or Mezz Mezzrow's *Really the Blues* (the most important examples of this rather new kind of jazz book), but by and large, despite their faults, they seem to be a healthy and important innovation.

Now this may seem a fairly strange statement. Mezz's book was a weird job about a reefer smoker who deliberately sought to turn his back on the white race; Condon's was a tale of a happy-go-lucky product of the Prohibition era; probably neither man is one you'd like to bring home to mother. So the statement does need to be qualified a bit. There are those who consider Mezz's book one of the worst things that happened to jazz during the decade, serving only to solidify the feelings of people like the previously mentioned sensation-mongers who goggled at the excesses of bop, people who believe that the whole damn thing is pretty loathsome.

But despite the frightening, and the corny, aspects of such writing, the fact remains that this is a way of indicating to a fairly wide audience (and both these books, selling some twenty to thirty thousand copies, must have reached many who knew very little about jazz) something of the vitality and individuality and appeal of these jazzmen and of others with whom they were associated. With the aid of two very adept professional writers (Bernard Wolfe for Mezz, Thomas Sugrue for Condon), some start along these lines was made. It was only a beginning, only a very partial and debatable achievement, but surely *some* people came away from these books with an increased understanding. And that's worth something. You run the risk, of course, of losing forever those people who really weren't ready to be exposed to rough and unprettied books like these. But it's our guess that it's worth the gamble, that in the long run it will be books of this sort (and better) that will make jazz and jazzmen more widely and more accurately known in this country.

There is one other set of published efforts to make jazz "popular" that deserves some comment, although it's not easy to say just what conclusions can be drawn from it. When the decade began, *Esquire* magazine seemed likely to do great things for jazz. Articles by Charles Edward Smith, Paul Edouard Miller, and others, indicated that here at last was a mass circulation publication with good intentions and vast potentialities. But things soon got very confused; the subject matter became diluted and over-popularized and faddish. The magazine's approach to jazz soon indicated the effects of unsubtle, high-pressure propagandists. For a while it was wild propaganda for bop; at other times, press-agentry bent on making Eddie Condon into a cute living legend. Finally, it all fizzled out. Today, jazz in the slick, mass-circulation magazines appears limited to occasional breezy articles describing what odd characters the more character-like jazzmen are. Perhaps it all boils down to just one more object lesson, the moral being that jazz never benefits from being served up pretty for the people.

The Professors: In somewhat sober contrast to much of what has been described above, towards the latter half of the decade came a surge of academic interest in jazz. There had always been some interest: occasional jazz courses in universities, but it wasn't until Professor Marshall Stearns (then of Cornell, now of N.Y.U.) came to New York about three years ago that the new momentum became apparent. Perhaps it was just a part of the upsurge reflected in the "serious" books by Blesh and others; but more than likely it was substantially due to Stearns's great energy and solid reputation. He had been a professor (of English, not music) for several years, and important in jazz-criticism circles for many more years, and he rather suddenly began to get more results than anyone else ever had before. His most notable achievement was to start a lecture course on jazz at N.Y.U. (with the able assistance of George Avakian and John Hammond) that now has at least a dozen well-established imitators.

It was not a one-man surge, of course, but Stearns is unique among educators in that he began with an interest in jazz and has worked deliberately towards recognition for it. The others who have done work in jazz have, for the most part, merely come across it in the course of their work in general. But this does not minimize the importance of their efforts. In many universities, a substantial number of sociologists, musicologists, and others, have become strongly interested in jazz. (Most famous of these is probably Northwestern's anthropologist, Melville J. Herskovits.) It is true that their emphasis has largely been on the origins and folk-sources of the music, its African roots, rather than on contemporary aspects—although Stearns, for one, has paid considerable attention to modern jazz forms. It is also true that some long-established jazz writers and critics find an over-balanced emphasis on "Africanism" in their work.

But it cannot be denied that much valuable work has been done, and it seems safe to assume that much more will be done. It would appear that we can expect from the social scientists, in the decade to come, important contributions to the existing body of knowledge of jazz backgrounds, and perhaps equally important studies of the sociological aspects of jazz.

It surely seems as if the universities are well on their way towards accepting jazz as something more significant than whorehouse music. If introductory courses, plus the respect that other professors show for the music, can bring more awareness and understanding to the college students of the next few years, a tremendous amount of good will have been achieved, and the pioneering work of men like Stearns can certainly be counted as among the most significant events of the past decade.

A survey such as this one must inevitably be arbitrary. There are undoubtedly gaps and omissions; some points that have been hurried through at great speed surely deserve more extended treatment. But despite the necessity of skipping about in time and in subject matter, a more or less clear picture does seem to take shape.

It can be summarized briefly: jazz is still very much of a social step-child in America, but here and there are impressive signs of progress. It would seem that more people are at least being given the opportunity to understand jazz and the peculiar half-world it inhabits, that people who read books or go to college and even people who just occasionally listen to the music are at least potentially in a better position to appreciate the role of this music in America. Undoubtedly it will never completely emerge from the shadows until the Negro is allowed to emerge (not that the Negro's problem doesn't involve a great many things that have no connection with jazz), and there's no cause for great optimism about that. But at least we can take note, with thanks, of the gains, and consider that in the past ten years some part of the job has been done.

Humor in Jazz Writing
1954

Jazz is obviously a very serious business to most readers of this magazine, as it is to us. None of us would have poured all the time, money, and enthusiasm that we have into this music, its recordings, its history, if we didn't have strong feelings about the value and importance of one or more of its aspects.

All this can be taken for granted. But the subject for today is not the importance of jazz, or the dignity, seriousness, and respect with which it should properly be taken. Instead, it seems high time to look at things from a slightly different perspective.

The word "fan," we should never forget, is simply a shortened form of "fanatic." It's also a pleasanter form: fanatics are grim-faced, cold-eyed men who burned witches at the stake or broke non-believers on the wheel in less subtle centuries than this. Fans are presumably just people with an enthusiastic capacity for enjoying what they believe in, and an easy-going scorn for those who don't share their enthusiasms.

But there are times when the longer form of the word shows

through. In jazz, its more extreme applications can bring about such sorry spectacles as the name-calling of the early years of bop. But the extreme manifestations are fortunately fairly rare. It's one particular chronic symptom that has begun to bother us. We are slowly being forced to the sad conclusion that far too many jazz fans lack a basic human ingredient known as a sense of humor.

From time to time this magazine has published pieces that we considered truly funny. Sometimes we've run such a story simply because it made us laugh and we thought you'd like to share the joke. Sometimes we've felt that a piece had the kind of penetrating insight that can be humor's most valuable quality. The foremost American humorists of the century—writers like Mark Twain, Ring Lardner, James Thurber—have all had that insight, that ability to make us laugh at ourselves, and at those things we're most likely to get pretentious about.

Their most effective weapon tends to be satire, a form of exaggeration that can, paradoxically, be more accurate than reality. For the exaggeration of skillful satire is only one short step beyond reality—and by showing us the sort of things we might almost say and do, it can often point out the pomposity and self-importance of the things we actually say and do.

Now, no writer ever published in *The Record Changer* is, to our knowledge, going to be placed on a plane with Twain or Lardner or Thurber. Perhaps the satire we've published just wasn't very good, after all. But we think it was deserving of less weird reactions than it has gotten. A couple of years ago there was a piece titled "Kenton Goes Righteous," which straight-facedly purported to be a review of a new record that "proved" Stan Kenton had seen the mouldy light and been converted to two-beat. The record, a two-sided creation called "Blues in Burlesque," was actually just a rather clever take-off on jazz-concert Dixieland, a chunk of satire in itself (although, coming from Kenton, its motives were questionable). The review, which made some strong (and, we thought, funny) comments, seemed to us to take some interesting cracks at both the weaknesses of Dixie and the pomposities of criticism. But an alarming number of readers felt it necessary to (a) gently inform us we were mistaken, that Kenton had only been kidding and we hadn't known it; or (b) gleefully report that Kenton's conversion was wonderful news.

We tried another hunk of satire just a few months ago, a piece submitted by a young man we've never met who strikes us as a truly witty fellow. His dead-pan article proclaimed that it was really the Swedes of Minnesota who invented jazz, that the music went *down*, not up the Mississippi. His proof involved tieing traditional jazz tunes to logging terms ("Snag It" stemming from log jams on the river, and the like). We had no real doubt that *Changer* readers would find this a highly amusing poke at the extra-serious researchers after unknown facts—very worthy people, but sometimes a touch lacking in perspective. We were wrong; letters have arrived arguing the point in shocked tones. This Minnesota theory is impossible, they say, because. . . .

This month we're at it again. On page 9 you will find an article, actually written by Weldon Kees—a talented author and critic in non-jazz circles—but also carrying the pseudonym Hilda Hopworth (which sounds just like the name of at least one syndicated movie columnist—get it!). The article gives details on a forthcoming movie based on the life of Jelly Roll Morton. Since this is satire aimed more against the Hollywood concept of jazz than against any members of the jazz fraternity, its obvious non-literal nature may not need any explaining. But just to make sure, let us inform you before you inform us: we *know* there is no such movie.

Thus has grown the suspicion that jazz fans don't know how to laugh at themselves, that we (and "we" can on occasions include the *Changer*'s editors) take ourselves with such seriousness that the very idea of humor based on our thoughts or activities is inconceivable. Maybe it's just that the *Changer* is viewed as so dedicated a journal that it seems impossible we could *want* you to laugh. Let us state flatly that this is not the case.

(The fault, dear readers, is not yours alone. A recent issue of *Down Beat* contained a front-page box explaining to all who had written and phoned that the *Beat* had *not* printed as fact the statement that the Ellington and Kenton bands were merging. It had been part of a humorous column detailing several impossibly "utopian" musings.)

It's a little difficult to understand all this dead-seriousness. Jazz musicians have never been bothered by any deficiency of humor. The examples are endless: just about anything Fats Waller ever did; the sardonic lyrics of many blues; the clowning of Louis; the devices of trombonists like Ike Rodgers and Roy Palmer; the "hokum" clarinet Johnny Dodds could play; and much more. Why, then, the inability of the jazz fan (or at least the inability of a surprising number of our readers) to know a laugh when they see it. If the gag is a poor one, that's another matter; but even the poorest surely should be recognizable as such.

We may be libeling a good many of you by these remarks, and we recognize also that you can't scold anyone into having a sense of humor. But this was a gripe we had to get off our chests. Comments (and old jokes) from readers would be appreciated.

Bucklin Moon
1953

This magazine usually does not concern itself with the problems of the world outside our own special interest in jazz. Arguments over what cornetist actually appears on what rare record are our standard fare; the confusions of current affairs are left to others. But every once in a while the anxieties and stresses of that outside world strike close enough to us to demand comment.

Bucklin Moon has for several years been a contributor and reviewer for *The Record Changer*. Until last month, he worked as an associate editor in the fiction department at *Collier's* magazine. Then, in a shocking display of the sort of hysteria and fear that now seem to be gripping even the presumably sanest organizations, Moon was abruptly fired, as a result of some incredibly flimsy charges.

The facts of the matter are these: *Collier's* had published an article. "I Was Called Subversive," telling of the attacks made on a Los Angeles housewife who had briefly testified at a local Board of Education hearing, arguing against a ban on study of UNESCO (the United Nation's Education, Scientific and Cultural Organization) in Los Angeles schools. Moon had no connection with this article, but those Californians who apparently consider the U.N. to be subversive dragged his name into the matter. In angry letters to *Collier's* advertisers, protesting the article, attention was called to the presence on the *Collier's* staff of Moon, described as a man with "a long record of active membership in Red-front organizations." The editor of *Collier's* then confronted Moon with some "evidence" apparently gleaned from Washington sources. It was charged that Moon had been listed as a sponsor of a "Peace Conference" held in New York in 1949, and that he had been a member of the "Writers' Board for Wallace" in the 1948 elections. It was further charged that his most recent novel, *Without Magnolias,* had been favorably reviewed in the Communist party newspaper, *The Daily Worker,* and that another of his books had been included in an ad listing books for sale at a bookshop operated by the *Worker.*

According to Moon's immediate superior at *Collier's,* fiction editor McLennan Farrell (who bitterly opposed the firing), this report on Moon was "incomplete, . . . fragmentary and misleading." Moon's own answer to the first of the charges was that the "Peace Conference," which presumably *was* of Red-front sponsorship, had used his name without either his knowledge or his con-

sent. As for *Without Magnolias,* a calm and non-sensational book
published by the very respectable firm of Doubleday and Company, it was reviewed favorably in a great many publications—
including several Southern newspapers, the New York *Times,* and
The Record Changer. Henry Wallace, whatever one may think of
him, was a legal candidate for the presidency. And as for the final
charge, surely any magazine should be aware that an author has no
control over where his book is advertised.

But this was all the "evidence" against Moon—accounts of the
firing that appeared in the New York *Times,* New York *Post,* and
Time magazine disclosed nothing more damning or more substantial. But it was enough to cause *Collier's* to get rid of an editor.
According to Moon, the magazine informed him that it would not
matter if the charges could be disproved: "the mere fact of their
having been made would be bad for the magazine."

That's the story. It is a story that shocks and distresses us immea-
surably. We happen to be particularly sensitive to this occurrence
because Bucklin Moon is known to us through his association with
this magazine. But even more shocking is the total picture presented. Bucklin Moon has stated: "What has happened to me can
happen to any man." The scantiness of the evidence that cost him
his job would seem to bear out this statement. It is certainly
enough to shock any jazz fan out of his secluded contemplation of
rare old disks.

This magazine finds itself numbed and bewildered by all this.
We recognize as sharply as anyone else the great menace of Communism. But panicky and arbitrary action like this, based on such
very dim grounds, scarcely seems to accomplish anything in the
fight against Communism. Very much to the contrary, all that
seems to be accomplished is a serious undermining of traditional
American concepts of democracy and individual liberty—and it is
these concepts that surely are this country's most important assets
and strongest weapons in any battle.

Can we really be living in such times of timidity and terror as this
story indicates? Does such a representative of our free press as
Collier's now automatically turn and run when threatened by any
sort of accusation? All we can think of to do at the moment is to
offer a piece of advice to *Collier's* and to the self-appointed California vigilantes who felt that Moon did not conform to their personal
definition of 100 percent Americanism. There's another book by
Bucklin Moon they ought to read: or if they are too busy for
reading, they might at least ponder the implications of the title. It's
called *The High Cost of Prejudice.*

The Great Victor Bootleg Exposé

Late in 1951, a long-standing cultural, ethical, and (to some extent) commercial issue in the jazz world exploded into a most unlikely exposé. Sensational journalism was hardly consistent with the normally staid and scholarly personality of the *Changer,* but I'm afraid we didn't even try to resist temptation—it was one of those rare opportunities to play the part of David beating up on Goliath, and we made the most of it. Our October issue carried on its cover the screaming headline "Victor Presses Bootlegs!" followed by the opening paragraphs of my rather strident story.

The two related articles and editorial reprinted here are of lasting importance to me because they managed to change the whole course of my life. Their direct aftermath was an offer from RCA Victor to lease early jazz masters to us for reissue. We really had not had any such goal in mind but were quite willing to consider it. Eventually there was a corporate change in plans, and instead Bill Grauer and I found ourselves producing a reissue series that was released on a new Victor subsidiary, the oddly named "Label X" (that had been its designation in the planning stages, and they were never able to agree on anything else!). But in the meantime we had jointly made the irreversible personal decision to go into the record business, had acquired the rights to other old jazz material, and had even come up with a name for our venture: Riverside— that being the name of the telephone exchange at the magazine offices. Even without being able to use the Victor catalog, we plunged ahead.

Victor Presses Bootlegs!

November 1951

RCA Victor, sworn enemy of disc piracy, is currently engaged in pressing illicit Victor and Columbia LPs for one of the most blatant of the bootleggers! Documentary proof of this startling disclosure is now in the hands of *The Record Changer.*

The bootlegger makes no attempt to disguise his true colors and his association with piracy. He sails under the revealing banner Jolly Roger. Yet he apparently has encountered no difficulty in persuading Victor to process and press for this label four bootleg reissues of jazz classics.

These are the facts: One facet of the vast RCA operation is to do custom pressing for independent labels too small to maintain their own presses—which is a totally legitimate business venture. But, beginning in June of this year, they have been accepting material to be processed and pressed on the Jolly Roger label. Without exception, this material has consisted of master acetates made from old Victor and Columbia sides strung together to form long-playing records.

Of late, one of the biggest headaches to the sales departments of the major record companies has been the unauthorized issuance of their material by a number of small outfits. Paradox Industries, Inc., is one of the most prolific of these disc pirates; Jolly Roger is their best-known bootleg label.

All this can best be pointed up by a simple analogy: it's as if Seagram or Calvert were operating a custom bottling service for the benefit of Kentucky moonshiners.

Not only have the responsible parties at Victor been so incredibly naive as to miss the implications of the Jolly Roger name, but they also betray a surprising ignorance of the record industry. Everyone in the popular recording game could be expected to realize that Louis Armstrong is a star of sufficient magnitude not to be found making a long series of sides for a comparatively obscure independent. (Actually, he has *never* recorded for any but major companies.) Yet two of the LPs involved consist of Armstrong recordings. One of these, Jolly Roger 7003, is dubbed entirely from big-band Victor recordings of the '30s; Jolly Roger 7001 is exclusively a Columbia bootleg. In addition, Jolly Roger 5027 and 7002 are made entirely from Victor records featuring Sidney Bechet and the late Jelly Roll Morton, respectively.

This preposterous state of affairs may prove seriously embarrassing to any legal stand against bootlegging taken by RCA Victor. Ultimately, it could even leave the entire record industry defenseless. If one company tries and fails to correct the bootleg situation through court action, the path could virtually be considered cleared for unrestrained, large-scale record piracy. For, of course, unless such a test case can stand up in court, no legal deterrent action would be possible.

And we had very recently learned, while investigating the overall piracy problem, that Victor had finally ended a long period of indecision and was about to proceed with legal action against bootleggers. One high RCA spokesman had heatedly informed us that they would "seek injunctions and damages, prosecute, throw into jail and put out of business" not only the operators of bootleg labels but also those processing and pressing plants that serve them (apparently considering the latter as guilty as the former).

In the light of these remarks, top-level RCA Victor officials certainly appear to be unaware of the present ludicrous set of circumstances. But this lack of knowledge may not save their case if they do go to court seeking an injunction. Two local attorneys, familiar with the record industry, offered us these reactions:

One felt that any corporation, regardless of size, is "responsible for the implications of the acts of its employees," and that the assumed ignorance of the top RCA brass as to just what its pressing plant was doing was, in effect, "gross negligence." The second attorney's opinion is that, if it could be proved that any responsible officer of RCA had the knowledge that they were pressing illicit Jolly Rogers, "such knowledge would be equivalent to a consent to the practice and would probably prevent RCA from getting court relief to which it might otherwise be entitled."

There is a possible parallel in the recent case of Sam Goody, New York record retailer, sued by Columbia for price-cutting. The case was lost by Columbia on the grounds that, by continuing to sell him records, they had lulled Goody into a sense of security. As a result, nationwide price-cutting on records became the rule. Conceivably, by servicing Paradox, Victor may have placed themselves and the entire record industry in the same sort of untenable legal position with regard to bootlegging.

Victor's injudicious assist to the bootleggers of Columbia records may well have unpleasant inter-company repercussions, too. It should be noted that it is generally—if unofficially—recognized that only a "gentleman's agreement" has kept the majors from raiding each other's catalogues. Columbia has been every bit as outspoken as Victor in its attacks on the theory and practice of bootlegging. Some months ago, George Avakian, speaking in his capacity as a Columbia record executive, expressed that company's attitude to us in these words:

"Let's face it—these guys are making money out of something that doesn't belong to them. That's cheating, stealing, or whatever you want to call it. The pirates are using anything they think they can make money on without attracting too much fire from the owners of the masters." Perhaps these remarks can be extended to the present circumstances. At the very least, Columbia is apt to feel it has been sold down the river.

Art and the Dollar

November 1951

At first glance, the ludicrous mess featured on our cover and on the facing page would not seem to have much connection with the moral and ethical issues involved in the continuing argument about the "right" and "wrong" of the unauthorized reissuing of unavailable jazz records by so-called bootleg labels.

The RCA-Jolly Roger situation would appear to be a fairly clear-cut case. Here we have a large corporation being so ignorant, or having its eyes so intently on the buck, or being so unaware of the activities of one of its departments (any of these is a *possible* interpretation of the matter) that it winds up in the rather pathetic position of having its mouth howl about what illegal monsters these bootleggers be, at the same time that its hands are busily engaged in a business operation on behalf of a clearly labeled pirate.

We will agree that the primary importance of the story is as a hell of a startling and fascinating piece of news. It surely does nothing to alter the basic facts of the over-all debate. But it does seem to us that there is a significant lesson to be learned from this tragi-comic situation. We find it to be a most striking object lesson in support of the entire basis of our stand on bootlegging.

The major recording companies obviously consider themselves to be solely engaged in a business. If it is profitable to keep a record in the active catalogue, do so; if not enough copies can be sold, forget about it. But it is our firm belief—this is the key to our position—that this is *not* the case. Whether they like it or not, these companies have made themselves custodians of an important American art form; whether they appreciate the fact or not, they have an artistic responsibility to keep the more important examples of this art form available to the public. When they shirk this responsibility, they betray a trust.

It is not a question of what they want to do; it involves a moral and artistic burden that they automatically took on when they first decided to make their money in part by the commercial recording and distribution of material that "belongs" (by virtue of its cultural significance) to the people as a whole—or to that portion of the public that recognizes and insists upon the aesthetic importance of jazz.

It was the major recording companies' failure to accept, or even to admit, this responsibility, that led to the beginning of "bootlegging." (It is a matter of record that several of the present bootleggers, and other interested parties, unsuccessfully attempted to lease the rights to reissue material that the big outfits clearly had no use for; they often weren't even able to get a civil answer from the companies.)

With this as background, we arrived at our conclusion that the early bootleggers were serving a worthy purpose, in filling in for the jazz collector and fan the areas that the big firms had disdained to touch.

Now we have this almost grotesque example of the extreme extent to which a major company is an unfit custodian of jazz—so unfit, to put it on their own commercial level, that they were unable to protect either their own interests or those of their chief competitor!

RCA's custom pressing service is an integral part of their overall operation. But obviously it is strictly a robot, geared only to put out grooved circular discs with holes in the center, and to take in money. Take a look at the many things that these people either overlooked, never thought about, or did not consider to be their concern (and bear in mind that they are engaged in the production of recorded music which is, to our way of thinking, part of a great art form, and that therefore naive idealists like ourselves might consider it desirable that they know and feel something about their work):

They apparently did not know that there is such a thing as record bootlegging going on, or did not know that it is carried on by small companies who must turn to large organizations to have their material processed and pressed. For they apparently did not react at all when confronted with a label that every schoolboy would know meant, by definition, "a pirate flag." Record bootlegging is just as often referred to as record piracy . . . catch on, Victor?

They apparently were not aware of the nature of the music on the records, or even of the names of the musicians (one dead, one the most celebrated name in jazz—neither likely to be currently engaged in recording for some little company that doesn't even do its own pressing).

They apparently did not listen to the music or note the titles—or if they did they were not equipped to understand that the style and the names clearly showed that the music belonged to a period when the performers involved were engaged in recording primarily for the RCA Victor corporation's labels.

All they knew, or all they acted on, apparently, was the simple fact that a guy had a job for them to do and had the money to pay for it.

Custodians of a trust? . . . These fellows are a long way from being at that status. And if they think that we're talking mere artistic folderol, let them ponder this undeniable fact:

A man who knows and takes a sincere interest in all aspects of his own business or profession is not likely to be caught red-handed and red-faced—as Victor has just been found—in the preposterous position of assisting a pirate in the job of picking *his own* and a neighbor's pockets.

Bootlegging: The Battle Rages
December 1951

The record piracy squabble, forced further out into the glare of the spotlight than ever before by last month's *Record Changer* revelations, continues to rage hot and heavy on several fronts.

Here are the key points that emerged from the most important immediate reactions to our disclosure that RCA Victor's custom record service has been pressing LPs for a bootlegger of Victor and Columbia sides:

> From Victor: a slightly apologetic defense ("no one in this world is infallible and that includes us"; "we are investigating to see if anyone in the RCA had the slightest knowledge . . . we will not willingly be party to any such scheme").
>
> From Columbia: support for the contention that the pressing could have been done without Victor "really realizing it," and the disclosure that Columbia—like RCA—is readying for possible legal action against bootleggers.
>
> From Dante Bolletino, head of Paradox Industries, who put out the Jolly Roger label, the clearly and appropriately named pirate in the case: a complete defense of his activities, plus a rather surprising proposal to terminate them ("we are essentially for an end to bootlegging").

And, as a most important sidelight, came independent statements from leading jazz figures, laying blame for the upsurge of bootlegging on the major companies. Their refusals to grant to interested individuals the right to lease jazz material lying idle in the files, it is clearly implied, left the entire area open for piracy.

This last development helps make it clear that the true importance of the Victor-Jolly Roger episode lies not in the rather ludicrous facts themselves, but in the underlying implications. In dramatic fashion, the situation has pointed out the wide gap that exists between "their" world and "ours"—between the commercial pursuits of the major record companies and the aims of those who regard jazz primarily as an important segment of American culture and only secondarily, if at all, as a means of making money.

Last month's editorial, "Art and the Dollar," took Victor to task for the colossal ignorance of the music with which they deal that apparently permitted them to process records by Armstrong, Bechet, and Jelly Roll Morton without the slightest hesitancy. In defense of this action, Walter A. Buck, vice president and general manager of RCA Victor, expressing the company's official position, wrote us that "it would be a complete impossibility for us to check every one of the thousands of selections we press to order each year for our customers against the hundreds of thousands of sides pressed since the record industry began."

This is, practically speaking, a reasonable defense as far as it goes. It does leave out of consideration the perhaps whimsical fact that a little general information or a slight sense of humor might have led *someone* to look into the connection between Jolly Roger and piracy. Much more important, it ignores the fact that somewhere in the mammoth Victor organization were people who knew that this was primarily a bootleg label—the statement made to us by Bolletino notes that Victor has been in correspondence with him on bootlegging! But presumably this knowledge never filtered over to the custom pressing department.

Bigness, then, is the excuse. But, on the contrary, bigness is the most vulnerable aspect of the major companies' operation. Obviously they are big, and obviously jazz as a commercial property is small. This is why the classic jazz performances were allowed to drift out of the active catalogues and are reissued only spasmodically and haphazardly.

No one can criticize a business solely for being big. But when that bigness means that an artistically valuable property like American jazz music gets lost in the shuffle, it is lamentable.

The Jolly Roger fiasco, or some similarly ludicrous affair, was almost inevitable, once you realize that Victor's huge set-up leads to automatic procedures, such as the automatic pressing of specialized music by employees who have no reason to know or care anything about it. Mr. Buck's statement notes that Victor is working on "new procedures which we hope will make any such situation impossible in the future." But the only possible remedy would be to recognize the existence of jazz music to the extent of having it handled by men with some knowledge of it, perhaps by the creation of a small department—an oasis some place in the huge corporation—devoted exclusively to the furtherance of this important and largely neglected "small" musical property.

But in the light of other comment we have received, this would seem to be asking a great deal. It cannot be denied that some jazz material is being reissued by the major companies, but usually it only serves to emphasize the gap between "their" standards and "ours." There is much more to jazz than Armstrong and Goodman and a scattering of sides by a few other people, although obviously you can come closer to breaking even or showing a profit with these names.

It would be interesting and enlightening to discover the logic behind the major record companies' attitude towards the frequent pleas from independent jazz figures for permission to borrow their masters on a businesslike fee basis. Having decided, undoubtedly quite soundly from their point of view, that there was no real money in large-scale production of jazz records, that this minority market product could not feasibly be fitted into their massive distribution set-ups, the majors might have been expected not to guard this material with much jealousy.

Yet such men as this magazine's publisher, Bill Grauer; the noted jazz writer John Hammond; and at least one individual who was to "take the law into his own hands" and become a prominent bootlegger, Sam Meltzer—to single out a few examples—were consistently rebuffed in their efforts to get permission to establish authorized reissue labels.

Hammond noted to us Columbia's "short-sighted" rejection of his independent reissue plans at a time when he was connected with that company. He also took a stand in agreement with our conditional defense of bootlegging activities. "An important American heritage is being preserved, even if perhaps illegally," he said; "insofar as bootlegging fills a void with records not otherwise available, it serves a social good."

2

The Young Biographer

In 1956, Nat Hentoff and his friend Nat Shapiro, who had jointly compiled a remarkable oral history called *Hear Me Talkin' to Ya* (entirely made up of reminiscences and commentary from a great many jazz musicians), came up with the idea for a volume of biographies. Titled *The Jazz Makers,* it was to be written as individual chapters by a variety of writers. I was invited to be part of this consortium—others included Leonard Feather, Charles Edward Smith, John S. Wilson, and the two Nats—and when the dust settled after we had argued out the territorial rights to the twenty-one chosen subjects, I appeared to have come up a winner. For someone who prided himself on his eclecticism, what better three-man gamut than Jelly Roll through Tatum to Bird?

The trouble was that, while I knew quite a bit about the long-dead Morton, a favorite *Record Changer* subject, I remained too much the traditionalist to be very knowledgeable about the others—particularly Parker, still a controversial figure who had died only the previous year. But since there was no way to duck the challenge, I just dug in, doing a highly disproportionate amount of research and interview work. (We had been firmly promised advance payments totaling just $100 per chapter; but I was, after all, a long-time expert on low-paying or even non-paying jazz writing.) Perhaps because I felt unsure of my ground, I did a minimal amount of artistic pontificating, concentrating on a journalistic-inquiry approach that included as much interviewing and quoting as possible.

Back then, I didn't yet know many musicians all that well, but I was able to work a few key contacts to the hilt. As one example: Billy Taylor was already a friend; he introduced me to Roy Eldridge and to a Harlem bar-owner, two invaluable and previously untapped sources of Art Tatum lore. And although I was just beginning to work with Thelonious Monk, he proved most willing to talk authoritatively about Bird and the Minton's period, and it was through him that I met the Baroness Koenigswarter. (I still remember that Nica's apartment was overflowing with musicians the evening of our appointment, so we talked for hours in her Bentley, parked on Central Park West—certainly a highly atmospheric interview setting.) On rereading these chapters three decades later, I am pleased, particularly by what turns out to have been a definite consistency of style and approach in building all three posthumous portraits.

Jelly Roll Morton
1956

> " . . .And when I die, you can bury me
> In a box-back coat and Stetson hat;
> Put a forty-dollar gold piece in my watch fob,
> So the boys'll know I died standin' pat."

The words of the old, traditional song refer of course to some anonymous gambler; but the sentiment expressed could not have been any more directly applicable to Jelly Roll Morton if they had happened to be among the very many words he spoke about himself during his turbulent life. Jelly himself did speak of a fervent early desire to own "a hat with the emblem Stetson on it." A photograph taken in Chicago in the early 1920s shows him resplendent in box-back coat; even when he was down on his luck, in Washington in the late 1930s, his watch fob was gold. When he died, however, he was buried in more conventional attire and, it is sadly and reliably reported, the celebrated diamond he had worn in a front tooth for many years was unaccountably missing. Nevertheless, there is no doubt that Morton died as he had lived: planning a big comeback, blaming only his ill health for holding him back, convinced that he was being cheated by music publishers, and doing all he could to show that he held—or at least shortly would hold—a hand with which he could safely stand pat.

"Good music," Jelly Roll had told perhaps the closest friend of his last years, Roy Carew, "doesn't get old." And there is reason to believe that he was right. At the time of his death it may have looked as if he had been bluffing and his bluff had been called: he was broke and embittered; his kind of music was largely being overlooked. But in the years since he died there has been a very extensive resurgence of interest in traditional New Orleans jazz, and Morton has been one of the principal posthumous beneficiaries of this movement. Many jazz writers have analyzed his recorded work and found it (particularly the best of the Victor Red Hot Peppers material) worthy of the highest praise; and his influence has been newly felt in the music of young players deliberately seeking to carry on in the spirit of the early jazz. It would be overdoing it to claim that Morton's greatness is unanimously accepted. There are those who consider him to have been a greater braggart than anything else; although he died in 1941, some musicians who disliked this unparalleled egotist with passionate intensity have not yet reached a state of being able to hear his music with anything like objectivity. But the consensus would probably go along with the statement once made by Omer Simeon, the New Orleans-born clarinetist who played on some of Morton's most celebrated recordings: "One thing . . . about Jelly, he would back up everything he *said* by what he could *do.*"

One other thing is certain. For better or for worse, like him or not, this Morton was an original. There are many musicians whose life stories have been legendized, embellished and refurbished—by themselves or by others. There are many whose abilities and contributions to the mainstream of jazz have been hotly debated. There are many who have praised themselves with brash self-confidence, many whose careers have taken them from obscurity to the top and back again. But there was only one Jelly Roll Morton. And, as has been true of "unique" individuals in many fields of endeavor, a good part of his uniqueness can be attributed to what might be called a sort of personalized universality. Gambler, flashy dresser, ragtime pianist, footloose traveler, band leader, pool shark, arranger, bordello "professor," ladies' man and composer of many tunes that became firmly established jazz standards, Ferd Morton packed into his approximately fifty-five years of life just about all the ingredients that are to be associated with the gaudy, bawdy, flamboyant, earthy, and richly musical aspects of the New Orleans red-light-district origins of jazz.

"Approximately fifty-five years" is about as close as one can hope to come to his precise age. He died, in Los Angeles, on July 10, 1941, but the date of his birth was variously given by Morton himself as 1885, 1886 and 1890. His name was, to begin with, Ferdinand Joseph LeMenthe; he has claimed that "Morton" was his own invention ("for business reasons . . . I didn't want to be called Frenchy"), but research by Alan Lomax has established that this was actually the family name of "a nice type of fellow who did portering jobs" (as an uncle of Jelly Roll's put it), and who married Jelly's mother after the irresponsible Mr. LaMenthe left her. It might be thought that when a man's spoken autobiography exists in sufficient detail to make up a dozen long-play records, his story would be in clear focus. But discrepancies like the rather basic LaMenthe-Morton matter serve to point up that the extensive recordings made by Jelly for the Library of Congress in May of 1938 are much more valuable for recreating the aura of early jazz as recalled by one of its most colorful practitioners than for determining cold, hard fact. Actually, it would appear that Lomax, who was responsible for the recording, was at first primarily interested in setting down a first-hand recollection of New Orleans in the days when jazz was first taking shape, rather than being concerned with the personality and career of his subject. But inevitably and characteristically, Morton took over. (A decade later, Lomax put together a book titled *Mister Jelly Roll,* which combines an edited transcript of Morton's words with the results of further search among family and fellow musicians for opinions and for corroborative—or differing—fact. Consequently, anyone who cares to delve into matters concerning Jelly Roll, particularly in his younger years, would find it both difficult and rather pointless to avoid being indebted to Lomax.)

Putting together the data available from Morton, Lomax, various veteran musicians, jazz historians and other first- and second-hand reporters on the Storyville scene, plus such documentation as the *Blue Book*s that advertised the better-type New Orleans houses of joy—putting together all this and no more than a grain of salt, one can arrive at a reasonably firm picture of the setting from which this controversial titan of jazz emerged.

"Storyville" was the legally fixed area within which prostitution flourished in New Orleans between 1896, the year in which Alderman Sidney Story unwittingly immortalized his name by sponsoring a city ordinance, and November 14, 1917, the date on which the mayor obeyed the close-down edict of Secretary of the Navy Josephus Daniels. The attempted solution of an ancient problem which had satisfied a city with a basically Old World culture and viewpoint had become untenable when war brought young men from all over the nation within its range. But during its twenty-one years of existence, the thirty-eight-block Tenderloin District adjoining Canal Street was obviously quite something. It was, as the 1906 *Blue Book* put it, "the only district of its kind in the States set aside for the fast women by law," and its gamut included, as Morton has said, everything from "creep joints (and) cribs" to "the mansions where everything was of the highest class." Photographs of the lavishly appointed dining room at Miss Josie Arlington's still exist, and they are as impressive as a *Blue Book* description of Madame Lulu White's establishment (". . . some of the most costly oil paintings in the Southern country. Her mirror-parlor is also a dream"). Inevitably, Storyville also housed a multitude of assorted saloons, gambling joints, dives and cabarets, and in all of these there was music. Jazz was obviously not "born" in New Orleans in any single sudden lightning flash; and there is no room here to do any more than acknowledge as accepted fact the myriad sources—religious and profane; African, European and indigenous American—from which this singular musical form slowly developed itself. But Storyville, although it undoubtedly couldn't have cared less, was clearly a vital catalyst. New Orleans, a bustling metropolis at the mouth of the Mississippi, drew to itself musicians (as well as a good many others) from all over the South. And New Orleans, a city with a rich French-Spanish "Creole" cultural heritage, was highly conscious of music. That tells the story quickly, but it should make it easy to understand how the young Creole LeMenthe boy, brought up with music all around him and fascinated by the sights, sounds, and mystery of the District ("I liked the freedom of standing at a saloon bar, passing along streets crowded with men of all nationalities and descriptions") needed little urging to use his ability as a pianist to make himself part of that surging, richly flavored life.

Morton has specified "the year of 1902" (when, by any count, he was no more than seventeen) as the time when he first "happened to invade" the District, and there is little doubt that he quickly became a figure of some musical importance. Bunk Johnson has been quoted as saying that Jelly was even more noted than a legendary pianist like Tony Jackson, because "Tony was dicty" (that is, a bit pretentious for some tastes), while Morton from the very first played "barrelhouse music . . . the music the whores liked." Jelly Roll himself was somewhat more diffident about comparisons with Jackson, a pianist from whom he learned much and for whom he appears to have had great respect. Years later, in a letter to Roy Carew, which is generally notable for its lack of the usual Morton self-esteem, he referred to Jackson as the "world's greatest single-handed entertainer," and claimed that he decided to concentrate on playing "something truly different from ragtime" because he felt inferior in that genre to Jackson and several other highly regarded piano men of the day, all of whom were. Jelly Roll wrote, "much faster in manipulation" than he. Jackson was a singer and composer as well ("Pretty Baby" was his best-known number although, typically enough, he reportedly sold it outright for a small sum long before it became a hit), and Morton, who remained quite proud of having once beaten him in a piano-playing contest, was given to explaining that he won by unnerving Jackson: he repeatedly whispered, "You can't sing now," while Tony was playing.

One early result of Morton's new career as a sporting-house pianist was the severing of family ties. His mother had died, and the grandmother who had raised him apparently refused to have anything more to do with him when she learned how he was earning his living. Also, pianists tended to be loners by trade: they obviously didn't march in parades; many bands didn't use them at all; and so the most usual job was solo work in the parlor of a house. Thus it was not surprising or unusual that Morton left New Orleans after a while and wandered throughout the South, playing piano and shooting pool. Jelly Roll himself would have reversed the order of listing those activities: in the Library of Congress recording he can be heared claiming—how seriously is anyone's guess—that he "wanted to be the champion pool player in the world," and only used the piano "as a decoy," getting jobs in honky-tonks with an eye to being invited into pool games by the local "suckers." He was back in New Orleans at times, but after 1907 apparently never returned there. It is not really possible to draw a clear picture of his itinerary during the next several years, since the only first-hand account is the one he supplied to Lomax long after the fact and, although this is sometimes full of minute detail, it is thoroughly convoluted and full of digression and not necessarily to be taken as gospel.

However, it is relatively easy to establish a general pattern and make certain basic conclusions. He played, gambled, hustled pool, and lived as high as possible (by his own account: "I had the bad habit . . . of being a big spender when I had money," and there was "a new girl in every town"), in a wide variety of towns, good and bad. The bad would include Helena, Arkansas, where, he said, a policeman told him, "A musician don't mean anything down here. We put more of *them* in jail than anybody else. . . ." The good would include Chicago where, in 1907, "there were more jobs than I could ever think of doing," and, about five years later, he managed and played at the Elite club until the Original Creole Orchestra hit town from New Orleans and was such a powerful attraction (its trumpet player, Freddie Keppard, was rated by Jelly as superior to King Oliver and Louis Armstrong) that business at Morton's place "went to the bad."

In between, before and thereafter he turned up in New York (James P. Johnson recalled hearing him there in 1911); Memphis (he had a run-in there with W. C. Handy in 1908); Houston, where he ran a tailor shop for a while; St. Louis; Los Angeles. He was writing music—enough musicians have recalled hearing his "Jelly Roll Blues" way back then to support his statement that it was originally written in about 1905; and he was working in vaudeville and in minstrel shows. This last point has its significance: Morton's greatest success, in the '20s, came as a band leader; the standard and generally accurate picture of him as a solo pianist in earlier years does not supply any real explanation of what should actually be considered a marked change in musical *thinking*—from soloist to bandsman. Morton himself credited the depression of 1905 for his having "learned the band business." In that year, "the work in the high-class mansions fell off" in New Orleans and he had to take a variety of "small-time band jobs," sometimes even playing trombone or drums in those endless streams of parades organized, by the countless societies and clubs supported by the city's Negro population, to celebrate all manner of social events (including the funerals of members). That background, plus a reasonable amount of formal musical training as a boy, apparently made it easy enough for Jelly Roll to pick up band jobs as he moved about—something that would not have been that easy for most sporting-house "professors."

In about 1917, Morton was in Los Angeles, which was to be his base for the next five years. According to his story, he was a fabulous success, not only musically but as the owner or manager of cabarets, a gambling palace, a dance hall, and other enterprises. Anita Gonzales, a girl from New Orleans (her brother was Bill Johnson, who played with King Oliver's Creole Jazz Band), became his wife during this period. Anita obviously had some money of her own (some stories have it that she paid for the famous diamond that adorned his gold front tooth), and she bought a "hotel" in Los Angeles. There are quotation marks around the word because the difference between her mention of it (when Alan Lomax interviewed her years later) and Morton's description seems to cast a revealing ray of realism. As noted by Jelly Roll, it seemed a part of a grandiose pattern of business success; Anita's words indicate something more like a small rooming house that didn't pay off too well. Unquestionably Morton worked regularly, up and down the coast, probably as far north as Canada and certainly as far south as Tijuana (his "Kansas City Stomps" is named for a bar in that town, and "The Pearls" was inspired by a waitress at the bar). What can be questioned is whether his playing actually attracted the "movie trade," whether he actually vacationed in Alaska with "diamonds pinned to my underwear," whether "Anita had three or four fur coats and I had plenty clothes, plenty diamonds," whether it was really the politically powerful enemies and jealous rivals he later complained of so darkly who cost him bookings and squeezed him out of ownerships.

But if one is inevitably moved to question and minimize, it must be done carefully and within limits. The man did build an impressive musical reputation; he did wear diamonds and the sharpest of clothes; a decade later, in New York, he did keep a thousand-dollar bill (or at least some very large denomination) on hand to flash at anyone who wondered out loud if he were doing well. These things were not inventions, and if the way he dressed and spoke was designed to advertise himself and magnify his success to the utmost, it was no more than an inevitable and readily understandable outcome of the way of life he followed (a self-chosen way, it is true) since he was barely out of short pants. Wilbur de Paris, who knew him well in New York in the '30s, is emphatic about describing him as "sensitive, a gentleman," who, although he had lived in a sporting-house environment, "was no roughneck." If this description seems at variance with the standard picture of a flamboyant, argumentative Morton, note that de Paris knew him better, and differently, than most. He rarely worked for Morton; primarily he knew him as his neighbor in a brownstone rooming house on a Harlem side street, a man with whom Morton could talk about other, more casual things than music (such as the obscure fact that Jelly Roll's second wife had once worked for a "plantation show" run by Wilbur's father). In short, a man Morton might have felt little need to dazzle and impress. The only other person to know him in something of the same way in his later years was Roy Carew, a white man who had worked in New Orleans in the early part of the century and had known Tony Jackson then. He met Jelly Roll in Washington in the late '30s, and the first basis of their close relationship was that Carew could "talk to him about Tony and about the old days." To Carew also, Morton was a sensitive, relatively quiet man: "He was no braggart to me."

It is certainly reassuring to anyone who feels that there is depth and warmth in Jelly Roll's music to find evidence that the face he turned to the outside world was not his only face. As for the nature and derivation of that public face, de Paris provides an important clue by pointing out that the diamond in the tooth, the extravagant dress and mannerisms, were by no means an indvidual affectation limited to Morton alone. They were, on the contrary, more in the nature of a uniform: it was by such means that all "sporting gentlemen—and that included pimps" of the early 1900s announced to the world that they were in a state of affluence. Morton, in 1902, had surely not become a professional musician solely because of some abstract love of music. It was rather that this was the way of moving into a setting that this teenage boy found immensely glamorous and attractively free and easy. It began by being all mixed together—the music, the gambling, the women, and all the rest of it—and there was never any reason or occasion for things to become much different. Young Ferdinand Morton went into that world alone; his grandmother quickly made it impossible for him to back out (in the unlikely event that he would have wanted to back out). So the only place to try to go was up, and the only standards to use were those of his environment. (Jelly Roll's manner of speaking, it has been said, had its only counterpart in the rococo prose style of the advertisements in the Storyville *Blue Book*.)

He took on new names: he was known as, or called himself, the Winding Boy (*not* "Wineing," which was what he tried to tell Lomax many years later) and, of course, Jelly Roll. Both terms have clear connotations of sexual prowess. When he was setting himself down for posterity via the Library of Congress, it may have seemed somewhat more respectable to claim that one nickname was associated with drink and the other with a bakery, but in Storyville, where sex was the pivot point, how better to proclaim yourself a man among men than by being called by names like these? In his travels this pianist-gambler-pool shark had to ply his trades in the toughest joints in town; in most cases he must have come into town a stranger and alone, and (judging both from his own stories of encounters with men like Bad Sam, "the toughest Negro in Memphis," and from what is known about such towns in those days) if he were to thrive, or even survive, it was clear that he had to talk, bluff, or play—or perhaps all three—himself into a position of acceptance.

Pianist Don Frye recalls meeting Jelly Roll in 1923, when Morton was briefly working in Kentucky with Fate Marable, most celebrated of riverboat band leaders. This would have been when Jelly was first making Chicago his base of operations, after leaving California; and Frye remembers that he "made a big splash in the Midwest," as much because of his singing, his clothes, and his personality as because of his playing. "He was a big talker, with stories about gambling in buffet flats, and music and everything else" all mingled together; "he jumped about in his conversation as if it was all the same in his mind. . . ." As, of course, it was. Although, in all fairness, even if music had not necessarily been his sole motivation at the start, it was by this time rapidly becoming the key to his whole existence. Alan Lomax, in his book, attributes Morton's great productivity during the Chicago period largely to that city's being too well gang-organized to enable Jelly Roll to get into his usual business sidelines of running gambling joints, managing clubs, and the like—which may have truth in it, but seems sorely to overdo the sociological-realism approach. To credit nothing more than the absence of business distractions for the intensity of the most successful Red Hot Peppers recordings is to take far too dim a view of musical creativity.

Of course, as far as "business" is concerned, it was in Chicago in the '20s that jazz itself first became any sort of business: the era of the phonograph record was under way; jazz compositions were being published and sheet music sold; for the first time a musician could earn money from jazz in other ways than just playing in joints. Morton may have left Los Angeles because of a fight with Anita, or because of an awareness that Chicago was the new hub of the jazz world, or because (as he later told it) he wanted to straighten out the matter of his associates, the song-writing Spikes brothers, taking partial credit for "Wolverine Blues," which had been taken over for publication by the Melrose firm in Chicago. At any rate, that city became his home for the next half-dozen years.

At first he does not seem to have fitted in too well: for one thing, men like King Oliver and Jimmie Noone were already well established as top public favorites; for another, New Orleans musicians are a traditionally clannish crowd, and the newly arrived Morton was not only a known lone wolf but also a man who had been geographically dissociated from New Orleans for a good many years. It is a fact that he never had a band booking in Chicago itself (which may well be because this aggressive, vehemently outspoken fellow, the very antithesis of a "good darky," offended the local gang lords). But in all other respects, Jelly Roll was not to be denied. The Melrose brothers, who had done well with "Wolverine," were publishing and pushing compositions that many consider to be his real, lasting contributions to jazz: "King Porter Stomp," "The Pearls," "Milenburg Joys" and others, several of which he may have written years before, but which were now first being formally set forth, earning royalties and adding greatly to his reputation. Walter and Lester Melrose were probably responsible for his first important recording sessions, too. They placed quite a few of their tunes and artists with the Gennett company, in whose studios in nearby Richmond, Indiana, some of the most impressive early jazz records were made (Oliver, Morton, the New Orleans Rhythm Kings). Most of Jelly's major compositions were first recorded as piano solos for Gennett, in 1923 and '24. One of these sessions, on June 9, 1924, is notable as a monumental example of hard-working productivity: on this one day, no less than eleven numbers were recorded, ten of which (one was not released and the master has most probably been destroyed) remain treasured items to collectors of traditional jazz.

By the mid-'20s, the major record companies had discovered that jazz, designated as "race records" and aimed primarily at the Negro market, could be quite profitable, and a good deal of such material was being issued. It is open to question whether the powers at Victor, arranging for Morton to make some records, considered that they were taking a step of any great consequence. Omer Simeon, clarinetist on Morton's first Victor sides, has said that "Those people . . . treated Jelly like he was something special. . . ." On the other hand, Morton, who had been held back by a period of illness and had hardly been setting Chicago on fire, may have seemed no more than another local band leader of moderate fame and good publishing connections. (Significantly, all selections on the first Red Hot Peppers sessions, even those not written by Morton, were Melrose-owned, and the recording sheets list his address as in care of the publishing company.) But in any event, Jelly Roll appears to have approached the occasion like the momentous one it turns out, in retrospect, to have been. Ignoring the now-anonymous men with whom he had been playing club dates, he turned to the top of the New Orleans school: Simeon, Kid Ory, Johnny St. Cyr (on slightly later dates he used Johnny and Baby Dodds). According to Simeon, "I knew he was a big shot and one of the pioneers of jazz, so I was real excited," and even if that is a statement colored by the intervening years, the ten selections recorded on September 15 and 21 and December 16, 1926 (as well as several others made in the next few years) would seem to have been worth getting excited about. Accounts of those first sessions by St. Cyr and Simeon indicate that, on these occasions at least, Jelly was a master of tact. ("Very jolly, very full of life all the time, but serious," Simeon has said. "We used to spend maybe three hours rehearsing four sides . . . he'd give us the effects he wanted" but "the solos—they were ad lib . . . Jelly had his ideas and sometimes we'd listen to them and sometimes, together with our own, we'd make something better." To St. Cyr, "Jelly was a very, very agreeable man to cut a record with," largely because he would let them take breaks and choruses as and where they felt they best could: ". . . he'd leave it to your own judgement . . . and he was always open for suggestions.")

It may have been that Morton knew he could get nowhere playing the dictator with the men he had chosen, or simply that he had the taste to know these players had to be eased and gentled into the delicate combination he needed: enough skill and enough rehearsal time to do justice to his material as written, and enough improvisational talent and the right frame of mind to develop the right sort of solo work from the base he was providing. The results have been called the finest recordings of New Orleans jazz ever made: to cite one example, Rudi Blesh, in his book *Shining Trumpets,* devotes nine pages to the 1926 recordings without ever dropping below a superlative ("the qualities of classic jazz in their fullest development . . . incredible masterpiece"). Actually, this is not New Orleans jazz so much as it is Jelly Roll's jazz: obviously firmly based on the New Orleans pattern, but with a rich complexity, a showiness, a range from brashness to poetry, from naiveté to sophistication, that reflect this man and therefore cannot be exactly duplicated by anyone else.

During the rest of the '20s, Morton rode high. His records sold well enough for Victor to bill him as "Number One Hot Band," and he toured successfully through the Midwest, always using the Red Hot Peppers name, but never the same musicians as on his records. This distinction is no real matter of mystery: his recording bands were made up of men too much in demand in Chicago to go on the road; and undoubtedly too expensive, too unlikely to subject themselves to Morton's strict handling of his bands (unlike the cooperative spirit of the first record dates, Jelly Roll as an everyday leader was, according to Wilbur de Paris, a "disciplinarian," with "very little patience with out-of-line guys").

There is no doubt about this being a diamonds and rich clothes period for Morton. But, at the very end of the '20s, he moved his headquarters to New York, the new center of the jazz world, and then very suddenly he was on the down grade. "It was still good times when Jelly came to New York," de Paris has noted, but the music was beginning to change. "He was nothing special: Henderson and McKinney were *the* bands, and Jelly was just another leader making gigs." In New York the Peppers' records had not stirred up "*that* much fuss"—this was a city with its own Negro jazz traditions (Harlem stride piano; the big-band pre-swing style of Henderson and, later, Ellington), and New Orleans jazz and its practitioners were never really idolized in the big town. New York musicians were much more likely to note that, in terms of tech-

nique, Jelly was "a bit backward, like many of the old-line New
Orleans men." When the '30s came, Morton was in his mid-forties,
which is no age for change, even in a musician less supremely self-
confident than Jelly Roll. His Victor contract was ended after 1930
(he did make eight more sides for that company in 1939, but those
were nine long years); he was not working frequently enough to
hold together a regular band. This was the time of the Depression,
of course, and it was not merely that Morton's jazz was rapidly
going out of style: very few jazz musicians could say they were
doing well in those years. But Jelly took it all very personally: a
monumental bitterness took hold of him. Publishers were cheating
him on royalties, were stealing his tunes; ASCAP and the booking
agents were conspiring against him; an evil West Indian (he told
Lomax) had put a spell on him. By no means did he agree that he
or his music had had its day; de Paris describes Jelly's principal
feeling at the time as one of "frustration"—he did not have enough
chance to play, to express his ideas as a band leader, and he still
felt he had so much more to say.

Morton had always been disliked and feared by many people.
He was certainly not a considerate man. Little stories that could
sound funny must have seemed tragic to those involved: Lil Armstrong recalled how frightened she was, as a youngster demonstrating sheet music in a store, the day Jelly Roll came by and sat down
at her piano to give her "a lesson"; the three New Orleans musicians who were invited to join him in California (one was Buddy
Pettit, a trumpeter Jelly has rated as second only to Keppard) and
who soon "blew up, threatened to kill us" and headed back home
because Morton made fun of their "antiquated" clothes and their
down-home habit of bringing a bucket of red beans and rice and
cooking dinner right on the job. Now that he was on the way down,
more than a few people were ready to strike out at him and ridicule
him: Harlem musicians delighted in standing near him on the
street, making deliberate misstatements about the old days, knowing that this would quickly provoke him into futile rage.

In 1937 he was in Washington, part owner of a small and never
very successful club variously known as the Jungle Inn, Music Box,
and Blue Moon Inn. Here Roy Carew was aware of him as a neatly
dressed man who liked to talk about the old days. Carew was one of
the few who knew directly from Morton himself that he was badly
off. (He told of refusing offers of money from men who had known
him when he was on top: "I wouldn't let them know I needed help.")
But he still had not lost the habit—or was it the compulsion—of
being bluntly outspoken about other people's musical or personal

shortcomings; he still planned grandly for the future; and at times he could still play up a storm. Pianist Billy Taylor, then a student in Washington, tells of going with a friend to hear this relic, "mostly for laughs"; someone tipped off the fact that there were skeptical musicians in the house, and Jelly proceeded to put on a dazzling and impressive exhibition. And of course the 1938 Library of Congress recordings bear permanent witness that he could still talk of his own greatness with unflagging conviction.

One of the last instances of the old flair came earlier in that year, when Robert Ripley made the mistake of introducing W. C. Handy, on the "Believe It or Not" radio program, as "the originator of jazz and the blues." Morton had always been particularly contemptuous of Handy as a man who couldn't play jazz and who, above all, had made money by converting folk material to his own use. Jelly Roll's written rebuttal, which was published in *Down Beat,* branded Handy as "the most dastardly impostor in the history of music" and included the celebrated phrase that (even if it is assumed not to have been intended as literal truth) is breath-taking in its assumptions: "I, myself, happen to be the creator (of jazz) in the year 1902." This at least put Jelly back into the limelight for the moment, and he made another brief stab at New York. There were some records—some of them good, others indifferent or less—and a scattering of one-shot jobs. But it was all rather artificial; people seemed to be paying attention to Jelly, not as a currently active musician but rather on the somewhat unflattering premise that a surprisingly still-surviving founding father should not be ignored. This flurry of interest could not last long; Wilbur de Paris gauged its decline by noting that Morton could be found in the pool hall more often than in the nearby rehearsal hall. Then, too, there were asthma attacks; after one particularly severe one, he spent a month in the hospital.

In 1940, he learned that his godmother was dying in Los Angeles; there is reason to consider this just a good excuse for taking to the road again; in any case he did proceed to drive there from New York. There was a half year of little money and various plans: in January 1941, a royalty check for fifty-two dollars arrived from Melrose and he talked of suing them; he informed Roy Carew that he was going to appear on an Orson Welles radio show (part of the series that did succeed in sparking Kid Ory's considerable comeback). But he also wrote to Carew that "my poor health is spoiling everything"; he would be up and about for only a day or two at a time, and then the "heart trouble and asthma" that were the cause of his death would have him in bed again. He died in Los Angeles Hospital on July 10, 1941. Kid Ory and members of his band were the pallbearers, but the ceremony was a Catholic high requiem mass, which (although he had been nominally a Catholic all his life) hardly seemed the most fitting final gesture.

It is clear that Jelly had a great capacity for annoying people, and that at times it kept them from granting him his due. (Duke Ellington has been quoted as making the bitter statement: "Sure, Jelly Roll Morton has talent . . . talent for talking about Jelly Roll Morton"—which seems something less than a fair appraisal.) But it also is clear that all the traits and the trappings that disturbed many (though certainly not all) of his contemporaries were fundamental parts of the man and of the way of life he chose; they were a facet of the whole man, and he would not have been *himself* without them. Put it this way: a more sedate Morton, without diamonds or the name "Jelly Roll" or the bravado to have his business cards carry slogans like "Originator of Jazz—Stomp—Swing" and "World's Greatest Hot Tune Writer"—such a man could not have written "The Pearls" or "King Porter." And, all things considered, it was much better to have had it the way it was.

Art Tatum
1956

"Art was probably the last man left who had no trouble finding a place to play after hours."

That's the way Roy Eldridge put it, and the key words in his sentence—"after hours"—are ones that recur most regularly in the story of Art Tatum, and are inevitably stressed when one of his friends or old associates gets to reminiscing about the man who has been called the last, and perhaps the greatest, of the *big* piano players. "After hours" is a term that has a very specific, very evocative meaning in jazz. It is a bit outdated now, but not too many years ago there were places in almost any big city, not too difficult to find, where there was no curfew for the music short of exhaustion: back rooms where the emphasis was apt to be on the big man hunched over the battered, well-used upright piano. The world of after-hours jazz was, by and large, a private world. So it was altogether fitting that it was home for Tatum, whose personal world always had to be a physically restricted one.

For the other basic point to start with in any consideration of Art Tatum is, of course, his blindness. He was not totally blind—there was slight vision, probably no more than 25 percent, in one eye—

and he did not like being referred to as a blind man. He took pains to demonstrate how much he could do for himself unaided; he delighted in any situations that enabled him to participate as an equal or even to have an advantage over normally sighted people (Eldridge can tell of a mock fight in the snow, when Roy's brother Joe, another musician, and Tatum all joined in burying Roy in a snow drift; and he retains an equally vivid memory of Art leading him down a dark flight of cellar stairs). But the fact remains that Tatum was a man with a serious physical handicap. No other of the twenty-one performers singled out as greats in *The Jazz Makers* has or had a similar burden. Yet, it is important to note, these chapters surely deal with few if any lives on a more even keel than Tatum's.

It is not easy to set this down in cold print without seeming patronizing, either to Art or to others, but it might be put this way: his life was an apparently happy one, notably untortured, free from the ups and downs, the frustrations and maladjustments that so often batter the creative artist. "Calmness" is not the word for it; that doesn't come close to fitting a man for whom (as one obituary tribute aptly phrased it) life was "a vast maw of sound," a pianist whose talent placed him well ahead of his time. It must be granted that there is danger of oversimplification here: there certainly were specific areas and times of doubt and frustration. And it should also be stressed that this is no aesthetic value judgment: it is neither "better" nor "worse" for a twentieth-century jazz musician to be relatively non-neurotic, or to achieve quickly a widespread and lasting acceptance by both the public and his fellow professionals. Nevertheless, it seems highly significant that, unless there were secret torments that eluded the attention even of those who knew him best, Tatum can be described as fundamentally a confident and fulfilled, though never satiated, man.

It would seem that this can be explained undeviously in terms of the fact that Art's greatest problem was one he had to face early and deal with permanently. So nearly blind (he could distinguish colors to some extent and, by holding the cards quite close to his face, play an above-average game of pinochle, but that was about all his eyes could do for him), he had a tremendous adjustment to make. He found the way to accomplish this, through his music, while still in his teens, and it stayed with him all his life. His world was necessarily an inward-turned one; but it could very satisfactorily be just that. For he could know that he was supremely capable as a pianist; he need not doubt that he was deservedly a focal point of his self-chosen world of music. The people who mattered to him, who were similarly enmeshed in jazz as a way of life, came to him because his talent made him the man to come to. If this had not been so, if Tatum had not been a superior musician or if he had been one of those who have to struggle long, darkly, and alone for recognition, it would have been very different. But Art's dazzling technique and full, rich way of playing were appreciated almost from the first. Jazz had to be his life, and it was. There were very few occasions when it failed to work out just that well for him.

"Art was not an easy man to get to know," Roy Eldridge has said. Roy, who feels that he "knew him as well and as long as anyone," helps build the picture of a lusty, convivial man—his rather awesome drinking capacity was one, though not the only, point of similarity to Fats Waller—but a man who picked his friends with caution. "If he accepted you, that was one thing; but not just anyone could get close to him." Not just anyone could get to hear Tatum at his best, either. It is generally accepted (and in keeping with the pattern that has just been described) that his most formidable playing was displayed only in circumstances and before audiences largely of his own choosing. After hours a man played strictly as he pleased (when you're not being paid for your services, there are, after all, certain basic privileges you can expect). He played as long and as late as he pleased (while these sessions didn't necessarily *start* after closing time, many musicians literally came there after their regular night's work was done, and as often as not they'd keep going until long after dawn). And he played primarily for friends and fellow musicians. It was then, according to the stories, that more than a few performers reached peaks they could never duplicate under more normal and formal conditions. And quite specifically, it was in the after-hours spots that Tatum really came to life. (If there were other piano players on hand worth hearing, the owner of one such place recalled, "we could never let Art sit down until real late, because once he started, he'd never get up.")

The after-hours joints probably reached their peak in the 1930s; they lasted somewhat into the '40s, but not beyond that point; and their special aura and flavor will probably never be recaptured. In Harlem, and in the Negro districts of some Midwestern cities, they would seem to have been direct offshoots of the fabulous all-night "rent parties." Like them, they were at least semi-selective about admittance: they weren't exactly private affairs, but it helped if you were known. Like rent parties, such sessions were apt to have pianists as the center of attraction, and "cutting contests" of incredible length and intensity were the rule. You might say that legalisms brought about the virtual end of the after-hours club: tougher enforcement of legal closing times; or the musicians' union cracking down on the once-prevalent habit of unpaid "sitting in." (Tom Tilghman, whose Hollywood Bar in Harlem was practically home for Tatum for many years, points out that "no club could ever have afforded the going price for all the men I'd have in my place on a good night.") But you could also say that the temper of the times has changed, that there aren't that many musicians interested in playing all night just for the love of it and maybe a few free drinks, not that many who still feel it vitally important to prove their mettle in all-out personal competition.

In any case, after hours was Tatum's time as long as he lived. He could guard it jealously, too, against intrusions by outsiders who failed to grasp the distinction between it and the standard nightclub setting. Billy Taylor, the young modern pianist who was one of Art's closest friends during the last dozen years of his life, notes that Tatum "would usually sit around for quite a while before he'd feel ready to play"; sometimes he might wait until maybe seven or eight a.m., "when the others gave out," before starting. So there would be nights, Taylor recalls, when "someone in the audience would come up to him and ask, 'When do you play?' He might have been just about ready to start, too, but he'd say something like 'I play at the Three Deuces,' and hold off for maybe another hour."

Even the earliest stories about Tatum place him in this setting that he loved best. The basic statistics are that he lived forty-six years, having been born in Toledo, Ohio, on October 13, 1910; his father was a mechanic who had come north from North Carolina just before that. He showed an early interest in music, which his family encouraged with violin lessons when he was about thirteen, and then with piano lessons. His fully professional debut came at about the age of eighteen, when he was hired as staff pianist at a local radio station, WSPD, and, as Barry Ulanov puts it in his book *A History of Jazz in America,* he began "to get a reputation (when) his extraordinary fifteen-minute morning programs on that station were picked up and piped across the country by the Blue Network of the National Broadcasting Company. . . ." But that would have to be later than 1926, the year in which the NBC network was first formed, and there would seem to have been a basis for a Tatum reputation—built in less conventional surroundings, of course— even before that. June Cole, bass player with McKinney's Cotton Pickers, who played throughout the Midwest from the mid-'20s on, recalls first meeting Art in Toledo (he believes it must have been as early as 1924 or '25) when young Tatum was playing at "what we called chittlin' dinners, like house-rent parties, where the landlady would slip him maybe five dollars." Cole was doubling, after his night's work with McKinney, as a singer at a late-running gambling joint called Big Noble's. He remembers quite clearly the night when, just after he had finished "Dear Old Southland," with Todd Rhodes of the McKinney band accompanying him, "this young blind fellow came up to me" and, very quietly and shyly, asked, " 'Mr. Cole, could I play that number for you again later?' I said he could, and I can still remember just how good he was." According to Cole, the big, crashing chords, the sweeping runs, the richly elaborate fill-ins were part of the Tatum style even then. "He used to play behind me all the time after that, and he didn't have to ask permission again."

Art's local activities, including radio and night-club work, brought him to the attention of singer Adelaide Hall, and when he came to New York for the first time, in 1932, it was as her accompanist. His first records were made with her in that year, and in 1933 came his first, highly impressive, records as a soloist, for the Brunswick label. By then, Art had already begun to have a great impact on musicians, many of whom were making the most of their first chance to hear him at the Onyx Club on Fifty-second Street, which with the repeal of Prohibition was coming out from underground as a jazz center. It was also possible then, and only then, to spring Tatum as a devastating surprise on unsuspecting musicians. Roy Eldridge, who had met Art in Cleveland in about 1931 while working with the McKinney band, recalls the first time he, along with his brother Joe and the great tenor man, Chu Berry, took Tatum to the Rhythm Club, a Harlem musicians' hangout. The three horns jammed for a while, and then installed their unknown friend at the piano. "We turned Art loose, and goodbye. . . ."

Tatum next settled briefly in Chicago, leading a small band at the Three Deuces for a couple of years, but then switched to solo work. This was clearly the best procedure for a man who was, as Billy Taylor has put it, "a whole band, complete in himself," and whose preference was for intricate extemporaneous choruses that even rhythm accompanists often had trouble following. Until 1943, he worked alone: most often in New York, but in 1938 as far afield as London. The pattern was set; his reputation was firmly established; not only was he the idol of most jazz pianists, but it has been fairly reliably reported (although such items can sometimes be considered dubious) that his work was praised by Horowitz,

Godowski, and/or Rachmaninoff. (As for the opinions of his jazz colleagues, the largest chunk of statistics is to be gleaned from Leonard Feather's 1955 *Encyclopedia of Jazz:* of forty-six pianists who gave specific answers to a question about their "favorites" on their own instrument, thirty included Tatum's name.)

He was not exclusively a solo pianist; even while working in clubs as a single, he recorded with small bands, some of his most highly regarded work, for example, being a group of recordings made in 1941, on which he led the backing for blues singer Joe Turner on numbers like "Wee Baby Blues." And Eldridge's earliest recollection of Tatum is his jamming with horn men at a Cleveland after-hours spot called Val's Alley ("It's just too bad there weren't tape machines in those days; somebody should have taken down *those* sessions"). But Art belonged primarily to the early solo tradition of "two-handed piano players" who supplied their own rhythm with their own left hand. It was a tradition exemplified by Fats Waller, whom Tatum looked on as his basic influence. Barry Ulanov has written of a conversation in which Art insisted, "Fats, man. That's where I come from." (Waller, for his part, had immense admiration for Tatum, once stopped playing to introduce him to a night-club audience by saying: "I play piano, but God is in the house tonight.") An important part of that tradition of the earthy "big" piano men of the '20s and '30s were the "cutting contests." The first thing to do on arriving in any town was to look up the best players around and have at them. Thus, in New York in the '30s and early '40s, Tatum would head uptown for places like Reuben Harris's or the Chicken Shack (where, briefly, young Charlie Parker was a dishwasher). There, he knew, he would find men like James P. Johnson, the dean of the Harlem "stride piano" school, and Clarence Profit, and lesser-known (to the public) but scarcely secondary figures like Donald Lambert and The Beetle. Tatum's high regard for Waller actually extended to the whole stride style, elements of which could always be heard in his own driving pace. As Billy Taylor describes what he heard in the early '40s, Art was sometimes a bit slow in getting under way: "He hadn't played much stride for quite a while, but once he got warmed up . . . look out!" Taylor also recalls one particularly amazing encounter between Tatum and Clarence Profit, when both men decided to play straight melody, varying only the harmony, each improvising five or six choruses of a number at a time that way! Staying power was inevitably an important part of all such rivalries, and Tatum was apparently always proud of his stamina. Guitarist Everett Barksdale, who worked with Tatum in his

last years, had known him back in the early Ohio days. He insists
that young Art was once involved in an argument with a drummer
who felt he could keep playing longer than any pianist. They decided to battle it out, each using only one hand, and according to
Barksdale, it was five hours before the drummer quit. Tom
Tilghman claims that Tatum once battled a pianist for a full day—
"from two a.m. to two a.m."—in his back room, and he also says it
was not uncommon for Art to stay up for forty-eight hours at a
stretch, playing most of the time and taking only occasional cat-
naps. (On the other hand, when he did sleep, it was with unusual
soundness—although "you could always wake him up just by touching one of his hands.") And, of course, even if there is exaggeration in such accounts, or in Barksdale's estimate that "ten shots
and ten beers" was not an unusually heavy night's drinking for
him, the point remains that Tatum was a man regarded by his
associates as larger than life-sized, as truly capable of such feats.

It was not all a matter of bravura competition, of course.
Tilghman's bar was, from 1936, a home port for Tatum, a place
where, among other things, the nearly blind man knew every foot
and every angle well enough to move about without tension. It was
Waller, Tilghman notes, who first "coaxed" him into the spot, at a
time when just about every bar in the city was trying to persuade
him to be a regular visitor. Waller, it seems, had arrived unan-
nounced at dinner time one day, and began playing. Tilghman, not
recognizing him, and deciding that his dinner customers should be
protected from annoyances like this, tried asking Fats to stop.
When that failed, he resorted to turning on the jukebox, and
loudly. Finally Fats, on the way out, got into conversation with the
owner about the trouble he'd had "with that guy who kept playing
the juke box" and, Tilghman recalls, "we got to talking and I
admitted I hadn't known who he was, and we got pretty friendly.
He told me he liked the place, but he was going out of town, so he
was going to tell his friend to come by." The friend, Tatum, kept
coming, "because he got to know he wouldn't be bothered here.
He'd play cards here, or fall asleep in that booth over there, and
we'd kid him—you could always get his goat by calling him a *jazz*
piano player. He didn't like to be called that; said he was a *piano*
player, a *musician.*"

In 1943 came the formation of the Art Tatum Trio, with Slam
Stewart on bass and Tiny Grimes on guitar. It was a move that
seems to have been dictated by commercial considerations, adding
two showmanlike performers to the act. Both men were capable
musicians, particularly Stewart, who was far more of a driving

rhythm man and far less a clown than he was later to become, and there were even those who felt that for Tatum, no less than for any other current pianist, the newly prevalent idea of working as a trio in order to relieve the pianist of a part of the rhythmic burden was a sound one. Others, however, felt that Art, the "complete in himself" piano player, needed no such thing, and Billy Taylor (who, like virtually all modern pianists, consistently uses the trio format) sees Tatum's going along with this idea as the first instance of musical conflict and of compromise in Art's career. But, whoever had had the idea seemed fully supported by results. Tatum, playing as well as ever, became even more of a drawing card. Whether it was because of a general wartime boom, increasingly aware audiences, or the appeal of the lightning interplay between Tatum and his two colleagues, is difficult to say, but in any event Art became a very major Fifty-second Street attraction, equaled only by Billie Holiday. If there were changes in Tatum, they could be considered almost inevitable ones. His playing style became somewhat more florid in its intricacy; his personal attitude became somewhat more detached and Olympian. He remained a very warm man to those he accepted. To Taylor he was "so much like a big brother . . . I played way over my head when he was around, and it was the same way with lots of young musicians." But in place of the lusty, direct rivalries of the old-style cutting contests, there were scenes like some in Los Angeles that have been described by Taylor, who was there briefly at the same time as Tatum during the mid-'40s. "I was with Eddie South, and Art would come by the place we were working, pick me up, and take me to sessions at Ivie Anderson's and places like that." Tatum would still search out the top local man, but his procedure after that was different. "He'd know the fellow's best number, and he'd ask me to play it, to sort of bait the guy. I wouldn't know what was going on, so I'd play it. . . . Of course if I (or any of Art's boys) were getting carved, he'd just step in and take over."

Still very much in evidence was an innate politeness towards other musicians. Only to his very closest friends did he ever have anything negative to say about others, Everett Barksdale has reported; and, as Tom Tilghman has put it, "he could correct someone's mistakes without ever seeming insulting." Taylor notes that he "listened to everyone, even the worst," and he was apt to find something for himself to develop in the work of the most unlikely third-raters. There was one really bad pianist around in California, as Taylor tells it, of whom Art would do a devastating imitation. But then Art would play "straight," using touches adapted from this fellow's playing, "but most people just don't listen closely to the bad ones, so they never did catch on to what Art was doing."

By the late '40s, however, came a period that Ulanov has written of as "disillusionment, diminishing audiences, declining interest." Ulanov attributes this to an eventual awareness among critics and fans that Tatum was really not full perfection, that he had "several limitations as a pianist and musician," among them "excess of hyperbole" and "the quotations, endless interpolations of the familiar phrases of Gershwin's 'Rhapsody in Blue,' perhaps; Sousa's 'The Stars and Stripes Forever,' maybe." Actually, there had always been those who objected that Tatum's style was overly ornate, lacking in taste, more concerned with effect than content, shallow, even (an inevitable complaint against any performer with an inordinate amount of technical virtuosity) "not really jazz." There was nothing very new in what Ulanov refers to as a discovery of the late '40s, the feeling that "Art was taking himself more seriously than he should have." And there was undoubtedly some truth in this; yet on the other hand a doggedly traditionalist critic like Fred Ramsey has referred to Tatum's "easy, lilting style wholly suffused with a refreshingly humorous approach." However, Ramsey, too, wrote in his *Guide to Longplay Jazz Records* that "his tendency to display his accomplishments sometimes gets in the way of a performance."

Such negative comments, though, must be considered a minority report. The majority would go along with a musician like Barksdale, who worked alongside Tatum for the last few years of his life and stresses the "ease—no apparent effort at all" with which Art developed his "startling" ideas, the sort of seriousness that led Tatum, even in the 1950s, to work "long hours at home, by himself," and the "far out dissonances and harmonic variations, the augmented elevenths and thirteenths that others are just now beginning to get to." Barksdale's emphasis is on the awe so many musicians have felt: "He leaves you with a sense of futility. . . . What you've studied maybe years to perfect he seems able to perform with such ease" and "He'd always say he didn't 'hear' what he was going to play in advance, he'd just feel it; and since so much of what we did was extemporaneous, not routined, sometimes he'd get off on something and just leave me out in left field. . . ." To Billy Taylor, the so-called floridity came about because Tatum "heard so much. There was always a desire to fill in all the other things he could hear besides just a normal piano part. But he was basically a melodic pianist; not like some other pyrotechnic pianists: his playing was always melodic, not just exercises."

Nevertheless, it is fact that the period from about 1947 to '50 represents the one important dip in the otherwise even plane of Tatum's popularity. One theory—which has also been advanced in the cases of Eldridge, Coleman Hawkins, and other greats of the pre-modern jazz idiom—is that their confidence was actually shaken by the fact that supposedly aware and opinion-forming writers, as well as much of the jazz public, were paying attention to nothing except bop and its variously named successor forms. Everything else was being down-graded; there was no room for what it later became fashionable to refer to favorably as "mainstream" jazz.

One story belonging to this period tells of a duel that never came off, but which might conceivably have been a basic test case. Bud Powell, Tatum, and Billy Taylor were all on the same bill at Birdland, and Taylor tells of an overheard conversation between the other two. (It should be obvious by now that Taylor's views and recollections were vitally helpful in the preparation of this chapter.) Billy recalls that Powell, "who was pretty juiced," said in effect that Tatum wasn't *that* great, that he didn't do as much as it was claimed he did. Unquestionably Tatum could scent the prospect of the sort of contest he loved so well. "I won't take you on now," he said, "but tomorrow come in sober and anything you play with your right hand I'll play with my left." Powell was in early the next night, practicing with his left (admittedly the weaker) hand in anticipation of a two-handed battle, but the duel never took place. Actually there was great mutual admiration, and it is not far-fetched at all to suggest that a lot of Art can be heard in Powell's solo work, such as "Over the Rainbow."

By 1950, Art was back up near the top again. There was club work and there were concert tours; he recorded for promoter Norman Granz, who issued eleven long-play records forthrightly titled *The Genius of Art Tatum*. But the years of full living were catching up with him; the all-night sessions and the prodigious drinking were taking their toll. Everett Barksdale went with him to Washington, D.C., in 1953, for a check-up by a doctor who was a long-standing friend of Art's. Although Tatum was told nothing specific, it was made clear to Barksdale that the end was just a matter of time. The pianist must have been aware that all was far from well with him, though, for Barksdale notes that a joint three-day binge following a Birdland engagement in 1954 was the very last time he saw Tatum drink.

The clearest indications, though, were in his playing, which normally was of impeccable accuracy. "He's absolutely infallible," Barksdale once told a British interviewer. "With a man like that there's no such thing as a mistake. The only time I ever heard him goof was when the piano was at fault—a mechanical flaw." And Tatum had once suggested to Taylor that it was helpful to practice deliberately making mistakes, "to see how quickly you can recover." Tatum himself, Billy notes, could be playing arpeggios at great speed, hit a wrong note ("playing that fast, you're past it as soon as you hit it"), and nevertheless make so swift a recovery that the flaw couldn't be detected and thus, in effect, couldn't really be considered a mistake. Yet in the *Genius* set, recorded in 1953, Billy noted, to his surprise, places where he could actually hear Tatum falter.

The first time Barksdale heard him falter was also the last. It was during their final engagement, although it was supposed to be the middle of a tour. One night in mid-October of 1956, Tatum was almost too tired to continue after the second set, and the guitarist knew then that the end was near. Tatum returned to his Los Angeles home, "to rest for a while," telling Barksdale he would be in touch with him shortly as to when they would resume. No such word ever came. On November fourth, Tatum was rushed to a hospital. Six days later he was dead. The cause of death was uremia, a kidney ailment.

There were many sincere tributes from musicians, but most seemed generalized, inevitably rather standard stuff. The sorrow and the respect were genuine enough, but the trouble is that once past the statements about his having been a great pianist of far-reaching influence (and in how many different ways can that possibly be said?), you've covered all that most people knew. It is surprising that a musician of his stature was scarcely ever interviewed; but it is not so surprising, at that, when the musician was Art Tatum. He would probably not have enjoyed having his personality pieced together as it has been done here. He might have enjoyed the fact that, since the Tatum story must be assembled from the not always mutually consistent, quite subjective views of associates and friends, there are unreconcilable loose ends. More than one source, for example, has said that he was a tight man with money. Yet Tom Tilghman has said that "no one could buy Art a drink without his buying another right back"; Roy Eldridge recalls Art flashing a five-hundred-dollar bill, the first time Roy had seen a bill that large; and Tilghman tells of his pressing a thousand dollars on a once-well-off man who had befriended him when he first hit New York. There is, from one source, a story of his reluctance to be helpful to white musicians who asked how he played something (unless it were a close friend, like Nat Jaffe, he might say, "Why should I show him my stuff so he can go use it at a place I can't get to play at?"). But from another source comes vehement denial that color, rather than talent, was ever a consideration with him.

However, although there are areas of contradiction, the pattern as a whole seems to be knowable. Two final points can help pin it down. Once, rather late in his life, he was told of an operation that might improve his sight considerably but might also, if it were unsuccessful, cost him the small percentage of sight he did have. He was afraid to try it: he would not risk being literally and entirely a blind man. And, although it remained possible for him almost always to find a place to play as long after hours as he wished, he resented the passing of the era in which those high-spirited but deadly serious "cutting contests" were the rule. They were both the symbol and the reality of the world he wanted and needed: the world in which Art Tatum, a winning pinochle player and a truly awe-inspiring piano player and a man with good, chosen friends, need never be alone or entirely in the dark.

Charlie Parker
1956

Charlie Parker died quietly, shortly before nine o'clock on the evening of March 12, 1955, having been seriously ill for only three days. The doctor attending him had seen him no more than a half hour earlier and had expressed the opinion that he was much improved; and Parker was propped up in an armchair watching television when death came. He was not yet thirty-five years old, but considering that he had led a physically punishing life and had a poor medical history, it was not notably surprising that he should die so young. Described this way, then, it was the sort of death whose circumstances must have been duplicated countless times.

But it must also be noted that this man was very probably the most significant jazz figure of his time, that he died in the New York apartment of a wealthy and titled woman, that his body lay unclaimed in the morgue for two days, that the precise cause of death is still open to argument. With such additions, the passing of the man known as "Bird" (a nickname of at least three supposed derivations and no vital significance, but consistently used), can be seen as mysterious or even sinister, as part of a contradictory, colorful, seething legend about a foredoomed folk-hero.

Actually, there are rather unsensational explanations for most of the elements of "mystery" associated with Parker's death, but the really important point may be that most people have automatically elected to accept at face value the assumption—and this is true with anecdotes about his life as well as his death—that the weirder stories were the truer ones. There is no question that Bird is going to be one of the larger-scale jazz legends; he was well on his way to that status long before he died. It cannot be denied that Parker himself, by his attitudes and by many of his quite verifiably non-standard activities, did much to help create and build the legend. But it is equally undeniable that a great many people (including many who knew him closely, in addition to those who merely knew *of* him as a public figure) seem to have shown a positive *desire* to turn him into legend as quickly as possible. In part, this tendency can be seen as no more than the very familiar urge to romanticize the "artist." Bird is just one, and certainly not the last, of a very long line of writers, painters, musicians, and what-have-you to be quickly converted into myth. But it may also be that it is more comfortable to accept Parker as fiction, rather than as reality. It is not without importance that at this writing there are at least four people or sets of people reported at work on books about Bird and that, of the four, the only one that has been completed is a novel! (Its author is Ross Russell, who in the 1940s operated the independent jazz label, Dial, for which several of Parker's first important recordings were made. Russell, on the other hand, is today reluctant to reinvolve himself emotionally with the facts by discussing such rather strained circumstances as Bird's committal to Camarillo State Hospital in 1946, immediately following a Dial recording session in Los Angeles. For the record, the other three Parker works currently in progress are by his last wife, Chan, with a collaborator; by a musician-turned-writer friend who also helped handle Bird's business affairs in his last years; and, jointly with a professional writer, by a New York librarian who has doubled as a jazz night-club operator and promoted a number of public "jam sessions" that were among Parker's last appearances.)

The diversity of approaches to the man's life that can be assumed as forthcoming from such a list of potential authors is a fair clue to the diversity of opinion, fact, and pseudo-fact that currently exists about Bird. There is, by now, little argument about his position in jazz history: he was a (very possibly *the*) major force in the creation of current modern-jazz forms; his approach, his tone, insofar as possible his musical ideas have been followed, adopted, understood, imitated, aped, unintentionally parodied and misunderstood by performers on all manner of jazz instruments in a way that far transcends any cliché about "the sincerest form of flattery." Musically, there is near unanimity. But concerning the man, it is something else again.

The major problem faced by any researcher into Parker lore is a problem of overabundance. It is almost literally true that everyone involved with modern jazz in the '40s and thereafter feels, whether justifiably or not, that he really "knew" Bird and is entitled to make definitive, strongly felt statements. Asked for suggestions as to helpful subjects for interview, one musician, who actually did know Parker well, came up with a list of twenty-two names almost without pausing for breath, and then apologized that with a little thought he could make the list much longer. And, no matter how many or how few sources are actually turned to, there is such a welter of conflicting report and reaction that it hardly seems possible that everyone is discussing the same man. Of course, to a great extent there is truth in that contradiction: few men are fully consistent; the sensitive creative artist is apt to be far less so than most and far more inclined to be reshaped over and over again by subjective pulls; and Parker, addicted to narcotics for a substantial portion of his life, could easily be considered to have been several men.

Do you accept French jazz critic Charles Delaunay's impression of him as a sort of Rousseau-ian Noble Savage: "a big, dreaming child; a natural inspired force . . . good-natured, shy and quite boyish, (with) curiously juvenile thoughts?" Or do you turn to other writers who have been impressed with the "searching clarity" of his comments on music and have quoted him as discussing with considerable insight why Bartok had become his favorite composer or the possible similarities of aim between his own work and Hindemith's? How much attention do you pay to friends' reports on how intelligently he could discuss philosophy or science? What valuation do you place on Chan Parker's conclusions that "he was very mature and wise about the world and life; just immature about himself," and that "Bird was a very gentle man, although he hid it much of the time"? There are stories of his having been crudely cruel and openly contemptuous towards musicians he considered not up to his standards; but there are other stories to balance against those. Pianist Randy Weston recalls a night in the late 1940s—he was not yet even a professional and Bird had heard him play only once—when he was literally snatched up from the bar at one New York club, hustled over to another on Fifty-second Street ("where, of course, they treated Bird like a god when he walked in") and installed on the bandstand with Parker for almost an hour of playing with the band—"the most wonderful thing that could have happened to me." And Bird's close friend, alto player and arranger Gigi Gryce, insists that his awareness of music was so strong that he could "hear right *through* to something good" in the most unlikely places. "We might be walking along and pass someplace with a really terrible rock and roll band, for instance, and he'd stop and say 'Listen to what that bass player's doing,' when I could hardly even hear the bass. And then he might go inside and play with that band and try to teach them things."

There are stories that can't be ignored of his borrowing money and even instruments and never returning them ("You had to pay your dues with Bird"), but Gryce, who says simply, "I lent him my horn plenty of times and always got it back," can tell of Parker's visiting him in Boston with a little money in his pocket, finding a bar in the "really poor" part of town and spending all he had on whipping up an impromptu party for the patrons there. "Of course, then he'd have to find someone to lend him the money to get back home. . . ."

Doris Parker, who met him in 1945 (when his impact both on musicians and on the jazz-listening public was at its first high point) and thus was with him both during that "up" period and the extreme "down" period that followed it rather closely, expresses deep, hurt surprise at a number of prevalent attitudes and stories. She is an admittedly prejudiced source ("To me he was Charlie, not 'Bird,' not the fantastic character . . . but the guy I loved . . . gentle, soft-spoken, withdrawn") but presumably not interested in whitewashing his memory ("Really, he did so many things that were bad, they don't need to manufacture any"). Commenting on an article in one of the shock-value men's magazines, a piece that claimed in reasonably lurid, if non-specific, anonymous-quote detail that Parker "may have had the most advanced case of satyriasis ever known," Doris has remarked: "This I find very hard to believe. For long periods of time I'd be with him twenty-four hours a day. . . . At no time did I know Charlie to be vulgar about sex . . . and I can't believe he could ever change so completely." She similarly discounts stories about his inventing "new" ways of drug-taking: "Let's not let anyone kid about that. He didn't invent addiction—everything he did has been done many times before, even the destruction."

If the stories fail to balance, there is at least little difficulty in setting forth the basic facts of Parker's life (although there is some clouding at both ends). He was born in Kansas City, Kansas, and brought up in the larger city of the same name across the river in Missouri. The usually accepted birthdate is August 29, 1920. There has been some claim that he must have been born earlier (trumpeter Harold Baker has been quoted as saying he recalls Bird playing with a Kansas City band in about 1931), but Doris reports that his mother verified the 1920 date. His mother bought him an alto saxophone when he was about eleven. He subsequently told interviewers that he had become interested in this instrument by hearing Rudy Vallee on the radio, but it's questionable that this should be taken seriously, particularly since it later seemed important to him to stress that he was not influenced by any of the noted horn players of his youth, Lester Young in particular. Parker has also spoken of taking up the baritone horn in high school because "it was loud and boisterous and dominated the band so much the judges could scarcely ignore it" in awarding prizes, another comment that can be taken as indicating more about Bird's later cynicism than about early motivations.

At about age fifteen he left school and decided to take up music professionally. As much as has ever been stated about his reasons was set forth in a 1949 *Down Beat* interview, in which he noted the necessity of earning a living and that music "seemed easy, looked glamorous, and there was nothing else around." But it doesn't call for much guesswork to add to this another reason, one that can be equated with his mother's motives in so readily buying a saxophone for an eleven-year-old presumable Rudy Vallee fan. This was Missouri; as in the Deep South, then and earlier, a great many Negro parents were more than willing to encourage any musical leanings in their children: however dubious its moral reputation, at least the entertainment business was one of the very few open avenues leading to other than menial jobs.

But if music "seemed easy" to young Parker, that decidedly was a wrong impression. It is clear that he was not much of a musician at the start. Bassist Gene Ramey, who came to know Parker very well in later years, has written that when he first met Bird, "he was barely fourteen years old (and) wasn't doing anything, musically speaking." Ramey wrote of one early humiliation when Parker began to play during a jam session with members of Count Basie's band. "Jo Jones, . . . as an expression of his feeling, took his cymbal off and threw it almost the complete distance of the room. . . . Bird just packed up his horn and walked out." Parker himself has told of a similar incident at the High Hat club when "I tried doing double tempo on "Body and Soul." Everybody fell out laughing. I went home and cried and didn't play again for three months."

Parker's main reaction to all this, according to Ramey and others, was a "just you wait and see" kind of determination. Bird has noted that he had first seriously learned to read music at about this time, and Ramey has written of the "unbelievable" transformation that came about during his sixteenth summer, which was spent at a summer resort with George E. Lee's band, where a guitarist named Efferge Ware ("a great chord specialist, although he did no solo work") educated him on "the cycles—the relationship of the chords and how to weave melodies into them. . . . After which, of course, Bird expanded on his own. . . . After this sudden development in his style, Bird began to get lots of work."

There is a theory that Parker was a "natural genius." Gigi Gryce, for example, believes that he just "happened" to take up music, and would have made an important mark in any field. ("If he had become a plumber, I believe he would have been a great one.") In support of this, there is his late enthusiasm for painting. (I have seen an impressive sketch of his friend Baroness Nica Koenigswarter and have been reliably informed of highly interesting, more ambitious work.) The accounts of his rough start in music might seem to weaken this natural-genius theory, but under the circumstances perhaps the wonder is not that Parker did not play better, but that he played at all well. He lacked any sort of formative jazz background: he had heard little if anything of the music of early jazz greats; it seems clear that the swing of the mid-'30s meant little to him musically; and his immediate reaction to the heavily vibrato-filled style of just about all jazz saxophonists of the time was simply, "I didn't like it." In addition, he had been introduced to narcotics almost as soon as to music. The accounts vary, but whether it was "an actor friend (who) told me about a new kick," or older musicians, or "a stranger in a washroom," the fact is that, by 1935, he was firmly addicted. Bird's own statement to writer Leonard Feather was that "It all came from being introduced to night life too early. When you're not mature enough to know what's happening—well—you goof." Perhaps that doesn't really say it *all,* but there seems no need to get overly devious about a sensitive fifteen-year-old, working as a musician in the heart of Kansas City (then in its Pendergast heyday and probably the most wide-open town of all), trying to be as hard a guy as the next and accepting heroin as part of the "glamor" of it all. Very little is known about Bird's childhood. (Doris Parker, denying that he was particularly "closemouthed" about his youth, makes the point that "he didn't have much youth to talk about. What can you say about being 'hooked' at fifteen? That rather limits the conversation.") It does seem reasonable to take the known teenage circumstances and add to them whatever you care to accept of the sexual-appetite stories and also his later strongly demonstrative affection for children—his own or those of friends—and conclude that he was looking for a warmth and acceptance he had been unable to find in childhood. Chan Parker has been quoted as saying, "He had been hurt early and he had been hurt bad. He was cynical sometimes as a result, but he was also sentimental. When he came home, whether he had much money or barely any, he'd bring presents for the kids."

As for the practical problems of addiction, Parker later commented forcefully that "any musician who says he is playing better either on tea, the needle, or when he is juiced, is a plain straight liar." For a Bird who was just learning his trade, this must have been true many times over.

Nevertheless, he was developing as a musician, accepted by that time at the plentiful jam sessions, and working briefly with Jay McShann's band, a top local group. Then came a now-cloudy unpleasantness involving his refusal to pay a cab fare. Apparently his mother refused to help him out, and he spent twenty-two days in jail, after which he abruptly left town—leaving his horn behind. One story places him briefly in Chicago in 1938, where (as singer Billy Eckstine has told it) he walked into the Club 65 during a "breakfast dance" and sat in, using a borrowed horn and looking "like he just got off a freight car, . . . but playing like you never heard." A short time later he was in New York, still without an instrument. For three months he was a nine-dollars-a-week-and-meals dishwasher at a Harlem after-hours spot; then he just "bummed around awhile." He had been in town eight months when some by-now-anonymous musicians bought him a horn (presumably after hearing what he could do on a borrowed alto at some session); shortly thereafter he was hired at Clark Monroe's Uptown House, soon to become known as one of the key breeding grounds for the new jazz.

This was in 1939, which seems to have been the year in which things really began to jell. On one subsequent occasion (during a *Down Beat* interview ten years later) he was inclined—or induced—to pin it down to a specific month (December 1939) and place (the back room of a Harlem chili house, where he was jamming with a guitarist named Biddy Fleet). Bored with "the stereotyped changes being used then," Parker is quoted as thinking "there's bound to be something else. . . . I could hear it sometimes, but I couldn't play it." Then, while playing "Cherokee," "Charlie suddenly found that by using higher intervals of a chord as a melody line and backing them with appropriately related changes, he could play this thing he had been 'hearing' . . . and bop was born."

This somewhat technical version is a good deal more apocalyptic and less plausible than the way Bird told it on other occasions, when it was merely that he used to "hang around with Fleet at . . . spots uptown" and "we'd play around with flatted fifths" and the like. But both ways of putting it have their merits. The assumption that Parker's new approach came about gradually jibes with accounts that trace at least some elements of his eventual style back to his Kansas City days. Both Jo Jones and Ben Webster have mentioned an alto player named Buster Smith, who played with Bennie Moten and then with Count Basie's earliest band, as being (in Webster's words) "the only man I ever heard to whom you could attribute anything Bird ever did." Jones has flatly called Smith "Charlie Parker's musical father." Doris Parker recalls Bird telling her of "a tenor (?) player who influenced him greatly" at the start, and some of Bird's friends have cited mention of "a guy who played alto in an old band." Unquestionably, Parker's "modernism" did not suddenly spring into full-blown life one fine day; but on the other hand, the *Down Beat* sudden-flash account does have the virtue of dramatically indicating that, by the end of 1939, Parker had found himself. For by early 1940 he had returned to Kansas City and rejoined Jay McShann; and his sound on his first records with McShann, as well as stories of how he was a leading force in the band, make it clear that he had come a long way since he ran home and cried in 1935.

It does seem strange that Bird found himself during a period of rootless wandering and odd jobs, not even owning a horn most of the time, but it is simply a fact that must be accepted. It must also be kept in mind that he was certainly on narcotics at this time, that this was part of a period in which, as he once put it, he was "always on a panic." Pain, poverty and loneliness were among the ingredients— whether because of them, in spite of them, or both, Charlie Parker was about to become a focal point of the new jazz forms that were just beginning to take shape.

For many reasons, among them various personal jealousies and some musicians' tendency to supply interviewers with answers they think are the ones wanted, regardless of accuracy, the precise beginning of the music first known as "be-bop" will most probably always be shrouded in confusion, contradiction, and double-talk. It was not necessarily recognized by the participants as a glamorous period of creativity: as Thelonious Monk puts it, "Nobody was sitting there trying to make up something new on purpose. The job at Minton's was a job we were playing, that's all." But at Minton's Playhouse, the number-one proving ground for bop, the job was at least one where men could play as they pleased, with a sympathetic club

manager (ex-band leader Teddy Hill) and a growing crowd of interested musicians eager to listen or to sit in. There, and at Monroe's
and at other side-street Harlem spots, Monk could play as he had
always wanted to; drummer Kenny Clarke, another member of the
Minton's band, could work on the ideas that had been frowned on
when he was with Hill's band; Dizzy Gillespie and guitarist Charlie
Christian and so many others could come by. (Monk does not recall
Parker having been there at the very start, nor that there was any
single memorable moment when he first appeared; but he does say
that Bird's ability and authority were immediately accepted as exciting and important additions.) Their various new concepts were similar enough to merge—or perhaps it was something like the classic
stories of inventors separately, but almost simultaneously, achieving identical results. Clarke has been quoted on this subject of
mutuality, noting that he, Monk, and Gillespie would often end up
at Monroe's after Minton's closed for the night: Bird had left the
limited confines of McShann's rather routine Kansas City riff-and-
blues outfit and returned to New York, and "we went to listen to
Bird," although at first it was "for no other reason than that he
sounded like Pres." ("Pres"—Lester Young—was perhaps the only
no-vibrato sax man before Parker, and Bird had spoken of admiring
his "clean and beautiful" sound, although disclaiming any influence
from Young's jazz ideas, which "ran on differently" than his own.)
But they found, Clarke added, that Bird also had something new to
offer: "Things we'd never heard before—rhythmically and harmoni-
cally," and it aroused the interest of Dizzy and Monk because they
"were working along the same lines" (my italics—O.K.).

Earl Hines's band was becoming a home for several members of
the bop clique; men like Eckstine and Gillespie helped persuade
Hines to hire Parker. The only opening was on tenor, so Bird
played that instrument exclusively during the ten months of 1943
he spent with Hines. But, although there is a story that Ben Webster was moved to open admiration the first time he heard him,
Bird was never at home with the tenor; and when he joined Billy
Eckstine's big band in 1944, as one of several ex-Hines men involved in that musically ambitious but short-lived orchestra, he
was back on alto for good.

After 1944 bop broke out into the open, beginning its rather
brief, hectic, and heavily publicized period of more-or-less acceptance by the public. Parker was making his first important records
with small groups for the small jazz labels and no one since Louis
Armstrong's early heyday had ever had so overwhelming an impact on his fellow musicians. Parker was working on Fifty-second

Street, first with Dizzy and then heading a group that included eighteen-year-old Miles Davis. He was, everyone around him agreed, playing wonderfully well. He was also living hard; but so were most of his coworkers, and so have most jazzmen of most eras, particularly when times are good for them and the clubs are crowded. When you spend each night working hard at playing what you want, when your work is being enthusiastically received, and when your setting is a place that does nothing but serve drinks all night long—well, the atmosphere is hardly conducive to sedate living, or to rationing either your emotions or your appetites. There are stories of eccentric behavior (with the Hines band he had once missed a theatre show because he arrived early and was asleep under the bandstand throughout the performance), and it can be said with hindsight that Bird was close to a breakdown late in 1945 when he went to Los Angeles with a group that included Gillespie and vibist Milt Jackson. But the unanswerable question is whether he would have gone over the line at that time if Los Angeles had not turned out to be a terrible place to play. "Worst of all," Parker told Leonard Feather in an interview a few years later, "was that nobody understood our kind of music out on the Coast," in sharp and bitter contrast to the Eastern scene, where he and Dizzy were the newest of idols. And through it all there was the narcotics habit, which among other things is expensive, so that even when he was working regularly, he was painfully unable to "buy good clothes or a place to live."

It all came to a head on the night of July 29, 1946. At a record session for Ross Russell's Dial label, Bird, despite having drunk "a quart of whiskey to make the date," was beset by uncontrollable muscle tics. He cut only two numbers, one of them an almost incoherent "Lover Man." (Parker's later comment was: "Lover Man" should be stomped into the ground," but it was released, and an embarrassing number of listeners didn't seem to know enough to dislike it.) Later that night he broke down completely, was arrested and then committed to Camarillo State Hospital. He was released seven months later, seemingly quite recovered: he was playing well on records made in February 1946. There are contradictory details concerning his release; although he worked for Dial again, there was some feeling that Russell had taken advantage of him by insisting that he sign a recording contract before agreeing to help gain his release, although, according to Doris's account, they later determined that he could have been released, and even sent back to New York by the state of California, without outside aid.

In any event, the next few years were successful and seemingly happy and stable, although by taking a long hindsight view again it is possible to say that the road was leading down towards its end. Bird was in demand at New York clubs, and was a big enough name to make it a commercially appealing idea for a club that opened in 1950 to be called "Birdland." He was in Paris and the Scandinavian countries in 1949 and '50, was featured on several of promoter Norman Granz's "Jazz at the Philharmonic" tours, and eventually recorded (for Granz's Clef label) an album with a rich string background. This, Doris Parker says, "had been one of Charlie's pet dreams . . . for so long."

But the with-strings recordings can be taken as marking another turning point. Although some have found these selections, especially a version of "Just Friends," among his most moving work, others considered them a sign that he was going "commercial"—always the most insulting word in jazz.

Bird had for some time been talking about the potentialities of the "variety of coloration" and "new sound combinations" offered by strings and other primarily symphonic instruments, and several friends were aware that he was deeply disturbed by the negative reactions. He went ahead with plans for a tour with a string group, but it was unsuccessful. Entering the '50s, he was moving into a period of personal confusion and erratic behavior. Bookers and club owners were growing impatient with his unreliability; there was a falling out with the management of Birdland (in his last years he played in "his" club only twice; both times with disastrous results). He apparently was fighting to keep "straight" as far as narcotics were concerned, but there are conflicting reports as to how successful he was. One prevalent self-cure among musician addicts has been to drink heavily as a sort of substitute (what medical authorities might say about the effectiveness of this is another matter), and it is a fact that Parker drank more heavily at this time than ever before, to the point where he was hospitalized by a serious ulcer attack. For the first time (except for the actual breakdown in 1946) his physical condition was affecting his playing, and although he was still vastly appreciated and widely copied by musicians, many of them placed him in a sort of *emeritus* status that didn't sit at all well with him.

Bird had left Doris, and Chan had borne him two children. Early in 1954, the girl, Pree, died of pneumonia. Many people consider this tragedy to have been the real finisher. Leonard Feather has called the next few months a "pattern of apparently intentional self-destruction." The immediate culmination came in September of that year, when he was booked into Birdland with a string group. The strings began playing one tune; Bird began on an entirely different one, screamed wildly at the musicians, and fired them on the spot. Later that night he drink iodine in an apparent suicide attempt.

There was one last attempt at regeneration, sparked by Chan. She rented a house in Bucks County, Pennsylvania; Bird attempted to stop drinking and for a while actually commuted to New York, over an hour away, almost daily for sessions with a psychiatrist. But this rather demanding routine didn't last too long. He went back to work, usually as a "single," backed by a local rhythm section. It was an oddly unreal existence; Baroness Nica Koenigswarter (in whose apartment he was to die), who came to know him well during his final months, insists that he was not moody—except when Pree was mentioned—but was for the most part quite cheerful, warm, and witty, But she also notes that he told her, "I've been dead for four years." And there were times when he would ride the subways all night long, alone.

There was no question but that he had deteriorated badly. Frank Sandiford, a Chicago writer who was a close friend for several years, tells of a night at The Beehive in Chicago, "just before he left . . . to go back East and die."

"It began with the owner begging me to go to the room behind the bar to get Charlie to go on the stand. It was a small room used to store cases of beer and other things. . . . Bird met me at the door by throwing his arms around me as though I were the only person left in the world to whom to plead for rest. He couldn't go on, he said. Didn't want to, was in no condition. He looked it. The house was packed. I reminded him that there were many people out there who had come just to hear him play. I opened the door and . . . he glared at them. 'They just came out here to see the world's most famous junky,' he grumbled. I will always feel guilty about this, but I did get him to get up and face the crowd. He couldn't play. All he did was to make a few awful bleating sounds . . . spilling out his disgust, his fears, his frustrations. He made a pitiful figure. . . . He was a beaten man and he knew it. That made it most painful."

Birdland tried him again, on March 4, 1955, but someone misguidedly arranged to have his group include pianist Bud Powell, who was far from fully recovered from his own mental illness. It was, according to eyewitnesses, a thoroughly painful experience, with a full-scale verbal battle between Bird and Bud on the bandstand the first night.

The following Wednesday, just before he was to leave for a

Boston engagement, Parker stopped at the Baroness Koenigswarter's apartment. While there he had a bad coughing spell that
brought up blood and left him breathing with difficulty. The baroness called a doctor, who asked a few briskly routine questions
(including "Do you drink?," to which Parker answered: "Sometimes I have a sherry before dinner") and recommended hospital-
ization. Bird refused insistently, and the baroness agreed to keep
him there; she and her daughter could nurse him. He was very
weak for two days, tried to eat only a few canned peaches during
that time, couldn't retain even that, but drank great quantities of
water from a jug at his bedside. He remained very alert, however.
The doctor knew, if somewhat unclearly, who he was, and there
was much discussion as to which of Bird's records would be most
suitable to play first for the doctor. (Parker finally decided on
"April in Paris," from the with-strings album.) He also talked,
near the end, about the future: about forming a large new band
"that would knock them all dead." "On that third day," Nica
Koenigswarter says, "he seemed much better; then he died." (He
died while watching the Dorsey Brothers' television program; he
had always admired the Dorseys as technicians.) As the baroness
recounts it, the doctor was called three minutes later; he immediately sent for the medical examiner; and thereafter it was out of
her hands. She says she was most anxious that Chan not learn of
Bird's death from the radio or newspapers, but it was more than a
day later before she could locate Chan. (Bird had refused to tell
her Chan's whereabouts, saying that he didn't want her or anyone
else to know where he was until he was better.)

As for the cause of death: the baroness knew of no heart attack
or pneumonia, which were mentioned by most newspaper accounts, and says that the doctor specified ulcers and cirrhosis of the
liver. Doris Parker, on the other hand, says, "The district attorney
told me they did a very thorough autopsy on Charlie and he died
from lobar pneumonia and nothing else was mentioned." This
mystery may never be fully clarified, but there is no doubt that it
can be said, without excessive sentimentality, that Charlie Parker,
like more than a few others before him, died of being a naked,
inevitably unadjustable genius.

"Genius" has become a rather cheapened word in our times, but
it tends to have its old, formal dignity when musicians talk about
Bird. What might be called the omnipresence of music in his life is
something on which several have commented. Gene Ramey has
been quoted as saying, "Everything had a musical significance for
him. He'd hear dogs barking, for instance, and he would say it was

a conversation and . . . he would have something to play that
would portray that thought to us." Similarly, Gigi Gryce has noted
his ability to "augment anything. You might be humming a couple
of bars of something, without thinking about it, and in a couple of
minutes he'd be giving it back to you so changed and developed
you wouldn't even recognize it."

Yet, like many artists to whom creativity is, at least in part, a
sort of natural function, he tended to minimize his own abilities.
This might have been simply a not-uncommon urge toward perfection. "Basically, he was never satisfied with what he did," Doris
has said. "There wasn't a record he didn't think could have been
better." And Bird himself once answered a question as to what
he'd recommend to anyone wanting to buy his three best records
by saying, "Tell him to keep his money." Gryce, however, feels
that he was bothered by his lack of formal training, that he
thought, incorrectly, that the fact that he could write and arrange
so readily without schooling did not just mean that it came easily to
him, but rather than he wasn't doing it as well as he might. Yet,
Gryce notes, he had a phenomenal ability to read, and even to
transpose, music at sight.

The extent to which he was disturbed by imitators, or made
unhappy by varying degrees of non-acceptance by the public, is
hard to define and obviously was itself quite variable. Gryce believes that part of the unhappiness of his last years stemmed from a
feeling of "What's the use? People didn't really dig him," and there
is agreement that he felt his "disciples" were overdoing it to the
point of stultifying their own creative potentials.

But any opinions about Parker must be looked at with an understanding that, to an amazing extent, people saw in him what they
wanted to see. Take even so apparently simple a matter as whether
he was more, or less, reliable during his best periods. Doris says,
"When Charlie was on his feet, he made time" (i.e., showed up on
time for engagements). But Gigi feels that he was simply unable to
adjust to business routine—"he wanted to create like a painter,
when he wanted to; not like a commercial artist working on
schedule"—and that, when he was feeling best, he was most apt to
get wound up in a session someplace and just neglect to show up
for work.

Of one thing there can be little doubt: he had given up the fight
towards the end. He spoke often about his death as close and
inevitable ("I'm just a husk," he told Nica Koenigswarter); and in
1954 he sent Doris a poem, which he may have written but more
probably had copied down (judging from the rather ornate style),

and which he seems to have considered fitting. In part it sets forth a credo that might easily have been his own ("Hear the words! Not the doctrine. Hear the speech! Not the meaning. . . . Don't look at the sun! Feel it!") and in part is concerned with dying ("death is an imminent thing"), though also with hope ("My fire is unquenchable"). There can also be little doubt that he was a tortured man, and there are several who emphasize the loneliness. One friend of the last years, Chips Bayen, never thought it unusual that he had long talks with Bird, and discovered only after his death that most people considered it something unique. Gigi Gryce puts the blame on Bird's position of eminence: "The pressure of being on a pedestal, which he didn't like at all." Gigi feels that he wanted and needed companionship, but that many musicians were wary of approaching him on a personal level: "People wouldn't talk to him because they didn't know what to say—but, really, all they had to do was say 'Hello.' "

Although so many writers of fiction have turned the concept of the artist as a soul in torment into something approaching a stereotype, it still seems the clearest way to sum up this man. The basic paradox must be that the same qualities that made him play as he did made him unable to find "normal" happiness and acceptance. Frank Sandiford calls him "a man of violently opposing urges: one towards greatness . . . the other towards defeat." In a letter, Sandiford tells of seeing him at his worst: ". . . when he would beg dimes and quarters, anything, from those that came to hear him play . . . sweaty and looking sick and tired [and trying] to keep his words together so as to make some sense. There were times when I would see him sneer, trying hard to believe in the cynical statements he made, when I knew he made them only to keep pain at a safer distance." This is a friend speaking, of course, and perhaps being considerably more tolerant than, say, someone at whom the cynicism was directed or from whom the money was begged. But at the very least a man is entitled to have a friend speak the final words. And there is another portion of Sandiford's letter that seems a suitable epitaph for Bird (and probably for more than one other musician whose living presence was sometimes less than pleasant for those who knew and worked with him):

"He was an artist who paid a great price to be able to get out of himself some of the things that most disturbed him. He might have cheated a little, he might have stolen from some, he might have hurt many. But he cheated, stole and hurt himself more than anybody. And he did give us something far more wonderful than he took from us."

3

Transition

It is never easy to understand exactly how tastes and attitudes about any art form can undergo drastic change. Even though I recognize, as an empirical fact, that over the years there has been more than one major alteration in the way I hear jazz, I still have trouble with *why* such changes in me have taken place. I'm also aware that, almost without exception, the other producers who took part in the heavy modern-jazz creativity of the '50s and '60s also had begun as firm traditionalists and then experienced a definite metamorphosis—which must mean *something*.

One key element surely is a dissatisfaction with the older forms, and their lessening ability to remain fresh and valid. That seems to be what I was complaining about as far back as 1948, in a *Record Changer* editorial that dared to be vehemently negative about a Louis Armstrong performance. (In that same early issue there appeared my first positive thoughts about Thelonious Monk—reprinted in the next chapter. Obviously, a seed had somehow been sown.)

Eight years later, I was a very different man, and had the rare opportunity to be specific about it, in a piece written for a monthly jazz section that ran in the *Saturday Review* back then. By way of intriguing coincidence: that section regularly featured capsule album reviews by Whitney Balliett. On the page facing my confessional article was Whitney's report on the second Monk album produced by me, "The Unique Thelonious Monk." He found it "subtle, beautiful" and "an essential record." Confirmation, apparently, that I had made my transition.

A Louis Armstrong Review
1948

The Record Changer does not ordinarily concern itself with reviews of specific concerts and night club or theater shows. Performances of that sort are generally only of timely interest and forgotten long before any review by us could get into print. But a recent stage show at a New York movie theater has caused us to break this rule. Sadly, it is not to shout anyone's praises that we do this, but rather to point out with some anger the unmistakable signs of commercialism and tawdriness in a most unlikely and unseemly place—the band with which Louis Armstrong is now touring the country.

This is a band that includes Jack Teagarden, Earl Hines, Barney Bigard, Sid Catlett, Dick Carey and Arvell Shaw. Presumably so many talented musicians must produce pretty good jazz at times when they play "concerts," but their most recent New York appearance, as the feature act of a Roxy Theater stage "presentation," found them at a shockingly low ebb. It is obvious that after all their years in the business, these men would find it hard to be inspired three times daily by a movie theater audience, but the least that could be demanded of them, if they were bored, was that they play it straight and get it over with.

Instead, what you got (after sitting through the chorus line, the tap dancer, the juggler, the ventriloquist) was a pointless humor spiel by WOV's disc jockey, Fred Robbins, who dragged in the names of his principal radio sponsors and then went into one of those gooey routines about the Only Real American Cultural Musical Contribution ("He didn't study singing in Milan; he learned it in a newsboys' quartet in New Orleans").

Then on came the band, with Louis in a white suit. They have standard small-band instrumentation, except that the absence of a guitar is made up for by the inclusion of two pianos—snow-white Steinways. It's hard to figure out a reason for this (perhaps they weren't able to break Carey's contract when Hines joined the tour, who knows?), but on the night we heard them, the two together didn't play enough piano for one man and didn't have much success in staying with each other.

The program ran like this: A bored, jumpy, band version of "Muskrat Ramble." A fluid, empty solo by Bigard that started as "Tea for Two" and ended sounding for all the world like Artie Shaw's "Concerto for Clarinet," except that it ended in a tasteless lower register instead of a tasteless upper. There was a ghastly

vocal by a very plump girl named Velma Middleton, after which
Louis joined her in a vulgar, mugging duet of "That's My Desire."
When you consider that Frankie Laine is a bad imitation of Armstrong, a bad imitation of Laine by Louis is really something. Sid
Catlett then demonstrated that he, too, could throw drumsticks in
the air and catch them, while the band fumbled through that old
New Orleans classic, "Mop, Mop." Hines faked his way through
something that was announced as his "famous boogie-woogie on
the 'St. Louis Blues.' "

The only happy note in the proceedings was the presence of Jack
Teagarden, who diffidently announced that he 'would like to play
and sing one of the oldest known blues," and then did "St. James
Infirmary," complete with water glass solo. Tea couldn't have been
any more "inspired" by that audience than anyone else, but his
performance only substantiated what I have always felt about him:
Teagarden doesn't have to try; he can be good without trying. Or,
conversely, it is almost impossible for him to be bad. He has so
much jazz feeling, so much good taste, that he has to be good. And
Jack either feels the pain and pathos of the blues every time he
plays them, or else he is one of the finest actors of our times.

It cannot be denied that Louis is the greatest. His exuberance is
unbounded; when coupled with his superb talents it makes him the
greatest experience in jazz. But unfortunately, on the Roxy stage
he brought nothing with him but his exuberance, and a pretty
commercialized, Uncle Tom version of it at that. Occasionally, in
ensemble (like the brief chorus of "Saints" with which that show
closed), when he wasn't pressing, the beautiful quality of tone
shone through, but most of the time he not only didn't care, but
converted himself into a parody of himself. His singing, in particular, sounded like a bad and cruel take-off on Armstrong vocals.
The last number found him singing "Shadrach," backed up for no
good reason by the whole damn Roxy chorus; it sent me racing up
the aisle, where I paused only to listen to the wonderfully ironic
organ music that came after the curtains had closed. The organist,
intentionally I hope, was playing a currently popular ditty entitled,
"Some Things Money Can't Buy."

Now, there is no excuse for this sort of thing. I'm willing to grant
that the whole idea bores the boys and is only a fine way of making
money for some otherwise unemployed-at-the-moment jazzmen.
But why then can't they just play some straight, shallow but
unphonied music and get the hell offstage. (I am assuming that
most of the shows were about like the one I saw. It was all done in
a well-arranged manner, and they did substantially the same num-

bers as in the show reported on by *Variety,* so the assumption seems warranted.)

People like Armstrong and Hines can't argue that you have to pretty it up for the audience; these men are the living proof that sincere jazz, all by itself, brings money and fame. And, whether they realize it or not, the kind of fame and stature that a man like Louis Armstrong has achieved brings with it certain responsibilities. Not that he is "responsible" to any particular audience, or should play only the way I would like to hear him play. His responsibilities are to his art, and to all of jazz. Without getting unduly stuffy or arty, I'd like to insist that these men, whose names are synonymous with "jazz" to a multitude of people, have no moral right at all to let their names be used to drag both fans and curious outsiders into a shoddy exhibition of pseudo-jazz.

I don't want to get maudlin about it, but a man could almost cry remembering that it was really "the greatest name in jazz" giving that phony exhibition. Teagarden, though he obviously thought the whole thing as laughable as did the rest of them (My, but Earl Hines has such white teeth!), at least had the decency to play music when he was supposed to. There's no reason to expect sincerity or taste from Catlett (advertised on his drums as "Big Sid, Esquire Award Winner 1944–45") or from the jivey young bassist, Arvell Shaw, but the rest of the boys deserve a slap on the wrist. Maybe it gets better on the road, but doesn't New York deserve a break?

A Jazz-Pilgrim's Progress
1956

Way back in the fall of 1945, when I had very recently returned from the Pacific and was only vaguely aware that all sorts of new currents were supposed to be swirling about in jazz, a very bright-eyed young man whom I had just met insisted upon playing some new records for me. He gave the impression of being about to produce the Holy Grail, or at the very least a live rabbit out of an old top hat. But all I could hear was a screeching, exhibitionistic trumpet, a whining alto saxophone, very little discernible melody, and no sort of reliable beat. I hated it, and informed the young man, in a patiently paternal way (I was at least three years older than he), that this noisy fad could never take the place of The Real Thing.

For I was, by exposure and inclination, strictly a Louis Armstrong-Jelly Roll Morton man, and what I had heard was something called "be-bop"—early-1945 recordings by Dizzy Gillespie and Charlie Parker.

Such an experience was actually not too uncommon then. I may have had the new music thrust at me more abruptly than most, but quite a few traditional-jazz fans were, at about that time, more or less forced to listen to a couple of "far out" selections. Almost invariably, they recoiled several feet and then spent the next few years either trying to ignore or loudly preaching against all forms of modernism. There has been much written and spoken argument in the past decade about this antipathy, but I don't recall any notice having been taken of what I now consider to have been the core of the problem for myself and for a number of other defenders of early jazz. It was, simply, that we were not ready, were not at all prepared to listen to modern jazz.

Since only the really one-dimensional myths have any staying power, a great many people accept that fantastic oversimplification about jazz having been rather suddenly "born" in New Orleans. Quite similarly, it is almost as customary to accept bop as an instant revolution that was hatched overnight at Minton's Playhouse in Harlem. But of course, just as a good many years and a wide variety of pre-jazz influences preceded New Orleans, the modern-jazz revolution has been gestating for a long time. You can go back and hear its first stirrings in, for example, some of Duke Ellington's records of the period when Jimmy Blanton was on hand, in Lester Young's work with Basie, in other big Negro bands, and in some of the small, nominally "Swing" groups of the late 1930s.

But the very important fact is that the typical traditionalist jazz fan was not listening to such music. I undoubtedly can no longer qualify as "typical," having sacrificed any such claims when I turned a hobby into a livelihood and turned myself into jazz writer and magazine editor, record producer, etc. But I was once, I suspect, a very typical sort of specimen: my interest began in the late 1930s, when I heard some records from the '20s; it was fanned by hearing live jazz at New York clubs like Nick's and the Hickory House (recommended by friends primarily as notably inexpensive places to take a date, and secondarily as places to hear good Dixieland). Thus the music that I absorbed was, roughly speaking, homogeneous. Armstrong, Jelly Roll, King Oliver, Bessie Smith, Bix—these were the records; in person, at the Greenwich Village and Fifty-second Street clubs, there were such as Wingy Manone, Jack Teagarden, Red Allen, Joe Marsala, Bud Freeman, Pee Wee

Russell, and the rest of the Eddie Condon mob. While all this certainly can't be called the *same* music, both the recordings and the live performances were specifically either in or closely derived from the original New Orleans tradition. Furthermore, although I wasn't particularly aware of it at the time, that live jazz had something else in common with those records: the musicians themselves, both in their way of life and in their music, were firmly rooted in the late 1920s, which was "their" time.

There was probably also a degree of snobbishness mixed in with such jazz tastes: not everyone knew about such things as recordings of the "pure" early jazz, or those small jazz groups playing in rather out-of-the-way places. Big bands and Swing meant "commercial" music, readily available to just anyone. Thus insulated, people like me had no need for the new snobbishness of the insiders who first adopted modern jazz. All in all, with my listening background, it would have been incredible if, at first hearing, I had (as the saying goes) flipped for Diz.

My personal alteration began with some rather accidental touches. In 1948, because I was newly involved in editing a music magazine and was potentially malleable, the head of a small jazz label spent an evening playing and explaining the very earliest Thelonious Monk records. Finally (possibly in self-defense), I found that I could at least feel and enjoy the beat. A year later, on a night when I had specifically gone to hear Armstrong and had been disappointed by a routine act, I reacted extremely hard to the other group in the place, which was the first George Shearing Quintet. (I remember being strongly impressed by his vibraphonist, Margie Hyams. Perhaps it was her effective use of an instrument that doesn't exist in traditional jazz—thus making comparison impossible—and that I had previously disliked—I've always considered Lionel Hampton a drummer gone wrong—that really began to turn the tide for me.)

In the next few years, I listened with increasing frequency to the newer jazz forms, began to feel able to have my own pro-and-con opinions, began (I believe) to have greater understanding. At first it was frankly a matter of professional necessity for the most part, but eventually I began to realize that I had unknowingly passed some point of no return and was enjoying the music for its own sake. This sort of thing is impossible to pinpoint, I'm afraid: you can never really re-understand the tastes of the man you used to be, or retrace the gradual transitional steps. I have listened again to those 1945 Gillespie-Parker numbers and have been doubly amazed; both by how melodic and warm this music can be and by how narrow and musically immature was that other me (the one who was so totally deaf to its considerable merits).

This may seem a contradiction of the points I've barely finished making in explanation of my original 1945 attitudes, but I don't think it really is. It is, simply, that being "unprepared" in 1945 is no excuse for remaining that way forever. I am quite glad that I was first a "moldy fig," for I am very dubious about the likelihood of anyone's reversing the process and, after entering jazz by way of the music of the 1940s and '50s, being able to progress back to King Oliver and Jelly Roll Morton. And I would hate to have missed out on hearing the wonderful and exciting music of such men. I certainly propose to keep on listening to my Creole Jazz Band and Red Hot Peppers records, among others, and to continue to find them meaningful. But, on the other hand, I can hear no voices in them that tell me to stay away from the Modern Jazz Quartet.

As I am far from unique in this matter of broadening one's jazz tastes, I imagine that all I gained from virtually forcing myself to listen to modern jazz was to achieve a device for overcoming ingrained projudices. Others less stubborn-minded than I, or with more willpower, ought to find it even easier. I can also recommend the use of a simple paradox: concentrate on both the differences and the sameness. By the former, I mean that there's no use looking for absolute parallels: New Orleans jazz sprang from a particular time and place (that it can be enjoyed outside that context is quite true, but irrelevant to my present point); current jazz expression belongs to here and now. This is *not* a value judgment: there is some inferior modern jazz, of course, but there was also some pretty bad music played in Chicago in the 1920s, too (you just don't bother to listen to *those* records any more, and let it go at that). There is also a lot that is wrong with the world of here and now, and a lot of that is in the music, too. But it is *our* time, so that at the very least it has immediacy on its side. I'll go so far as to say that I can't understand any serious listener, unless he is in love with archaism for its own sake, not finding something of value for him in some aspect of modern jazz.

As for the sameness, the major link lies in the aims of jazz musicians: roughly, in working from "popular" musical frameworks to create valid individual and group expression. There are some modernists, like Gerry Mulligan, whose innovations have fairly readily discernible traditional roots. There is the continuing important use of instrumental blues. Finally, there's even occasionally a tendency to think in the same way. I've recently been listening to the work of an extremely far-out musician whose trio is experimenting with something completely novel. He described it to me as "collective improvisation." The term had a strangely familiar ring that had me puzzled for a minute. Then I remembered. The first time I had heard it used, quite a few years ago, was to describe the music of King Oliver's Creole Jazz Band!

4

Three Separated Views of Thelonious

I have been writing about Monk almost as long as I've been writing about music; he was quite possibly the most important artist I have been associated with and undoubtedly a primary influence on my career as a producer. I've tried to show both his initial and continuing roles in my life by the three-part selection of material included here.

To begin with, there is the published result of the night when I first met Monk in Alfred Lion's living room and rather naively proceeded to interview him. Considering all circumstances, the article is nothing to be ashamed of, and several of my observations remain impressively acute. The piece is reprinted almost without change—with one repeated exception. In the original his first name was invariably misspelled; the error is a common one about which I have for many years sneered at many other people: omitting the final "o" in Thelonious. I insist on correcting it here.

Seven years later, I began a six-year period as Monk's record producer. The second segment consists of excerpts from my liner notes for half a dozen of our albums together; these comments and observations have the unique immediacy of having been written very shortly after the fact by someone who was very much involved throughout the recording process.

In recent years, I have written liner notes for a variety of Monk reissues, as well as several magazine remembrances after his death. Spread through all of these were a number of points that I considered important and, inevitably, a certain amount of repetition of thoughts and anecdotes. But I remained somewhat frustrated;

there was never enough room to bring together in one article everything I had to say on this subject, and there very possibly never would be.

But there was to be a happy ending. Eventually I was asked to assemble an ultimate reissue—a twenty-two-record boxed set with the awesomely definitive title, "Thelonious Monk: The Complete Riverside Recordings." (It's worth noting that, although it was subsequently released in this country, the project was initially commissioned by the company that has leased the *Japanese* rights to the records! Actually, the highly informed and rather possessive attitude of those fans towards American jazz is in itself a most fascinating subject.) In addition to compiling the set, I undertook to write the suitably extensive accompanying booklet. This material, a reminiscence followed by a session-by-session review of all my recording experiences with Thelonious, makes up the third and by far the longest portion of this chapter. In its own way, this overview is itself a "complete Riverside Monk," and it comes very close to being that hoped-for full recapitulation of my thoughts and remembrances and conclusions about this nearly incredible man. So it was particularly gratifying when the reissue set as a whole, and the booklet on its own, were both honored with 1987 Grammy awards as, respectively, Best Historical Album and Best Album Notes.

(The session recollections have been edited in places, but only to remove what would otherwise be rather cryptic and confusing comments referring directly to the recordings.)

The Original Interview
1948

Modern music has been rolling along these past few years, converting a number of young jazz men and often making for them a good bit of money. Sometimes it seems like a very sincere, if immature and frenetic, jazz form; sometimes it gives off strong hints of un-artistic neurosis, commercial power-politics, and childish clowning. I have always been ready to concede, without too much enthusiasm, that bebop might well have a bright future, but until recently had found nothing in it capable of commanding interest or respect.

Very recently, however, what looks very much like the first ray of light has broken through the clouds. A thirty-year-old New York pianist named Thelonious Monk has cut several band records (only four sides have been released as yet) containing music that is more interesting and worthy of far more serious listening than anything else that has yet been produced by a modernist. Monk, who has been a legendary and little-known figure in bebop circles, plays in a style that bears a strong superficial resemblance to standard bop. But there are indications that his music may represent a huge forward step towards discipline and coherence in this newest form of jazz.

Comparison with past jazz greats is probably pointless; the various "schools" of jazz may go through similar periods of development, but each has its own peculiarities. However, it may serve to clarify Monk's relative position along the main stream of modern music to point out that he is engaged in developing an essentially original piano style, as men like Pinetop Smith and CowCow Davenport did for an earlier style. In his current record he has created a band style molded around his own ideas and shaped to his own manner of playing, much as Jelly Roll Morton and Duke Ellington did before him.

Monk was unquestionably one of the very first to play in the modern style that came to be known as bebop. In 1938, while playing in a quartet at Minton's, in Harlem, he and drummer Kenny Clarke began "thinking" in that vein, and even before that Monk had been picking up a meager living by playing around town in his natural style—a strange style that most musicians found incomprehensible.

For reasons to be touched on later, Monk's conception of jazz has developed along somewhat different lines than his Harlem contemporaries—stronger and more mature lines, in our opinion. Possibly because Thelonious is the first pianist with his own set of ideas to come along in a type of jazz thus far dominated by horn men like Parker and Gillespie, his recent sides are the first "modern" records in which the piano and the rhythm section play important roles. Monk himself complains that bebop pianists have a habit of trying to imitate Dizzy's trumpet or Bird's alto; a piano that fulfills a piano's function in the band is a rare thing, but Monk's strongly rhythmic style is pure piano, beautifully integrated into a unit with his bassist (Eugene Ramey on some sides, Bob Paige on others), and with a powerful, steady and complex drummer named Art Blakey.

A great weakness peculiar to recorded jazz, and a weakness common to all schools, is the haphazard and casual business of bringing together men relatively unfamiliar with each other's styles in a hastily arranged pick-up session. Sometimes this produces great jazz; more often the product is rather disorganized music. Even if it includes great solo work, it still sounds like what it really is—a group of individuals playing in the same room, but *not* a band. On the occasions when units composed of men who understand each other's styles and ideas and peculiarities are able to get together, the results are likely to be superior, even if the individuals involved are not "all-stars." New Orleans jazz has many examples of this; the Ellington band is another case in point. Modern music thus far has been largely pick-up; the fact that Thelonious chose the men he wanted to work with, and rehearsed carefully with them, may be a major reason why his current records are an outstanding example of unified small band jazz, and sound purposeful and coordinated instead of like a cutting duel between comparative strangers.

Unfortunately, it seems to have been easier for Thelonious to find rhythm men able to adapt themselves to his style than to find suitable horns. Trumpet and tenor sax on his current sides are played by men who seem too steeped in standard bebop; their solos sometimes fail to follow the complex pattern being established by the rhythm unit, and the ensembles tend, on occasion, to fall into standard bop clichés. But one man, a seventeen-year-old alto player named Danny Quebec West (nephew of Ike Quebec), does some remarkable work. He has a firm, clear, driving style, and, apparently because he is young enough not to have fallen into current stylization, he is able to coordinate with the line along which Monk's playing moves.

Whether Monk is to become a "great," and whether his music is really as far from the beaten path of bebop as I believe it is, are things that only time and continued playing can prove. But, as of this moment, considering only the present batch of far-from-perfect records turned out by this still-young jazz man, these points stand out:

Thelonious is a talented musician, with a fertile imagination and a firm rhythmic sense; his band jazz has a feeling of unity, warmth, and purpose that contrasts sharply with the emotionless, jittered-up pyrotechnics of Fifty-second Street "modernism." And—although this is a point that cannot be proved in writing but only heard in the music—he is capable of a sly, wry, satiric humor that has a rare maturity. Monk's playing may be considered as "neurotic" as the rest of the jazz produced in the '40s, but it at least serves to indicate that the music of a neurotic era does not necessarily have to be a collection of cold, rhythmless and pointless sounds.

One of the principal reasons for Monk's "differentness," aside from the man's own probable genius, can be found in the way that choice and necessity have combined to keep him on the fringes of the bebop movement. Raised in the semi-isolated San Juan Hill district near the Hudson River in New York's West Sixties, he has lived there, away from Harlem, ever since. He started taking piano lessons at eleven, and two years later was playing solo dates at local parties and speakeasies. From the first, Monk says, "no written music sounded right" to him, although he obviously listened intently to the Ellington band of that day. His unconventional style and his unwillingness to play standard orchestra piano kept him from band jobs and led him to develop his style his own way. Those early years were undoubtedly not pleasant ones; Thelonious is a quiet, self-contained, and soft-spoken man, who doesn't seem too anxious to recall those first jobs in "juice joints," where he made $17 a week, and where people kept wanting him to "play straight."

"There are a lot of things you can't remember—except the heckles," he says.

Finally, in 1938, he went into trumpeter Joe Guy's quartet at Minton's. In those days, when "everybody was sounding like Roy Eldridge," he and Kenny Clarke began "thinking out" the style that was to be promoted into a big thing called bebop. ("Thinking" is a word Monk uses a lot in talking about his music, and to me the word seems fitting.) A great many men drifted into Minton's and into that style in those days: Charlie Christian, Coleman Hawkins, Dizzy Gillespie (whom Monk remembers as having been there only "very rarely"), Charlie Parker.

In 1940 Thelonious recorded an album with Hawkins, on the Joe Davis label. It's interesting to note that, although the balance and the arrangements on those sides were set up to feature only Hawk, what can be heard of Monk's playing is in the same vein as it is today. Not as sure or as forceful, perhaps, but clearly along the same lines. Then came two years with Hawkins's band, in Chicago and on the West Coast, which meant that he was not on hand during the period when "bebop" (which incidentally is a term he dislikes) was first being stylized and strongly plugged.

Then he returned to New York and comparative obscurity. Always appreciated by fellow musicians (like Mary Lou Williams, Ellington, Nat Cole—who says he sat "spellbound" the first time he heard Thelonious), but never quite in harmony with the kind of jazz that was being sold, he was completely without the qualities of showmanship and self-promotion in which so many others abound. A careful craftsman and an artist, he is obviously not a man who would be at his best in a quick recording session or be happy playing chords on a six-night-a-week job with an outfit that considered the piano a half-necessary background for some free-wheeling horn men.

His current sides, on which his particular variation of modern music is played with varying degrees of success, but with not-infrequent greatness, may or may not move him from obscurity to a position as a big name and big influence in modern jazz. But they do show that at least one modernist is capable of a maturity and soundness and brilliance that leaves room for much optimism for the future of jazz.

Some Notes from the Trenches
1955–60

A good part of the problem of the jazz artist who is considered excessively far-out is tied in with the playing of material that is unfamiliar to the "average" ear. This is not to deny that original compositions are an important part of jazz creativity. But it can be extremely helpful to know the precise structural and melodic starting point of a musician's improvisations. It can often mean the difference between following the unfolding of a performance with awe and delight or finding yourself just groping, bewildered, and almost inevitably somewhat irritated. Communication between performer and audience is, after all, rather essential; and to perhaps more listeners than might care to admit it out loud, the initial identification of knowing the tune can be something more than half the battle.

(from "Thelonious Monk Plays Duke Ellington"; Fall 1955)

Monk concerns himself here with standards—popular tunes that have demonstrated sturdiness and above-average quality by remaining popular for a good many years. The present group of numbers are decidedly personal interpretations, strongly colored by Monk's highly individual approach and ideas. But the starting point in each case is a familiar melody.

This is a departure from the procedure on his earlier recordings, where the emphasis was invariably on the pianist's own compositions. Monk's originals, it happens, are among the richest and most inventive of modern jazz writing. Nevertheless, the decision to bypass them temporarily is a quite deliberate one. It stems from a desire to deflate a myth that has gotten somewhat out of hand. For a variety of reasons, and starting (as most legends do) from a basis of moderately accurate fact, this pioneer modernist has gained the reputation of being a rather forbiddingly difficult-to-understand musician (the "High Priest of Bop"—whatever that might mean). As a result, there are those who shy away from Monk's music almost automatically, who have decided without *really* listening that it is something they can't expect to grasp or enjoy. It is our very strong belief that such people are cheating themselves, and missing out on valuable and compelling musical experiences.

If it were their loss alone, there might be no great desire to divert these people from their self-imposed fate. But some part at least of the measure of an artist's "effectiveness" must lie in the extent of his impact on an audience. Thus Thelonious—whose influence on fellow-musicians and on the whole basic framework of modern music is, by contrast, vast and almost universally recognized—must also be considered as losing something.

In this album and its immediate predecessor, there is no attempt to "change" Monk. (There could be no possibility of doing that even if anyone wanted to: this is a mature and properly self-confident artist whose fundamental musical concepts are by now quite firmly established.) But Thelonious is highly capable of working with the material furnished by the standard pop composers. More than that, he happens to enjoy (as some jazz artists do, and others do not) the challenge this can present. So it is possible to put into operation the theory that the likelihood of communication is greatly increased if the listener can start from a firm, familiar position. *You* know the tune of "Liza," or "Honeysuckle Rose," as well as Monk does. So everyone at least begins even. Thelonious can never be made to seem too "easy"; he is a forthright and uncompromising creative artist whose style and concepts remain non-conventional even by the standards of today's jazz. He is *not* easy, but neither is he a mystical or perverse wanderer in a private universe. And when the point of origin from which he moves on out is clearly understood, it should be a lot easier to feel that this music, intricate and unusual though it may be, is nevertheless knowable.

(from "The Unique Thelonious Monk"; Spring 1956)

Monk's music is not only not the easiest listening, it is also not the easiest to play. Musicians could save themselves a lot of trouble by *not* recording with Thelonious—but it's a form of trouble that a great many of the best have long considered a privilege (as well as an education in itself). The men—Sonny Rollins, Max Roach, Oscar Pettiford, Ernie Henry, Clark Terry, Paul Chambers—struggled and concentrated and shook their heads with those half-smiles that mean: "Hard? This is *impossible!*" Because Monk's creativity never stands still: during a preliminary run-through of a number, between takes or even during one, changes of phrasing or detail will evolve, as a constant fusion of arrangement and improvisation keeps taking place.

Monk is a severe task-master at a recording session, a perfectionist—"I've never been satisfied with one of my records yet," he says, and means it—who knows just how he wants each note bent and phrased and who drives the others as hard as he drives himself—which is possibly a little unfair of him.

In the end, it wasn't "impossible"—merely far from easy, and in the end everyone else was satisfied and Monk probably almost satisfied.

(from "Brilliant Corners"; January 1957)

Any musician who has had the experience can verify that it is hard work to play with Thelonious; even the many who admire him deeply do not always find it possible to grasp fully or execute perfectly the intricate and demanding patterns that Monk's mind can evolve. This does not mean that Monk playing by himself is a "perfect" situation, but what *is* special about this album is the rare opportunity to hear Thelonious as he thinks and sounds when he has chosen to be temporarily complete in himself.

The overall tone is reflective, and there is a good deal of a sometimes deceptive feeling of searching, while playing, for an idea to explore, of almost unexpectedly finding in a single note or phrase the impetus for a full chorus that follows. This is a feeling that often gives Monk's playing here a quality of thinking-out-loud. It isn't that he sounds unprepared, or surprised by the directions he takes; it is rather as if he were constantly discovering and rediscovering within himself both new and remembered patterns of music.

(from "Thelonious Himself"; Spring 1957)

One of the most important points to be noted about this debut performance by the Monk Orchestra is that it celebrates the fact that Thelonious is still at it—still creating and building as ever, still refusing to stand in one place and let the world catch up with him. More precisely, he is refusing to let the world, once it has caught up, *stay* abreast of him for very long.

In this respect, Monk is merely justifying the frequent description of him as a "pioneer." If I remember my history, it was the habit of that noted frontiersman, Daniel Boone, to establish a new settlement and then, when it had developed into a properly domesticated village, to strike out into the wilderness again, in further search of new territory and sufficient elbow-room.

Like many analogies, this puts things a little too patly. However, it is quite accurate to point out that whole cities of Monk fans and followers have now sprung up where once, not at all long ago, he existed almost in solitude within what many regarded as an impenetrable musical wilderness. For almost two decades, Monk has been developing a body of musical composition, performance, and influence that now clearly marks him as a truly gigantic creative figure. But for most of that period, the majority of listeners and critics, and even some musicians, considered Thelonious to be at best a frighteningly far-out and difficult artist, at worst an eccentric of small merit who played the piano incorrectly. Then, with a surge that made it seem as if a dam had broken somewhere, he was "discovered." Suddenly (and rather gratifyingly) things were turned around, and in most jazz circles it was the anti-Monk element and the shoulder-shruggers, rather than his partisans, who were considered the oddball minority. I think it was partly that a dam *had* burst: exposure to his work (in 1957, for the first time in many years, Thelonious became regularly available to New York night club audiences), and to the work of many increasingly popular musicians strongly influenced by him, had finally eroded the barrier that separated so many people from him. It was partly that Monk himself, seeming almost to thrive on public indifference, had been constantly growing as an artist until he reached a point where it was literally impossible to ignore him any longer.

At any rate, 1958 was a year of attention and honors: of good reviews and feature articles and high standing in popularity polls. Which made it quite fitting that at the end of the second month of 1959, Thelonious offered the first public appearance of something new. The full, pervasive sound of this orchestra seems to me a long overdue extension of his music, but as some concert reviews have indicated, there will be those who do not approve of this new step. I welcome the return of controversy to the world of Monk's music—I really think he belongs at least a little apart from overwhelming acceptance and may even function more creatively when he is out on the frontier building something that the multitudes of settlers can accept fully whenever they are able to catch up.

(from "The Thelonious Monk Orchestra at Town Hall"; Spring 1959)

The artistry of Thelonious seems to have an almost infinite number of facets. Each of his albums offers some combination of several of them, but none can show the total complex picture. This is of course all to the good: too many jazz musicians (as well as performers and creators in many other fields) show us their whole hand all too quickly and then show it to us again and again—possibly deepening and maturing, but inevitably repeating themselves at least somewhat and therefore becoming at least somewhat less surprising, challenging, or interesting. But the artist who can never be considered completely knowable or predictable always retains a touch of magic. He is a wizard, a poet, and so we always turn to his latest effort with a thrill of anticipation and wonder.

(from "Thelonious Monk at the Blackhawk"; Spring 1960)

The Complete Riverside Recordings
1986

Thelonious and Me

It should be clearly understood that the purpose of this collection is to present to the greatest possible extent the complete results of the six-year association between Thelonious Monk and Riverside Records. This is not at all the same as merely reissuing all the albums he made for that label, or even offering the material from those albums plus a scattering of alternates takes. The intention here is something I consider much more personal, more revealing, more historically and musically significant. This is, basically, all of my work with Thelonious, including several of the accidents and the failures as well as the highly important creative moments. Except only for the tapes that have vanished (and must be assumed to be lost forever, accidentally or unthinkingly destroyed), it is the full and naked truth about several pivotal recording years in the career of a very major jazz artist, which means that it is at times something quite different from the carefully packaged entertainment units that the public is usually allowed to purchase.

Therefore, this is also a very important segment of my life-long involvement with the creation of jazz records. Monk was the first artist of real consequence with whom I went into the recording studio. Although I have never felt there was any point in comparing one valid artist with others, I must admit that it is entirely possible that he was the most important musician I have ever worked with. Certainly he was the most unusual, probably he was the most demanding. Undoubtedly I learned more from him than from anyone else—at least partly because our association began so early in my career that at the time I knew practically nothing and therefore had almost everything to learn! It was in some respects a most rewarding working relationship, but it was at times extremely frustrating. We last worked together in 1960, and therefore I had two decades before his death in which to think with regret of projects we might have done or should have done.

Above all, however, I will always retain a feeling of satisfaction. Over the years it has come to be my personal definition of the role of the jazz record producer that he should serve primarily as a *catalytic agent*. In a literal sense, my dictionary refers to this as something that "initiates a chemical reaction and enables it to proceed under different conditions than otherwise possible." In a jazz sense, I mean that the producer's job is to create, in whatever ways he can, a set of circumstances that will allow and encourage the artist to perform at the very highest level. I first attempted to function in this way on my early sessions with Monk, and I do feel that at least some of the work I helped bring into being was truly different and lastingly valuable, and that without my involvement it might not have been quite the same.

Monk and I first met a very long time ago. It was early in 1948, only a few years after he had been involved in the pioneering bebop sessions at Minton's Playhouse in Harlem. As I like to point out in recalling that initial encounter, it was so incredibly long ago that I was still several years away from producing my first album, and Monk was poised at the very beginning of his recording career. Specifically, Blue Note was preparing to release his first 78-rpm single, and I had just made a formal (although unpaid) entrance into the jazz world by becoming the managing editor of a small and previously quite traditionalist magazine.

It was precisely this combination of roles—Thelonious as a new recording artist and me as a totally inexperienced jazz journalist— that was responsible for our being brought together one evening, thereby setting in motion a chain of events that eventually led to our intense six-year working relationship at Riverside and to the creation of all the recordings that make up this collection. I was twenty-five years old at the time and Monk (if his listed birthdate in 1917 is accurate) was just past thirty, but there was considerable difference between us. Even though the outside world was not aware of Monk, his reputation in certain jazz circles as the eccentric "high priest of bop" was already well established. I, on the other hand, was merely a beginning jazz writer who was editor of *The Record Changer* simply because my former college classmate Bill Grauer (who was later to be my partner at Riverside) had just become publisher of the magazine. But Alfred Lion, the guiding force at Blue Note, had seen an opportunity to influence us newcomers into publicizing his unusual young pianist. So I found myself sitting in Lion's living room, not only meeting this already-legendary musician but attempting to interview him.

My first real problem was to understand what he was saying. In later years I developed the theory that Monk had several different ways of speaking: to strangers, or if his mood was withdrawn, there would be a thick and murky tone that made it necessary to strain for each word. As he came to know you better and to accept you, his speech patterns gradually became clearer. I remain convinced that in speech (as in his music) Thelonious for the most part became easier to comprehend only when and if he wanted to. At our first meeting, facing an intrusive young writer that his record company had thrust at him, he retreated behind a wall of grunts and mumbles and one-word answers.

Nevertheless I kept at it and somehow—possibly because I have always been stubborn, or because I had the arrogance that can come from ignorance and was too inexperienced to be properly frightened of him—I succeeded in putting together what Monk later told me was the first article about him ever to appear in a national publication. He may have been wrong about that: there was a George Simon story in *Metronome* at about the same time, and that magazine certainly had a much larger circulation. But the really important thing was that Thelonious liked what I had to say and remembered it; seven years later, that had a lot to do with my becoming his record producer.

On re-reading that original *Record Changer* piece a great many years later, it is clear that I responded immediately and strongly to this man and his strange music. At that time I was still very much a traditionalist, with virtually no knowledge of the new jazz forms; I had not yet heard anything attractive in the bebop of Gillespie and Parker. As I wrote in that article, I had previously found modern jazz to be "frenetic, emotionless, and rhythmless." Nevertheless, I found myself highly impressed by the test pressings I heard that night from Monk's first Blue Note session. I remember most clearly the original version of the tune called "Thelonious" (which was to be recorded again for Riverside, almost exactly ten years later, in a big-band concert performance). And the total impact of what I heard led me to some initial comments that, quite astonishingly, I would still be willing to affirm today, close to forty years later!

Calling his first records "an outstanding example of unified small band jazz," I used such phrases as "discipline and coherence" and "purposeful and coordinated." I noted his "warmth," his "firm rhythmic sense (and) fertile imagination," and found him "capable of a wry, satiric, humor that has a rare maturity." Most remarkably, when you realize how much of a novice I was back then, I was able to perceive that "he is engaged in developing an essentially original piano style," and that in those first recordings he had "created a band style molded around his own ideas and shaped to his own manner of playing, much as Jelly Roll Morton and Duke Ellington did before him." I continue to feel that to appreciate properly Monk's work and his position in jazz history it is essential to understand that he stands in a direct line of succession from Morton and Ellington. The fact that I grasped this basic point on first hearing him not only speaks well of my jazz instincts but also points up the clarity with which Monk's message has always been delivered—to those who are willing to listen with open ears.

However, for seven years I had no occasion to make use of my early insights. Although I had begun to enjoy a good deal of the new music that was all around me in New York, and by 1953 had become professionally involved in the record business, the young Riverside label at that time was almost exclusively concerned with reissues of early classics by Louis Armstrong, King Oliver, Jelly Roll, and Ma Rainey. Then, early in 1955, we received a momentous telephone call from Nat Hentoff, informing us of the possibility that Thelonious might be available for recording.

Monk's career had not been progressing well. He could not work to any extent in New York clubs; several years after a minor narcotics-related conviction, he was still unable to obtain from the police department the "cabaret card" that was required under the arbitrary regulations that were then in effect. He had moved from Blue Note to Prestige Records a couple of years earlier, but his records were not doing well with either the critics or the public—perhaps at least in part because of the rather overdone publicity emphasis on the weirdness and obscurity of his music. Monk was quite unhappy with Prestige, and they did not consider him at all important in comparison with the label's top-selling attractions like Miles Davis and the Modern Jazz Quartet. Prestige, we were informed, could easily be persuaded to release Monk from his contract.

Grauer and I responded with great enthusiasm. We had made the decision to get heavily involved in recording contemporary jazz; to sign Thelonious would not only be a strong starting point, but would certainly let the jazz world know just how serious we were. We met with Monk, and I was very pleased to learn that he knew exactly who I was and remembered quite clearly and approvingly what I had written about him. Having very little to lose, he was willing to take a chance with the fledgling Riverside operation, particularly since it was run by the men responsible for that article. It did take a touch of trickery to free him from Prestige. All that was required was repayment of an absurdly small sum of money that had been over-advanced to him, but the label might not turn the pianist loose quite so casually if they were aware that a rival company was standing by. So I personally lent Thelonious the necessary funds, and I still have on my wall a framed copy of the letter informing him that "with receipt of your cash for $108.27," Prestige was "releasing you of your exclusive recording. . . ." It was the start of a very exciting and significant period, the beginning of the first of my several long-term associations with major jazz artists. It opened the door for our many record sessions together, several of which were of great importance to his career and unquestionably to mine, and to the overall story of jazz in our times.

Signing this genius was not hard; recording him was never easy. When I entered a studio with Monk in 1955, for the first of a great many times, I was quite inadequately prepared for the task. Like many of my colleagues at the independent jazz labels of that era, I was a fan who had become a producer by the simple procedure of declaring that I was one. I was one of the owners of the company, so who could argue with my claim? But I know now that I, as an executive, would never entrust so important, difficult, and sensitive an artist to a producer as thoroughly inexperienced as I was then. I had handled a few sessions, with studio musicians and with pianist Randy Weston (who was a disciple of Monk, but has always been one of the gentlest of human beings). Such a background in no way prepared me for working with this erratic, stubborn, basically intolerant, and overwhelmingly talented artist. I was at the beginning of a massive learning experience!

Sonny Rollins, with whom I have often discussed the ever-fascinating subject, shares my belief that Thelonious was a great teacher, and that we both have absorbed very important (although certainly very different) lessons from him—despite the obvious fact that he was undoubtedly the most unorthodox and indirect of teachers and never in his life gave either of us (or anyone else) a

formal lesson. Sonny, who has spent some time in India, has referred to Monk as his "guru," and this is perhaps a more accurate
term than "teacher," since he functioned less as an instructor than
as a guide who helped you bring out the very best qualities within
yourself. As examples, I am aware of how he aided Rollins in
developing both his musical sense of humor and his ability to play
ballads in a way that combines beauty with emotional strength; I
also know how greatly John Coltrane's several months with
Thelonious at the Five Spot in 1957 accelerated his transition from
a rather interesting young bebop tenor player into an unconventional, boundary-extending giant. Above all, I remain deeply conscious of the extent to which my early sessions with this brilliant,
difficult, and demanding man literally forced me to learn very
quickly under pressure a great many necessary and valuable skills
and attitudes and some essential truths about dealing effectively
with a great variety of jazz artists.

My first problem—and it was an almost symbolic preview of
what my future as a producer would include—came on the scheduled first day of recording with Monk, and involved the absence of
a reputedly quite reliable musician. Kenny Clarke and Oscar
Pettiford, both already recognized as among the elder statesmen of
the new music, were the carefully chosen sidemen for this initial
album. We were all to gather at the small Riverside offices in
midtown New York and travel together across the Hudson River
to the New Jersey studios of Rudy Van Gelder, the most celebrated of jazz engineers. I was relieved when Monk arrived almost
on time, just after Pettiford, but Clarke was nowhere to be found.
We waited with growing impatience and concern; we telephoned
everywhere; eventually Thelonious suggested using a substitute.
Ironically, his choice was Philly Joe Jones, who in later years was
to be Riverside's most frequently used drummer, but I had barely
heard of him, and did not want to begin by being pushed into using
an unknown in place of an acknowledged master. Van Gelder
agreed to give us a one-day postponement; Kenny, when finally
located, insisted quite convincingly that Monk had told him the
date was scheduled for the next day. It was not the last time that
Monk was to indicate a lack of concern for such routine things as
time and place and passing on the kind of basic information that is
important to ordinary people.

Looking back on that album, I realize that the real problem had
begun long before. My partner and I had decided that our initial
goal was to reverse the widely held belief that our new pianist was
an impossibly obscure artist; therefore, we would start by avoiding

bebop horns and intricate original tunes. We proposed an all-Ellington trio date: certainly Duke was a universally respected figure and major composer with (as my 1948 article had noted) a valid musical connection with Monk. He agreed without hesitation, despite claiming to be largely unfamiliar with Ellington's music. I insisted that Thelonious pick out the specific repertoire, and eventually he requested several pieces of sheet music. But when we finally arrived at the studio, he proceeded to sit down at the piano and hesitantly begin to work out melody lines, as if he were seeing the material for the first time! I will never know to what extent he was actually learning on the spot, but I'm certain that at least in part he was deliberately testing, demonstrating that he was in command, and probing at this new producer to see how he would react. (There were a few very strong clues: it is clear from his performance that he was quite aware of the quote from Chopin's Funeral March that forms the coda of Ellington's original recording of "Black and Tan Fantasy." And he turned out to be an unbelievably quick study, moving from fumbling note-picking to intriguing improvisation in very little time—although it may have seemed an eternity to me.)

If this was indeed my first lesson at Monk's "school," I was somehow able to pass the test. I reacted calmly and patiently, although that was not at all how I felt. I was in the process of learning that the most important thing is to get the job done, *not* to be the winner in a clash of wills.

I was also becoming aware of the pervasive, though not entirely universal, attitude among jazz musicians that the operators of record companies (even including producers) are—like club-owners—members of another world. If we are not exactly the *enemy,* we are at least the *opposition.* I have always fought against this attitude, often successfully. I do happen to be one of the few jazz producers who can be found listening to the music in clubs with any regularity, and it remains true that some of my warmest friendships have been with people I work with. Thelonious and I never became close friends, but we had a direct and honest relationship throughout his Riverside years. We could talk at times about matters outside music (we had young sons of almost the same age, and compared notes on the difficulties of fatherhood; at this point in time—early 1986—my son Peter happens to be involved in researching and writing a biography of Monk). Above all, I take pride in the fact that Thelonious actively brought young musicians to my attention on more than one occasion. He was the first to tell me about both Wilbur Ware and Johnny Griffin, who became very important parts of the Riverside picture; and Clark Terry, whom I first met when Monk called him for the final session of the *Brilliant Corners* album, became a vital link in a most important chain— Clark introduced me to the Adderley brothers, and it was Cannonball who first made me aware of Wes Montgomery.

When we moved on from the relative calm of the first trio albums to the hectic sessions involved in the creation of *Brilliant Corners,* the pace of my learning process increased rapidly. Later in these pages I will deal in some detail with the actual circumstances of those and several other tense periods in the recording studio. What I want to emphasize now is that, working with this larger-than-life-size figure named Thelonious Monk, I was going through the most rigorous kind of on-the-job training. I was beginning to learn, under conditions of extreme pressure, the importance of being flexible, of instantly altering plans and schedules, not tightening up when faced with the unexpected, and remembering that a major aspect of the producer's role is to reduce the overall tension. Above all, I was beginning to grasp a fundamental lesson that I suspect many jazz producers never fully appreciate: it is the artist's album, not mine. My *only* objective is to achieve the best possible results, and I must juggle, move, and maneuver myself and everyone else in whatever ways are necessary to reach that goal. It took many more sessions and situations before I thoroughly absorbed these lessons, but my course of instruction most definitely began with Thelonious.

It was during the final day of work on the *Brilliant Corners* album that I first became aware of the value of listening carefully when Monk spoke. (I soon came to realize that he had a remarkable ability to convey deep truths through specific, seemingly casual or even comic comments.) On this occasion, Clark Terry was briefly rehearsing "Bemsha Swing" with the composer. "Don't pay too much attention to what I'm playing behind you now," I heard Thelonious tell him, "because when we record I'll probably be playing something completely different and it'll only confuse you. . . ." It is difficult to imagine a more concise and accurate summation of the fundamentally fluid, ever-changing, improvisatory nature of Monk's approach to music. Similarly, listening to a playback of the blues called "Functional," while making his first solo-piano album, he noted to me: "I sound just like James P. Johnson." Of course he didn't sound *exactly* like the master stride pianist (to whom he had listened often as a teenager; they had lived in the same New York City neighborhood). But it was both an acknowledgement that Thelonious was aware of some of his most important roots and an announcement that he was satisfied with the way he was playing.

That same solo album also was the occasion of our first major confrontation, from which I learned another major lesson: working on behalf of the artist doesn't mean you have to turn yourself into a doormat. The first scheduled session for this album never took place; after a series of phone calls announcing that he was on his way, Monk finally arrived at the studio well over an hour late and unprepared. I had waited in order to deliver a rather heavy-handed speech: there were certain necessary limits to what my self-respect could allow; I could accept perhaps a half-hour's lateness, but after that he needn't bother to show up at the studio; I would have left. We set a new date; I got there about fifteen minutes early—and Thelonious was waiting for me. He gave me one of his big, slow smiles and quietly asked: "What kept you?"

Monk's first contract with Riverside was for three years, which was a usual maximum period in those days. This meant that it ended in the spring of 1958, after his first Five Spot engagement with John Coltrane had thrust him into the spotlight, but actually before there had been enough fame to encourage a major record label to try to entice our artist away. (It was a common enough procedure to let a small jazz company run the risks of early development and then have the giants move in; Prestige, for example, had lost Miles Davis to Columbia, and the Modern Jazz Quartet and Coltrane to Atlantic.) After some not unfriendly negotiation, his advance payments were more than doubled and his royalty percentage increased, and Thelonious began a second three-year span with our live recordings of the 1958 Five Spot quartet. But long before the end of that contract it was clear that a change would take place. His advisors were convinced that it was time to move on; six years *is* a long time with one label, and Columbia, then in one of its active jazz periods, was beckoning.

I did feel badly about not being able to discuss the future directly with Monk, and I have always felt distressed by the fact that I can say, quite immodestly, that nothing in his subsequent recording career really approached the creativity and variety of the best of his work at Riverside. But the only specific unpleasantness associated with his departure derived from the fact that his second contract had called for several more albums than we had been able to make. I was never fully aware of the circumstances, but Bill Grauer had learned of the existence of tapes professionally recorded—perhaps by the concert promoters, perhaps by radio stations—during two major performances on an early 1961

European tour. The musicians' union had already agreed that we were entitled to further albums from Monk before his contract with Columbia could be approved. Since there is really no way to force an unwilling artist into the studio (particularly *this* artist), use of the existing tapes seemed the best possible solution.

Thelonious and I saw each other from time to time in the New York jazz world of the '60s, but our closeness had been tied to our work together. By 1973 I had moved to San Francisco, and not long after that he retreated into a period of total inactivity and seclusion that lasted until his death in 1982. My last contact with him came about two years before that. On a sudden impulse, during a trip to New York, I telephoned him; the conversation ran approximately like this:

"Thelonious, are you touching the piano at all these days?"

"No, I'm not."

"Do you want to get back to playing?"

"No, I don't."

"I'm only in town for a few days; would you like me to come and visit, to talk about the old days?"

"No, I wouldn't."

When I repeated this to Barry Harris, who was much closer to him in the last years than almost anyone else, the pianist told me: "You were lucky. You got complete sentences. With most people, he just says, 'No.' "

So I am by no means an expert on the last periods of his life. The Thelonious Monk of the years from 1955 to 1961 is the man I really knew, and learned from, and helped as best I could to express his creativity on records. *That* Thelonious was a very unusual human being and extremely good at what he did; I am glad that I was able to know him and work with him.

The Thelonious Monk Sessions

As I add it up, there were twenty-eight different occasions on which I went into a studio (or had a tape machine rolling under "live" club or concert recording conditions) with Thelonious Monk. The earliest time and place was in July 1955 at the legendary original Hackensack, New Jersey, location of Rudy Van Gelder's studio. The last was an almost-unplanned evening late in April 1960, at a San Francisco night club that many years ago was torn down and turned into a parking lot.

Recording Thelonious was never what could be called easy; at times it was almost literally impossible. Not including two post-ponements, which are *not* counted among the sessions listed here, there were four dates that at the time were considered totally non-productive—although all four resulted in some material that eventually turned out to be of measurable musical or historical value. (Not to keep you in suspense, they are the sessions numbered 10, 15, 18, and 26–27.)

All of my afternoons and nights of work with Monk are very important elements in my long and still-active career as a producer, and each of them is recalled in these pages. Some occasions are much more vivid and detailed memories than others—and in a number of cases I have been able to supplement my mental pictures with written documentation: my own recording information sheets or rough notes made during a session; the data on original tape boxes; musicians' union recording contracts; album liner notes. In preparing this complete Riverside collection, I have done some additional digging through vaults and old files, and have actually rediscovered some forgotten facts. I have even listened to bits of conversation and argument remaining on some very old reels of tape. All these things have in some cases supported or improved my recollection of how it went, and in others led me to change my mind. In still other instances there simply is no existing documentation, and so some specific points that are by now twenty to twenty-five years old can only be guessed at.

For this reason it hasn't been possible to assemble the collection in its exact original sequence. There is just no way of knowing or recalling the order of recorded performance on some days. But at least the sessions are all in chronological order, and wherever possible they have been accurately recreated as they were recorded.

Of course there are regrettable physical gaps: as will be noted as I describe the sessions, there are several dates from which no out-take material or original tape reels can be found. There are others where—even more frustratingly—some complete or partial tape boxes are on hand but others have disappeared. Over the years I have become quite philosophical about this. When you consider that the original Riverside organization went out of business in 1964, that its tapes were never very sensibly filed to begin with, and that this material has passed through the hands of three additional sets of owners and traveled from New York to California—the really remarkable thing is not that some of it has been lost, but rather that *any* has survived.

Sessions 1 and 2
(July 21 and 27, 1955)

My very first working encounters with Thelonious were relatively
uneventful, actually not providing too much warning of some of
the tough dates that lay ahead—except of course for that almost-
symbolic day preceding the initial session when, as already noted,
Kenny Clarke never appeared. So my first scheduled Monk date
really never took place—we began our association with a postponement!

I don't recall how Van Gelder was able to fit us in on the very
next afternoon. At that time he was doing almost all the engineering for the highly active Prestige, Blue Note, and Savoy labels on a
quite regular schedule. (We could not, for example, have gotten a
one-day delay of our second session; a full Elmo Hope album was
recorded there for Prestige on July 28.)

Once we got started, I remember a fairly steady progression and
no special feeling of panic; we undoubtedly completed at least
three and possibly four numbers on the 21st, and finished work on
the 27th sufficiently early and in good enough spirits to have all
three musicians willing to pose outside the studio for the photographs that were used on the original album cover. (The better-
known reproduction of the Henri Rousseau "primitive" painting,
The Repast of the Lion, is from a repackaging that was issued in
1958.) However, since there were probably no notes kept by me
during recording (or only scraps of paper that were not retained),
and since mid-'50s musicians-union contracts did not call for a list
of song titles, there is no paperwork to identify even which tunes
were taped each day. I can't remember ever seeing original tape
boxes from any of the early trio dates in the tape files at the
Riverside offices, so any unused material presumably was destroyed without a second thought. (It must be understood that in
those long-ago times we were considering only the problems of the
moment: our goal was to record an album; if more takes were
needed, it was because the number had not yet been played well
enough; such matters as reissues or the use of alternate takes were
not even imagined.)

It is actually quite possible that almost everything was completed
in little more than one recorded attempt. For I still recall with
painful clarity that a great deal of studio time first had to be spent
in basic preparation, with Thelonious sitting at the piano reading
sheet music and slowly picking out the notes of the Duke Ellington
compositions he had agreed to record. Those run-throughs proba-

bly didn't take nearly as long as it must have seemed to me; although Monk began each time as if the tune were totally strange, within a relatively short time he had carved out his own firmly individualized version. And he had also picked accompanists of great value: Oscar Pettiford had never previously recorded with Monk, but he had a specific familiarity with the music from his time as bassist with the Ellington orchestra; Kenny Clarke had first worked with Thelonious in the Minton's era and knew all his tricks. (I can also remember the drummer displaying his own impatience at Monk's making all of us wait for him; Kenny simply picked up the large color comics section of a Sunday newspaper he had found—Van Gelder's studio, you'll recall, was also the living room of his home—and sat there behind it, reading and pointedly ignoring the rehearsing pianist.)

Sessions 3 and 4
(March 17 and April 3, 1956)
Riverside's initial decision had been to devote Monk's first two albums to standard tunes, and we proceeded with this second project without hesitation, uninfluenced by some unfriendly reviewers who felt we had "forced" him to play Ellington (which should show how little they understood Thelonious and his artistic stubbornness). Oscar Pettiford was again the bassist; Kenny Clarke had left the United States to take up long-term residence in Europe, and Art Blakey was called on to replace him. I have always considered Blakey the most appropriate and sympathetic drummer for Monk—ever since first hearing them together on that Blue Note test pressing. So things in the studio were even calmer than before. The leader saw fit to arrive well prepared and apparently felt no need to test me. He had picked much of the material for specific reasons: "Liza" was part of his performance repertoire; the chord changes of "Just You, Just Me" had provided the basis for his composition "Evidence"; he knew and was fond of Fats Waller's "Honeysuckle Rose." I do recall lending him a music book, *The Rodgers and Hart Songbook,* in which he found "You Are Too Beautiful." (That also helps to date the fire that damaged the Monk family apartment early in 1956; the book became a casualty.)

The only musical problems resulted from Pettiford's insistence on bowing an entire chorus of "Tea for Two" as an introduction, even though he was unable to stay in tune. (I later learned that Oscar, for all his greatness, was always bothered by intonation problems when playing *arco.*) I finally convinced him to bow only the first half, switching to *pizzicato* thereafter; it was possibly my first forceful decision as a producer. What I found most unforgettable was a dramatic non-musical event after the first session. It had snowed, and the roads were frozen and slick as we returned from New Jersey in two automobiles. Pettiford and Blakey led the way; I was with Monk who, unsure of the route, was following them closely. Another car suddenly turned out of a side road into the space between us. Thelonious, alarmed at the thought of losing the others, swerved to pass the newcomer—and skidded sharply across the highway, stopping mere inches short of smashing into a telephone pole, and then calmly informed me: "It's a good thing I was driving. If it had been someone else, we might be dead now." I had never been his passenger before; thereafter I limited my time in that role as much as possible.

Once again there is no documentation of sequence (although again I am certain that at least three numbers were taped the first day), so the selections are presented as on the original album. And as a final note on these trio sessions: although the credits on these and several other early Riverside albums read "produced by Bill Grauer and Orrin Keepnews," this was strictly the result of an initial agreement that my late partner and I would share the billing; actually, he was not on hand on these occasions, and eventually it was made clear that he ran business affairs and I produced the jazz albums.

Session 5
(October 9, 1956)

In many respects this is the real beginning of my work with Monk. When some reviews of the first two albums demonstrated a strange backlash effect, with even writers who had attacked his earlier work as too odd and far-out now criticizing us for denying Thelonious full creative freedom, we felt that our first purpose had been achieved. Riverside could now safely turn to recording him with horns, in original compositions. I had no way of foreseeing how incredibly more difficult this would be for me. Basically, dealing with Monk in full-scale action meant that it was my job to supervise and control the creative flow of recording sessions that involved a perfectionist leader driving a group of sensitive and highly talented artists beyond their limits.

Actually, even this first session of the *Brilliant Corners* album was deceptively easy. The lineup was powerful: Pettiford again; the great Max Roach; young Sonny Rollins, definitely a rising star, with whom Thelonious had done some impressive recording for Prestige two years earlier; and an alto player who was already my friend and protégé. Ernie Henry had been recommended to Riverside by our first contract artist, pianist Randy Weston; he had already completed his initial album for the label—and had just become a member of Monk's infrequently working quartet. Thelonious did have some new material, but one was a lovely melody named for his friend and patroness, Baroness Koenigswarter, generally known as "Nica," whose full first name is Pannonica, and the other only seemed difficult. Despite its strangely spelled and pronounced title, "Ba-lue Bolivar Ba-lues-are" was only a blues, named after the Bolivar, a West Side apartment hotel where Nica was then living. Monk did make things a bit more difficult by an impromptu addition to the former piece; seeing a celeste in a corner of the studio, he had it set up at right angles to the piano—so that he could play the ballad on celeste with his right hand and, at the same time, on piano with his left. Both numbers were completed in reasonable time, but the seeds of trouble were there: on several occasions, Monk stopped the band at the end of the first chorus of "Pannonica." They seemed uncertain as to what was disturbing him; one of these fragmentary takes has survived and provides the answer. It includes his impatient reminder that they are forgetting the "tag"—the structure is more complicated than the players realize, and Thelonious expects quicker and better execution than he is getting from them.

We were also in an unfamiliar studio, with an engineer lacking in jazz experience. My partner had arbitrarily made long-term arrangements with Reeves Sound Studios and informed me that this was my new working "home." Over the next few years I grew to be quite comfortable there, but in 1956 this was not yet the case.

Session 6
(October 19, 1956)
This is of course a very celebrated session; I have written about it often over the years, and I can still feel the same sense of emotional exhaustion on listening to the recording—and a continuing feeling of surprise that we were able to issue a complete version of "Brilliant Corners." The facts are quite simple: we spent a full four hours in the studio that night, began this piece at least twenty-five times (again there is no written documentation, but I have no doubts about the number), and quit without the quintet having once played it to completion.

The composition is incredibly tricky; it has an off-center rhythmic pattern; and every second chorus is played at doubled tempo. The mere fact that such thorough professionals as Roach and Rollins and Pettiford were unable to satisfy Thelonious says all that need be said about the immensity of their task. As for young Ernie Henry, who tended to feel insecure under the best of circumstances, he soon came close to falling apart, even though Monk tried to ease the pressure by not playing during the alto solo. Late in the evening, Pettiford and the leader exchanged harsh words, leading to an amazing situation that perhaps could only have happened on this night. During one take, we in the control room were sure the bass mike was malfunctioning: Oscar was obviously playing, but not a sound could be heard. The unpleasant truth was that the bassist actually was not playing; he was merely pantomiming quite convincingly! (Not surprisingly, this was the last time Monk and Pettiford ever worked together.)

When we finally quit, I was aware that several portions had been very excitingly executed; I could only hope that the pieces could be welded together—in particular, that one abruptly concluded opening chorus could be used as an ending. Although I had no previous experience with such drastic tape editing, it all succeeded far beyond expectations. The finished product still sounds quite miraculous to me (although I would now like to improve the editing in a couple of places).

Session 7
(December 7, 1956)
Our troubles were of course not yet over. Schedule conflicts kept us apart for a while, and then allowed only one day in which to put Max and Sonny (who were together in Roach's very busy group) into the studio with Monk. Desperate to finish the album, I unwisely scheduled a 10 a.m. start. There were two substitute players; not only was Pettiford replaced—by Miles Davis's young bassist, Paul Chambers—but Ernie Henry was absent. He had accepted a job with Dizzy Gillespie's world-touring big band, which seemed to him an improvement over working occasional weekends with Thelonious. But to Monk this meant that his regular saxophonist had quit; his feelings were hurt, and he responded by replacing Ernie with an experienced young trumpet player (already a veteran of both the Ellington and Basie orchestras) named Clark Terry.

When I reached the studio, only the two newcomers were on hand; gradually the others drifted in, and they began work on a relatively simple Monk tune, "Bemsha Swing." But we were running short of time—by now I had learned that the studio was promised to another customer at 1 p.m.—and when Roach spotted some tympani in the corner and insisted on adding it to his equipment (possibly in emulation of Monk's piano/celeste pairing), things began to seem hopeless. There were only about twenty minutes left to us when we finished the quintet number, and we remained about five minutes of music short of a respectable total album time. All I could do was ask Thelonious for a once-through unaccompanied standard; he responded with a flawless five and a half minutes of "I Surrender, Dear," and somehow I had survived the making of the first major album of my career.

Sessions 8 and 9
(April 5 and 16, 1957)
I am of course aware that the original liner of the solo album *Thelonious Himself* lists the recording dates as April 12 and 16, and I can think of no reason why I would have misstated the day of the first session, but I am increasingly impressed by physical and logical evidence pointing to the two dates I have listed above. So I choose to take this occasion to change my mind about the recording structure of this album. Once again there are no existing data sheets (I could have saved a lot of mental anguish if I had started my longtime system of recording information sheets just a little sooner). But there are two union contracts, one listing only Monk, the other adding John Coltrane; there are also some original tape boxes. The only dates indicated are April 5 and 16. One box confirms that "Monk's Mood" was recorded on the latter day, and the announcement preceding the touch of false-start-and-talk that's included here reveals that this was "Selection 6" (of a total of eight on the album). I also remember Coltrane and Wilbur Ware arriving at the studio while Monk was at work on a solo number. Turning back to April 5, tape boxes bearing that date contain several alternate takes—for "Ghost of a Chance," "I Should Care," and " 'Round Midnight," respectively identified on tape as Selections 1, 2, and 3. Thus, if at least three belong to April 5 and if one (and probably two) more were made prior to the "Monk's Mood" trio on April 16, there is simply no room for an April 12 session! (If this type of research bores you, please accept my regrets, but surely it's a producer's privilege to attempt to sort out his own past.)

There are other memorable aspects to the making of this album.

It was recorded at my urging—his single solo performances on each of the three earlier albums had convinced me that there was something quite distinctive and important about Monk playing alone. But when he illogically proposed adding two players on one selection (was he duelling with me again?), I knew enough to agree, and consequently we do have this "Monk's Mood," which is unlike anything else he ever recorded and yet also foreshadows the original Five Spot quartet. Some time before the initial session, Thelonious and I had our first open clash of wills, as already described—so it must have been on April 5 that he was waiting in the control room when I arrived. It was on that day that we recorded the half-dozen remarkable "in progress" takes of " 'Round Midnight," which fortunately remained intact through the years to eventually provide a unique and fascinating study of this man at work.

Session 10
(June 25, 1957)

This is the night *before* the marathon *Monk's Music* date, an evening on which Monk is thought not to have accomplished anything. He had come up with the wonderful concept of writing some four-horn arrangements utilizing two close associates who represented the past and the future of the tenor saxophone: Coleman Hawkins and John Coltrane. (I claim important reverse input into this choice: I had proposed recording with several horns, and had mentioned some names that he rejected. But rather than merely saying "no," he had offered his own alternative suggestion, which was Hawk and Trane.) According to reliable sources, he had stayed awake for several days preparing his music, and he arrived at the studio on time for what was scheduled as the first of two consecutive evenings of recording. Almost everyone was there, but Art Blakey did not show up for nearly an hour. By then, Monk was close to losing his fine edge, but he boldly plunged into a new composition, the formidable "Crepuscule with Nellie." (The word means "twilight" and for some reason it was consistently misspelled at Riverside as "crepescule." Nellie was his wife.) I have always recalled that Thelonious collapsed almost immediately; I was quite wrong. The newly discovered first take of "Crepuscule" is not at all unsuccessful; the band is hesitant but seems to understand what is wanted from them, and Monk is full of energy. But it *was* quickly downhill from there. There still exists on tape a strange false start in which I can tell from the tone quality in my voice, when it is heard after the music breaks off, that I have gone into the studio to urge him on; then it becomes quite clear that he is finished for the evening.

(At this point I turned practical; aware that the band would have to be paid for their time anyhow, I requested a six-man, pianoless blues that was titled "Blues for Tomorrow" when it was later issued on an anthology album of that name.)

Session 11
(June 26, 1957)

"Tomorrow" turned out to be a quite literal reference. Again faced with the prospect of key players going off on tour (coordination of schedules was a major problem for a producer in those active years), we had to try to get the full album recorded the very next night. We succeeded quite well, and I think that on this occasion the feeling of pressure helped. This time we waited a while before tackling "Crepuscule" again, but it seems to have become even more troublesome for the horns.

The order in which this material was recorded reflects how we dealt with our limited working time. The trickier and more tightly arranged pieces came first; then the band could stretch out on a couple of blowing tunes. Fortunately, these didn't need many takes. "Epistrophy" broke down once after an excellent Coltrane solo (this fragment has been reissued more than once), and the second try stayed strong throughout. There was only one complete take of "Well, You Needn't"—the memorable version on which Trane, uncertain of the solo sequence, has to be reminded loudly by Thelonious ("Coltrane, Coltrane") that it's his turn. I'll take credit for not even thinking of interrupting the take at that point; another of the many lessons I learned from Monk can be stated as "when in doubt, let the music continue"—you might just end up, as we did here, with creative results that heavily outweigh the minor mistake.

Session 12
(probably July 1957)

These are of course the only recordings by the historic quartet that played a legendary six-month engagement at the Five Spot in the second half of 1957. That was Monk's triumphant return to the New York club scene; it was a magnificent pairing of two of the very greatest jazz talents; and it is one of my major regrets that the group was not extensively captured on tape. But pride and person-

alities were working against me. Coltrane was then under contract
to Prestige Records (it had not been easy to arrange for his appearance on the *Monk's Music* album). This of course was where
Thelonious had felt unhappy and ill-treated just before coming to
Riverside. When I spoke to Bob Weinstock (the founder and back
then still the owner of Prestige) about recording Trane with Monk,
he had no objections—provided we would give him reciprocal use
of the pianist as a sideman with Coltrane. Thelonious, however,
was stubbornly firm: under no circumstances would he *ever* do
anything for Prestige. I could not change his position; actually, it
was not hard to understand and sympathize with his attitude. Besides, at that time I was hopeful of soon getting Trane to join the
Riverside roster. So we did hold this one, technically improper
session; later, Coltrane was reluctant to do more; and after a while
he left Monk to rejoin Miles Davis, leaving only these three one-
take selections as the quartet's legacy.

I remain uncertain of the exact recording date, due to the complete absence of any helpful documentation. In the past I have
made some wrong guesses, but I now feel certain that it must have
been quite early in the Five Spot engagement. Otherwise, it would
not have included Wilbur Ware—for reasons noted in my account
of the next sessions with Gerry Mulligan.

Sessions 13 and 14
(August 12 and 13, 1957)
Thelonious had stopped into the Riverside offices one day and
casually noted that "Gerry" had left him at the corner. It was my
first indication that he and Mulligan were friends, and it led me to
investigate the possibility of an unlikely combination that might
have considerable musical validity. When both musicians agreed
with me, we quickly put together a session, using Monk's current
bass player and drummer. Our plan was to do one "simple" quartet
date and then later put the two stars into a larger, formally arranged setting. But the blowing session, with two older Monk
tunes surrounding the very recent "Rhythm-a-ning," went so
smoothly that (learning that the studio was available the next afternoon) we decided to come right back and finish up the same way.
There was no pre-planning: just " 'Round Midnight" (because
Gerry insisted he had to play it with Thelonious), a Mulligan original, and a standard. The only problem occurred afterwards. August 12, it turned out, had been the last night for the original
Monk/Coltrane quartet: at the end of the session on the 13th,

Ware brought his bass back down to the Five Spot, left, and never returned. There were conflicting explanations, but later that evening Ahmed Abdul-Malik was hired as a permanent replacement.

Session 15
(February 25, 1958)
This is another of the "non-productive" evenings mentioned at the beginning of these notes; and I must admit that the performance is largely interesting as a footnote to history. It is the only reminder of an attempted album that would have had Sonny Rollins and Johnny Griffin as a two-tenor team, with Art Blakey as the drummer. But we never even assembled that combination in the studio. I had notified Griffin, Wilbur Ware, and Donald Byrd; Monk was to have contacted Sonny and Art, but neither one appeared (and both later insisted to me quite convincingly that they never had been told). Mid-evening phone calls brought in Pepper Adams and Philly Joe Jones, but after two run-throughs of what was then a new Monk tune, Thelonious decided not to continue with this lineup. Interestingly enough, he had been quite willing to work with Wilbur (it was six months since the bassist had been replaced at the Five Spot), but what really broke up the record date was Ware's stubborn and lengthy insistence to Monk that the bass part on "Coming on the Hudson" was impossible to play.

Sessions 16 and 17
(May 7 and 12, 1958)
I really could not picture Thelonious Monk in the lesser role of a "sideman," and would never have asked him to play that part. But when Clark Terry, whom Thelonious both admired *and* liked, made such a request, the pianist agreed without hesitation, did not ask for a heavy fee (I believe he was paid no more than twice the union-scale minimum), and turned in the most relaxed, happiest, and funkiest Monk performances I ever witnessed. One reason may have been that Clark (who, after all, had worked for years with Duke Ellington) made no special fuss over him—and included only one Monk tune on the album.

Thelonious was particularly pleased with the work of Sam Jones, who was making his first Riverside appearance, and several months later asked Sam to join his group. But the bassist was actually a last-minute replacement. Wilbur Ware had been hired and we spent quite some time the first day waiting for him before making an emergency phone call. (Wilbur's remarkable and original talent caused many of us to try to overlook his immense unreliability, but that eventually became impossible.)

Session 18
(July 9, 1958)

When Thelonious returned to the Five Spot late in the spring of '58, his saxophonist was Johnny Griffin, a Riverside artist—so there were no contractual obstacles. Early in July we set up equipment in the club and recorded a full night's work. But when Monk listened a few days later, he began to express small objections, and finally decided he didn't feel right about the whole evening and asked me to set it all aside. By then I knew better than to argue with him about music, so I merely began planning a second attempt. (It took place, quite successfully, the following month.)

Many years later, reviewing the surviving tapes (about half the material remained, plus a complete though rather battered information sheet), I found myself in disagreement with some of Monk's original decisions, and eventually went so far as to include four selections from that night in an album of previously unissued items. Most notable among them was Griffin's only recording of " 'Round Midnight" with its composer. Most peculiar is an unaccompanied, unidentified piano piece. Monk often opened a set with a brief solo version of an old standard, and that's what this sounded like. But no one I asked (musicians, friends of Monk, old-song experts) could come up with a title or composer, nor has anyone come along since it was first issued in 1984.

One more previously unheard number is worth noting. "Bye-ya" closed out the final set that evening; it's an earlier Monk composition that was otherwise never recorded for Riverside, and it is distinguished by the presence of guest drummer Art Blakey. Overall, things are rather sloppy, and Griffin's solo goes on too long. But Thelonious follows with a wonderfully concise solo; this is a rare glimpse of the Monk/Blakey team in spontaneous live action; and above all it offers a unique chunk of jazz reality—some good friends hanging out together in a club very late at night, and surely paying little or no attention to the tape machine.

Session 19
(August 7, 1958)

On this return trip with recording equipment, everything went well at the Five Spot. I was hoping to get two albums from the night's work, and asked Thelonious to play a wide variety of material rather than just repeating a few throughout the evening (which is the safer and more usual way of recording under working conditions). The gamble paid off; the quartet was particularly close-knit, and we found ourselves with—in addition to the ever-present closing theme, "Epistrophy"—eleven fully acceptable selections. Once again (but for the *last* time), I can find no helpful paper work and almost no tape boxes—but it's hardly possible that there was more music than this, all originally divided between the *Thelonious in Action* and *Misterioso* albums.

Session 20
(February 28, 1959)

Three decades ago, it must be remembered, a jazz presentation in a major New York concert hall was still most unusual. Even with Monk's new-found popularity, the idea of offering full-band arrangements of his strange music was too daring for any professional promoter—this evening at Town Hall was put on by Monk's close friend Jules Colomby. And there was a full house!

The scores were the work of Hall Overton, in close cooperation with the composer. Six strong horn players were added to the current quartet (Charlie Rouse had just begun his eleven years as Monk's tenor player), and there was an unusual series of long and detailed rehearsals, rigorously supervised by Thelonious. So when we set up to record that night, there was no reason to expect trouble. Actually, we encountered only one problem, but it was a classic:

Staff engineer Ray Fowler and I were working just offstage, using a single tape machine. Accordingly, I asked Monk to glance at me before each number, to see if we needed a momentary delay to load a new reel of tape. He neglected to check only once—but it *was* during a reel change, so that the first several bars of "Little Rootie Tootie" were not recorded. At the first opportunity, I explained the problem to Thelonious, whose solution was direct, outlandish, and quite helpful. At the end of the scheduled program, with the audience screaming for an encore, he calmly announced that the recording engineers had "loused up" and proceeded to repeat the entire number. The start of the encore, of course, doubles as the opening of both versions here.

The concert actually began with three quartet numbers. At the time, knowing that there would be enough orchestral material for a full album, we used this first segment only to work on the recording balance. Many years later, I found that the unused quartet reel had survived. The performances were exciting (Monk was clearly full of enthusiasm on this triumphant night), and the sound actually much better than remembered. The material was easily put into shape for belated issuance. (There are frequent rumors about two additional quartet numbers. I do not remember any; I would very much doubt that there could have been as many as five small-group pieces on what was billed as an orchestra concert; and above all this is everything that was recorded that night.)

There has also been some confusion about "Thelonious." The original Riverside album begins with a shortened version; Monk was not happy with his chorus (which is the only solo), and we decided to use only the final ensemble chorus, presented as a sort of opening theme. The full version actually turned up on a late-1960s German reissue album; hearing about this finally led me to search for and uncover that tape in the vaults. Apparently it had survived without my being aware of it and had mistakenly been copied for that reissue. A very awkward edit was clearly audible in the piano solo—presumably the result of someone's attempt to repair whatever had initially bothered Thelonious. I don't recall whether it had been a technical recording flaw or a performance error. However, a few years ago I re-edited and basically smoothed over the original problem so that the best possible full-length version could be issued.

Sessions 21, 22, and 23
(June 1, 2, and 4, 1959)

A few months later, Monk's working group and one guest went into the studio for what almost turned out to be an uneventful group of sessions. This was an ideal way to record Thelonious—three men he was quite used to, plus the adventure of one newcomer. Monk had never played with Thad Jones before, but this was the kind of trumpet player who could meet his tough standards: like Clark Terry or Donald Byrd, Thad was technically capable of handling the complexities of the music and was also an imaginative improvisor.

My recording information cards tell me that we spent the entire first afternoon on the three versions of "Played Twice." It was a new composition, and Thelonious was obviously in his demanding mood: years later, I find all the takes to be of value (but they are far from identical, and I'm delighted that they all exist). Apparently we had only planned a short session; we were scheduled again for the next day, and this time ran easily through three relatively familiar Monk pieces. At this point he informed me that we "must have enough" for an album, and he was—just barely—correct. These four add up to almost thirty-eight minutes; but I felt that this much time and only four selections made up a pretty skimpy total. I insisted on one more piece, preferably a new work, and was willing to call another session just for that purpose.

Presumably the extremely tricky "Jackie-ing" (named for Monk's niece) was written, or at least completed, in two days. It was ready for the third date, but that one-tune session was by no means uncomplicated. To begin with, Thelonious showed up without the music; he had left the just-finished parts on Nica's piano, but was sure he could just show everyone what to play. After he struck a few notes and sang a few more, there was a rebellion. The musicians insisted on having it in writing, and I quickly agreed to the delay. It was at least an hour before he returned, and even then it was not routine. I can remember Thad, who had a reputation for being able to sight-read *anything,* struggling through a couple of unsuccessful takes—unfortunately, that reel of tape has not survived—but eventually they did conquer what is clearly one of Monk's most memorably difficult pieces.

Sessions 24 and 25
(October 21 and 22, 1959)

This turned out to be as peaceful as a Monk date could possibly be, with no other musicians involved and none of the friends and hangers-on that you'd find on the New York scene. It took place only because of a coincidence: I was scheduled to go to San Francisco for a "live" recording of Cannonball Adderley's new band, and learned that Thelonious was to make his very first appearance in that city the following week. Since he would have only a pick-up band (Charlie Rouse, plus a bassist and drummer from Los Angeles), it seemed a good opportunity for something we had been considering for some some—a follow-up to his impressive *Thelonious Himself* solo album of 1957.

I was in good spirits following the highly charged Adderley dates: Thelonious was subdued (his wife was recuperating in a Los Angeles hospital following major surgery) but in an unusually genial and cooperative mood. He had his material almost completely ready, including four of his earlier compositions and two new ones. The only oddity was a ridiculous item from the '20s that he had just come across in an old songbook: "There's Danger in Your Eyes, Cherie." His outrageous interpretation of this one did take some

preparation and two takes—making it the only one of ten selections that was performed more than once!

This was not because we were in any hurry. Having been unable
to find a suitable recording studio, we were using the stage of a
spacious meeting hall; there was no time pressure. It's just that
everything fell into place effortlessly; on the first of two scheduled
afternoons, six tunes (including the two-take number) were completed. Accordingly, we delayed the start of the second session so
that Monk could take me to lunch, which he ordered very knowl-
edgeably at a nearby Italian restaurant.

Sessions 26 and 27
(April 28 and 29, 1960)

My next encounter with Monk, however, was in sharp contrast,
even though it took place in the same city. This collection includes
the very first appearance of material from an ill-fated attempted
collaboration between Thelonious and the late Shelly Manne. It
had not been my idea. During a European trip, my colleague Bill
Grauer (who hardly ever interfered in jazz production) had run
into both men at jazz festivals and had asked Monk's opinion of
Shelly. "He can play," Thelonious said, which is about the same as
answering "I'm fine" when a casual acquaintance begins a conversation by politely asking about your health. But somehow Grauer
took this as approval, and went on to enlist Shelly's enthusiastic
agreement and to get our friend Les Koenig to accept the idea of
two co-leader dates, one for Riverside and one for his Contemporary label (where Shelly had been a big-selling artist ever since the
1957 Manne/Previn *My Fair Lady* album). I suppose I should have
resisted, but Grauer could be a *very* persuasive man, and Shelly
was a very good drummer and had been part of the early bebop
scene on New York's Fifty-second Street. I also trusted Monk and
his stubborn musical honesty; if he hadn't objected, how could I?

I did devise what I thought was a way of turning this into a fairly
normal Monk date. It would be convenient to record on the West
Coast, during Monk's return engagement at the Blackhawk in San
Francisco, so I decided on combining Charlie Rouse and John Ore
(Monk's bassist at the time) with two other horn players with
Eastern jazz associations who were then in Los Angeles. Harold
Land had of course worked with the Clifford Brown/Max Roach
band; Joe Gordon had the added advantage of being part of
Manne's current group. Since I still didn't have a preferred studio,
we arranged to set up in the Blackhawk itself and record during

the afternoon. (I had brought along Riverside's engineer, Ray Fowler.) But from the start we were in trouble. Thelonious had a bad cold and was irritable; Shelly was *too* respectful. When he kept insisting that Monk was the master and should make the basic decisions, I knew Thelonious well enough to visualize his thoughts: "If I'm the top man, how come we share the billing?"

There was never any open hostility, but neither was there any musical meshing. Let's just say that the stale air and beer of the Five Spot doesn't interact with California open air and fresh orange juice, or that Manne could not go back to swinging in the way he had on Dizzy Gillespie's first Guild date in 1945. On the first day we made an acceptable version of a new Monk tune and a rather rambling "Just You, Just Me"—which had been on the second trio date back in '56. On the second day there was an unexceptional " 'Round Midnight," and then Shelly asked to be excused. He knew it wasn't happening well enough, and thought the proper thing to do was to stop. I agreed. Over the years we made smiling reference to this occasion, and I never seriously thought about issuing the material. (But with both artists dead, and above all considering the special retrospective nature of what was billed as the *"complete"* Monk-on-Riverside collection, I did think it suitable to include these often talked-about but previously unheard performances.)

Session 28
(April 29, 1960)
At mid-afternoon of this day, I felt totally frustrated. My engineer and I had traveled cross-country, worked hard, and would have absolutely nothing to show for it. Then I turned to Monk with the beginnings of a salvage idea in mind. My first words were probably pretty angry: he had kept the date from happening properly by not even trying to compromise with his co-leader; more than that, he must have known all along that he really didn't want to do it, so why hadn't he spoken up and vetoed the project months ago? Then I cooled down and developed my plan: add Land and Gordon to the regular quartet as special one-night guests and, making use of the equipment already in place, record in performance at the Blackhawk. Monk agreed, picked out a handful of not-*too*-difficult compositions, and then was shipped back to his hotel room to fight his cold with rest and Vitamin C pills, with Rouse assigned the task of making sure the other two horns knew the required chord changes.

As could happen when Monk was willing to admit he had been in the wrong, he became incredibly cooperative. The club owner informed me that it was the only night all week Thelonious showed up on time; on the bandstand he was all business; between sets he sat down at the tape machine with headphones and checked out the performances; and at the start of the second set he actually spoke to the audience, advising them not to be "alarmed" if some repertoire was repeated, "because we're recording."

There is an explanation for the dual titling of the new tune he had written for this date, first issued as "Worry Later" but subsequently known as "San Francisco Holiday." During rehearsal earlier in the week, I had asked the composer if he wanted to name his new tune now, or worry about it later. "Worry later" was the response—and that, I decided, was an ideal title. But when Monk did worry about it some time later, he chose to rename the piece to commemorate the fact that Nellie and their two children had been with him on this trip, and it became "San Francisco Holiday."

5

A Not-Quite-Musician
I Knew

Lenny Bruce was a friend. Not a very close friend (there are no intimate secrets revealed here), but we hung out with some of the same people, and ran into each other frequently for several years, and appreciated each other. The article that follows ran in *Down Beat* as a kind of belated obituary; for reasons that the piece itself should make clear, that magazine seemed an appropriate place for it, although I could have done without that "existential jazz aura" title that someone there conjured up.

I find that a couple of my fondest small memories were not included. One is a phone call in the very early '60s. My younger son David, about seven at the time, answered; Lenny opened by asking, "Would you like to fly on my Bagdad carpet?," launching without introduction into his imitation of the movie actor Sabu— the perhaps forgotten star of epics like *Elephant Boy*. (My son was obviously unflappable—or just used to my callers. He listened patiently for a few lines, and then handed over the phone, saying only: "It's for you, Dad.") The other memory is of a night at Mister Kelly's, a Chicago club, at a time when Lenny was into the transition from more formal comedy bits to his later free-style approach. When I greeted him after the show (in which he had been coasting, using several familiar routines), he was genuinely upset. "I didn't know you were here," he apologized. "I wouldn't have done any bits if I knew you were here."

In 1974, I again asked *Down Beat* to publish me on the subject of Lenny Bruce, this time in rebuttal to a biography-of-sorts that had deeply disturbed me. I was impelled to transcend the vehemence

145

of even the toughest of my *Record Changer* reviews. I haven't
written another book review since then, and I like to think I quit
when I was ahead.

The Existential Jazz Aura of Lenny Bruce
1966

I first saw and heard Lenny Bruce in the spring of 1959, on the
night he made his New York night club debut. It was in "The Den
in the Duane," a comfortable basement room rather oddly located
in an otherwise sedate hotel on lower Madison Avenue. Bruce
appeared at this club several times during the next couple of years,
and it came to seem something like his natural habitat. (Come to
think of it, although there *must* have been other acts there between
his visits, I can't recall any of them.) You could say that it was here
that the Lenny Bruce who was successful, rich, and relatively easy
to take developed and flourished.

There was more than a hint of this on that opening night. I went
at the urging of drummer Philly Joe Jones, who had been talking
up Lenny's coming with all the fervor of a disciple. Jones had
organized a group, including my wife and me, that journeyed to
the Den that night, even though most of us had never heard of
Lenny except through Joe. (I had first heard his name while preparing to record Philly's noted odd-ball Bela Lugosi imitation, which
was issued as "Blues for Dracula"—Joe explained that it derived
from a routine by this fabulous and unknown comic he had met in
San Francisco.)

The Den was jammed. Lenny's first show had run long, and, I
recall, the large crowd queued up for the next show included such
jazz people as Ira Gitler and the late Eddie Sherman (a major
Bruce fan and long-time author of *Down Beat*'s "Out of My Head"
column, under the pen name George Crater). Both the size and
nature of the crowd were of some significance—not only had a
relatively unheralded event drawn an overflow crowd, but then
and thereafter Bruce attracted jazz people in particular and, for
that matter, a hip show-business crowd in general.

He attracted lots of just plain people too. It may surprise those
familiar only with the later succession of arrests (the charges
steadily alternating between obscene performance and possession
of narcotics), but in 1959 Bruce was becoming—just like the hero
of some clichéd show-biz movie—an overnight sensation, a big-

time entertainer. Something called sick humor was supposedly abroad in the land; it was very *in,* although on close examination this "school" of comedy turned out to consist of very little more than Lenny. But he made enough of an impact (and soon had enough imitators) to be a whole school. He made a couple of big-selling albums; he worked at big-minimum supper clubs like Mister Kelly's in Chicago and the Blue Angel on New York's East Side. He was known to be far out and very outspoken, but not "dirty" or taboo. When he appeared on Steve Allen's Sunday night prime-time network television show, Allen did ruin much of the effect by apologizing in advance to all those who might not like it. But the fact remains that he *was* booked onto such a show.

For this was the earlier, comparatively safe Lenny Bruce. A strange way to describe him, no doubt, when the impact he made was so largely based on his being a nonconformist attacker of graven images. But looking back with all the wisdom of seven years' hindsight, it's clear that *that* Lenny was nothing at all like the final Lenny. I suppose it's something like the way a 1945 Charlie Parker solo, startling as it was when it was new, is apt to appear quite formal and almost conservative (although by no means less valid) in the mid-'60s, when you've just been listening to, say, Archie Shepp.

In 1959 and thereabouts, Lenny was an entertainer and at the same time an artist—the same kind of tightrope-walking that many jazz musicians have come to accept as the unfortunately normal way of pursuing their trade. He was telling jokes and doing all the voices in a number of routines, the details of which varied only somewhat from night to night. He was also ripping the hide off a broad catalog of pomposities and social idiocies and hates with well-chosen punchlines and stabbing, seemingly incidental comments.

This is part of what I have always felt to be a similarity between his technique and that of at least some jazz musicians. Although I'm treading on swampy ground in making direct comparisons between something as strictly verbal as a comic's act and something as presumably nonverbal as music, Lenny's work at this time included touches that were clearly the equivalents of the brief but corny "quotes" from another tune and the sardonic, dead-pan mockery with which a jazz player can approach a very square set of chord changes. One good example of this came in a bit in which Eisenhower confronts Sherman Adams (if your memory stretches back to that presidential assistant and his questionable acceptance of gifts); it was funny, but strictly timely and almost Mort Sahl-ish political stuff until suddenly there was a fleeting phrase ("Just tell me the truth, and I won't hit you") that revealed the whole thing as a parody of the clichéd confrontation scene between the all-American righteous father and his naughty-boy-with-a-heart-of-gold son.

Above all, Lenny Bruce at this time came across as a very funny man, as a stand-up comedian capable of producing loud, break-up laughter from his audience—whether they dug the message behind the material or not. This was clearly the result of early show-business training of the toughest kind. Bruce had come up the hard way, starting in rough strip joints and tenth-rate clubs where the comic is generally regarded as an unwanted interruption in the show. He learned what musicians playing in the same kind of places have always had to learn in order to survive: first, you must use your skills just as hard as you can to get the audience's bare, minimal attention; if you feel equal to it, you then keep working hard to get them on your side. If you get that far and have some-thing special and personal and important you want to hit them with, then and only then do you dare display it.

That kind of background had a lot to do with Lenny's special appeal to jazz people. In addition to anything else, it meant quite directly that they had worked on the same streets, in the same clubs, at the same hours. He shared, for instance, that problem of leisure-hour time that all late-night show-business people face: the man whose working day ends at 5 p.m. has plenty of places to stop for an unwinding cocktail, but what do you do when you quit work at two or four in the morning? Many are forced to become experts on obscure bad movies, the kind that seem to survive only in all-night fleabag theaters and on the triple-late shows of TV. Thus the detailed and affectionate knowledge of the world of Bela Lugosi that Lenny and Philly Joe had in common.

One of Lenny's best early routines was a complex takeoff on a super hackneyed prison movie called *Brute Force,* which is also perhaps the best example of his jazz-like technique. The trite movie itself equals a trite standard tune. The normal improvised chorus (perhaps including the soloist's own favorite clichés) would be the equivalent of some straight comedy bits in this Bruce routine—like a recurring catch-phrase yelled by the leader of the convict riot ("Ya-ta, ya-ta, warden") that automatically reduced Bruce fans to hysteri-cal laughter. But the next chorus is more daring; maybe it mocks the limitations of the syrupy tune by playing the ballad double-time, which is what happens when the stereotyped prison chaplain self-righteously elects to face the men unarmed ("I have a weapon might-ier than guns . . . judo!"). Then Lenny keeps going further and further out until he passes mockery and hits a raw and shocking bit of twisted reality (although he's still getting laughs) that has nothing to do with the old movie and everything to do with the vicious facts of our penal system—the convict leader is talked into surrender by the prison's top homosexual.

I certainly do not want to imply, even remotely, that Lenny's act was in any way a series of equivalents of jazz solos. Nothing is that simple, and actually Lenny's kinship to jazz was probably more to be sensed in the atmosphere around him than in specific details.

I'd sat around in dressing rooms with him, had exchanged put-down glances with him as he carried on outrageous dead-pan conversation with stuffy and/or "important" visitors, had talked with him about musicians we both knew, had been involved in discussing thoroughly impractical schemes to record him (he was under contract to Fantasy, but he was going to be the world's first talking sideman, or something, on a Philly Joe album—and he once even sent me the beginning of a script for Joe and him). And most of this was *so* much like conversation with a jazz musician that it was hard to remember that I wasn't talking with one. I can think of no other non-musician about whom I can make that statement.

By emphasizing Lenny's ability to get big laughs, the off-hand nature of a lot of his tough lines, and his ability to work with topical material or create parodies, I don't want to make him seem too easygoing or to underplay his original material. (In general, I remember his "originals" as preferable to his work on "standards"— just as, say, Thelonious Monk playing something like "Nutty" is funnier than a Monk take-off on an Irving Berlin ditty.)

Even back at this time there were some obviously strongly felt routines built very directly around his views on organized religion—which were, to put it mildly, totally negative. A particularly savage one presented a meeting of a group of fast-shuffle promoters known as "Religions, Inc." This and other examples of his way of seeing the world we live in made a lot of people uncomfortable in his presence.

I have always figured that night clubs were places voluntarily visited by adults. Whenever they don't like the way a musician plays or the language or subject matter used by a comic, they can get up and leave—or they could have stayed away in the first place. But for reasons that require far deeper analysis than I have space for here, our Establishment has the opinion that such adults need more protection from certain dangers than any other class of citizen.

I do not know anything about the existence, nature, or extent of any narcotics problems Lenny might have had—except that they obviously were irrelevant to his work. I do not know if there was any organized conspiracy against him because of what he had to say. But it seems quite clear, and not only in connection with Bruce, that law-enforcement agencies in our country are apt to mark certain entertainers, or certain types of entertainers, as being, for one reason or another, "trouble." And it seems equally clear that if you are "trouble" in one city, you are someone they are alert for everywhere.

Lenny was first arrested and charged with giving an obscene performance in May 1960. Ironically, it was not only in San Francisco but it was at the Jazz Workshop. The late Art Auerbach, who owned that club, had known Lenny for a long time and had very much wanted to have him work there—to my knowledge, the only non-jazz act Art ever coveted. And what happened almost immediately? Lenny was arrested, for using a particular ten-letter word that was too rough for the detective who happened to be there.

Lenny was out on bail and back at work without delay, and he found it all pretty amusing—then. He was in fine form the next night. There was an even bigger crowd than before (with that kind of publicity, he said, he could outdraw the French art movies around the corner), and privately he was delighted that the previous night's performance had been taped, so that the case could be fought on its facts.

He won the case, but it turned out to be only the beginning of a long downhill slide. That there was police harrassment is obvious. That he died of "an overdose of police," as Phil Spector (on whose record label the last Bruce album appeared) said in a trade-paper ad, can be argued either way. That Lenny contributed hugely and inevitably to his own downfall cannot be argued.

Lenny was far too stubborn a man not to continue to give the Bruce-haters all the ammunition they could want. Call it "stubborn" or call it "dedicated," it comes out the same. Once he had been dragged in for obscenity, there was no chance whatsoever that he might watch his language—except to make it rougher all the time.

But eventually Lenny came to devote far too much of his performing time to what was nothing more than self-defense, which is obviously too limited a repertoire. The pressures he was under were clearly overwhelming; it's really not surprising that Lenny could not continue to handle the constant barrage. At the start of his legal troubles, he could turn it all into quick, concise, biting, and effective humor. Later, he was more apt to tell his audiences about his difficulties and little or nothing else.

Lenny's lawyer, a distinguished attorney with a brilliant record of defending people, books, and films against censorship, concluded that the obscenity charges had become an obsession with Lenny. Specifically, the lawyer told me, Bruce wanted to fight for a court ruling to the effect that Lenny Bruce was not an obscene person and, therefore, could not perform obscenely—he wanted the police to be permanently restrained from arresting him on such grounds.

It would seem as if Lenny's always imposing sense of his own importance had finally overstepped the bounds of reality.

I know that the last performances I saw suffered from the preoccupation with self-defense and from a generally undisciplined air that contrasted wildly with the cleanly arranged and edited foundations from which he had once launched his improvisations.

My last encounter with him was at the Village Vanguard; he was eager to play something on a portable tape recorder he had with him, but it wouldn't function—so he kept insisting that I fix it for him. Now it happens that I am irrationally intolerant of people who assume that, because I am a record producer, I must know where to buy a phonograph cheap and how to repair all types of recording devices (actually, my mechanical skills are non-existent). It is a small point, of course, but it is such a *square* misconception, and it pained me to have Lenny Bruce, of all people, be square about anything at all.

When I learned of Lenny's death, I thought back to that last meeting and was fleetingly disturbed that it had been so meaningless and negative, scarcely a fitting final memory. But on second thought there was really nothing wrong about such a small and very human memory—it was a good one to put alongside all the larger-than-life recollections of nights spent laughing at fabulously funny and penetrating routines. For I think it's important to remember about men like this both the large and the petty things, without leaning too hard on either end of the scale.

Lenny Bruce was an artist of importance and stature; he was also very obviously a man with his full quota of human failings. I don't know if he was a genius, whatever that might be. I do know that his combination of big artistry and distressingly small shortcomings reminds me, with painful immediacy, of more than a few jazz musicians. I also know that those smallnesses play their own important part in the creation of the whole artist.

I never directly knew Charlie Parker, about whom the same sort of comments are so often made, so I can only guess about the role that his shortcomings played in his total makeup. But of Lenny

Bruce I am certain that the creation of the master satirist and incisive iconoclast needed the fallible, egocentric man (so vulnerable to so many of the evils and monoliths he attacked) as much as it needed the incredibly daggerlike mind and the large heart. Together, all those elements made up someone vivid and valuable. He will be missed. I doubt if he can be replaced.

In Defense of Lenny (Against His Biographers) 1974

Ladies and Gentlemen LENNY BRUCE! By Albert Goldman from the journalism of Lawrence Schiller. Random House. 565 pp. Illus. $10.

This is intended less as a book review than as a public service announcement. A strange, contorted, vicious, dirty book, somewhat inaccurate as to facts and incredibly inaccurate in attitude, and dealing with the life and bad habits of Lenny Bruce, has recently been put together and published. My earnest advice to all readers who can be reached by my words is—*pass it by!*

My major objection is not simply to the desecration of the memory of a vastly talented, although certainly badly flawed human being. Lenny took enough lumps of all kinds during his life so that one more bum rap doesn't, I suppose, really make that much difference. But for some years I have been profoundly disgusted at the various people who have ghoulishly gotten fat by ripping off the dead Lenny. I guess one can almost excuse the comics who have freely appropriated his style and attitudes—who can really say where "influence" ends and moral plagiarism begins? But how can you excuse these men, the intellectually pretentious Goldman and the self-styled journalist Schiller, for having constructed around Lenny's name this deeply obscene, ill-written, mean-spirited, venomously jealous and highly unperceptive pseudo-biography.

The book does have a lot to say about the showbiz and jazz folk that Lenny knew and worked with, and it certainly has all sorts of hard-core language and activity and much detail about the ingesting of narcotics. However, if these are what you crave, may I recommend that you buy a record album or two, or go see an X-rated movie or two. These are surely more reasonable and honorable ways of spending ten bucks.

It should be quite obvious that I am not writing as your average objective, impersonal reviewer. I knew Lenny, responded strongly to his work, dug him as a man but grew very unhappy with him in his last years. But if I want to warn you away (and I certainly do), I should do something more than just inform you that I find this book offensive. I can't hope to do a complete job of detailing my objections—*Down Beat* has only a reasonable amount of space for this essay—but I can give you a modest sampling.

We might as well start at the beginning, with a first chapter that purports to be a "reconstruction" of some sort of average/composite "day in the life" of Bruce. Let's note the third sentence of the first page, part of a physical description of a "dirty gray morning . . . in Times Square" as Lenny arrives in town: "The glass aquarium sides of the papaya stands are all steamy, frankfurters floating on their bellies over waves of rolling heat like ailing tropical fish." Mr. Goldman, you have just flunked Freshman English! Or is it Mr. Goldman? You must try to understand that Goldman (who says he knew Bruce) has written the book "from the journalism" of Schiller, who only became seriously interested in Lenny when "prompted" by reports that his death resulted from a drug overdose. In addition, one "Richard Elman, the novelist" was called in to rewrite the first chapter, which goes on from that quoted opening bit of purple prose to a wild-eyed account of a day dripping with drugs and sex.

Elman and yet another writer (Schiller's rejected original collaborator) get fragmentary credit for other literary chores; but despite this gangbang approach to writing, we really must consider Goldman as the truly responsible party. So we'll have to fault him for all of this chapter, which not only gives us every possible physical detail, but also provides an inside-Lenny's-head view of the emotional impact of each pill and injection. This, I suppose, is the "new journalism" that feels entitled to invent dialogue and entire scenes and to guess at never-expressed thoughts and hidden motives. I'm afraid that this is too much like making up your own rules as you go along. Later, Goldman details a strip joint dressing room sex scene between Lenny and an unnamed stripper, with no witnesses (except invisible, omnipresent Goldman, I guess). Still later, we are bluntly told that Bruce, at the time of his New York obscenity trial, "felt a secret affinity with the judge and district attorney" and "a secret aversion to his long-hair hippie and short-hair libbie supporters."

Such free-hand inventiveness must cast doubt on the whole fact/fiction ratio here, doubts that I find underlined in Goldman's fumbling handling of situations about which I happen to have first-hand knowledge. I am also impressed by Goldman's tin ear. *Item:* Lenny's famous "Paladium Bit" includes a deliberately horrible pun by the tenth-rate comic he is satirizing, a reference to "Lost

Wages, Nevada." Goldman twice gives this as "Los Wages," which
has no point at all. I am amazed at the shoddy research that has
Lenny talking to *Down Beat* critic George Crater—when Crater
was merely a pen name for Lenny's good friend Eddie Sherman;
and that has him working in denim jacket and jeans at a period in
time when he was still strictly an Italian silk-suit dresser. (I'm not
being picky here: clothing is an important indication of where the
man's head is at, making this as misleading as to confuse Miles
Davis's current leather attire with *his* late '50s suit-and-tie phase.) I
am mightily amused when Goldman, a sometime record reviewer
yet, describes how a law suit by Lawrence Welk was settled (his
name had been used in an unkind sequence on the first Bruce LP):
"Fantasy had to go through all the albums beeping out the
bandleader's name with a funny sound." Dear Mr. Goldman, you
can't take a sound out of a *record* (although my mind insists on
seeing little men scratching thousands of discs in exactly the right
place with a metal beep-maker); you must throw away the bad
albums and change the master tape and then press new records!
   A major "attraction" of the book is its language. Goldman
seems to delight in being able to use *all* the slang, Anglo-Saxon and
men's-room-graffiti genitalia and bodily-function words. If this is
how he gets his jollies, I guess that's all right, but can he really not
have grasped the significance of his being able to write like that for
publication? It was Lenny's performances as much as anything else
that broke down those language barriers and led to the freedom
that is now commonplace in the arts. It's irony enough that such
freedom allows Goldman to write dirty stories about Lenny, but
it's too much when the biographer doesn't even faintly recognize
the connection.
   I have called this book mean-spirited and jealous—and this is
undoubtedly its strangest and most reprehensible feature. As I
read, I was increasingly bewildered by Goldman's antagonism towards Bruce. He elects to begin with a chapter totally concerned
with physical excesses; to go on at length about how Lenny copped
his whole comic approach from a non-performer friend named Joe
Ancis (you know, a legendary genius who was scared to appear
before an audience); to describe Lenny as a near-illiterate who
faked all his intellectual allusions, as a "dirty comic" almost from
the start and a copycat who "tailored his act . . . as soon as he
spotted the new trend" towards sick comedy—in short, to belittle
and demean and scarcely to give Bruce any points at all for originality or wit or social awareness. I must wonder why so brilliant and

witty a writer as Albert Goldman would bother to waste his time with the life story of this poor bastard, unless . . .

Unless there is some perverse form of identity transfer involved. Lenny Bruce, who was such a big swinger and user, and such an applauded stand-up comic and is now such a revered cult figure, he wasn't really anything much. Now, Albert Goldman, who is smart and urbane and writes well and can use every dirty word Lenny ever used, how come *he* isn't the cult hero? I am left with the uncomfortable feeling that Albert Goldman finds it a dirty shame that Leonard Albert Schneider got the chance to be "Lenny Bruce" when, if there were any justice in the world, Goldman could have done so much better a job of being Lenny Bruce.

6

What I Do for a Living

The descriptive piece about the functions of a record producer which opens this section resulted from the kind of direct question that is very rarely asked with any sincerity. When someone politely inquires as to what you *really* do in your line of work, they're usually no more interested in a detailed and clinically accurate response than if they had asked: "How are you?" But on this occasion *Down Beat* was putting together an issue focused on the jazz record business and, on behalf of their readers, actually was looking for a straight answer. I responded in considerable detail; despite the passage of two decades, most of the facts and virtually all the philosophy remain relevant. (In the interests of full disclosure, let me amend the reference to an unnamed "colleague" whose category puzzled the unemployment insurance people. In reality, that jobless producer was me.)

The even more detailed survey of my long working relationship with McCoy Tyner also resulted from the request of a magazine. Again the circumstances were unusual. *Keyboard* is aimed largely at professionals rather than fans, so I was being asked for candor, some depth, and a few moderately technical references. Of at least equal importance, I was allowed as much space as I considered necessary.

The remaining four selections were all written to accompany re-issue packages. The most extensive, from the booklet for the Bill Evans *Complete Riverside Recordings* compilation, parallels the format of my session-by-session recollection of comparable experiences with Monk. (Again, I have deleted some references that would be irrelevant or confusing because they are too specifically linked to the actual contents of various records.)

One of the other pieces deals with what has become a highly pleasing activity for me in recent years—resurrecting quite valid recorded performances that initially had to be ignored because of the rather rigid ground rules of constructing an album. Another combines one of my favorite people (the late Cannonball Adderley) and one of my favorite clubs (San Francisco's late Jazz Workshop) in a cautionary tale about the dangers of lack of tension in "live" recording situations. Finally, there's a brief tribute to the Village Vanguard, where—as already noted—my jazz writing career could be said to have begun, and where so much of my working and hanging-out life has continued to take place.

Inside the Recording Booth
1967

Let us consider the least understood figure on the jazz recording scene—even though his function is unquestionably one of the most important. He is known by a variety of titles, of which the most common (and perhaps the most confusing) is a&r man, a set of initials that means "artist and repertoire," which in turn means nothing much to most people.

As it happens, I know a good deal about this subject, having by now functioned in this particular capacity for more than a decade. For this very reason, however, it is quite easy for me to understand why this is an area of more than a little mystery and confusion. I won't really go so far as to say that even I don't always know exactly what an a&r man is supposed to be up to—but there *are* moments . . .

To put the problem into a specific setting: if the average jazz fan were to visit an average recording session (for present purposes, I allow myself the thoroughly unlikely assumption that either of these "average" items exist), he'd have little difficulty identifying practically everyone present.

In the high-ceilinged, microphone- and wire-cluttered recording studio would be anywhere from a handful of persons to a small crowd. There would be musicians, some of whom he would recognize because he had seen their faces in clubs or on album covers. Others on hand could be deduced on a simple functional basis (the man playing the drums is a drummer; the one in the control room fussing with a multitude of dials is likely to be the recording engineer, etc.). Even the few who might plainly be doing nothing at all would therefore be identifiable as friends of the musicians, or maybe as the star performer's manager.

But one participant would undoubtedly defy analysis or categorizing: a man scurring from control room to studio and back again, with something to say to practically everyone, and later perched in the control room listening intently while the music is being recorded and then out in the studio listening intently while it's played back over the loud-speakers there—but probably talking to someone most of that time, too; a man whose reactions vary from anguish to pleasure (and back again); a man who seems to be overseeing everything from the ordering of sandwiches to the sequence of solos. . . . In short, this man is clearly a person in some position of authority but one whose precise function would appear virtually impossible to determine.

For me to call this mysterious creature the key figure at this "average" recording session would seem immodest, but to be honest this is exactly what I must do. *Not* the most important figure, mind you; that role does have to be reserved for the soloist, leader, group, or singer whose performance will be what the record produced here is all about. But the *key*—the glue, the guide, the catalytic agent, often the instigator of the whole thing and usually the one who, at the end, puts it into suitable shape for presentation to the world. Something like father, mother, foreman, and scoutmaster all in one. Small wonder that it's difficult for anyone (including myself) to define the nature or spell out the details of the job.

To underline the importance (for better or worse) of this key man, let me pause for a moment to reflect that, in our time, jazz records have been coming into existence at an overwhelming rate. Clearly the phonograph record has become far and away the main method of disseminating jazz. Even in a city that offers virtually no in-person jazz, one can stay home and hear a dozen or more groups in a single evening, thanks to records.

And just about all those records exist because of the decisions and production activities of those men described as, among other things, "a&r."

I began by noting that there are several different descriptive titles and catch-phrases in use—and actually this variety of nomenclature offers a few helpful clues as to what it's all about. This fellow, then, is at times listed in the credits on the back of an album as a "producer." On other occasions the credit may read that a recording was "supervised" by him. Sometimes he is referred to as a recording director (although that usually means something closer to the realm of arrangers and conductors). Combinations of terms evolve as well: one major label describes these men as a&r producers. And I have noted gradations of titling all the way from associate producer up to executive producerr without really knowing what significant meaning was intended (except perhaps to indicate smaller or larger salaries).

I know of one colleague who, during a between-engagements period, threw the state unemployment insurance office into complete turmoil. The clerks couldn't process his file, because they couldn't figure out what his job classification was. He always referred to himself as a record producer, which didn't seem to help them at all; finally, they listed him as "director, recording," along with the code number used for "director, stage and motion picture."

It also seems relevant to note that another colleague likes to compare us all, rather sardonically, with baseball managers. What he has in mind, it turns out, is a long-standing baseball-fan bromide to the effect that managing is a negative art: a manager can never really win a game, but he can be responsible for losing it. The best manager, therefore, is the one who louses up least often, who loses the fewest ball games.

One additional set of general observations may be called for:

I cannot describe for you a "typical" jazz a&r man, or even indicate any sort of basic-minimum attributes or qualifications. Because there is *no* typical producer, there is actually little or no similarity of techniques or attitudes between any two of us. There is no school at which a person can get formal training for this occupation, no set of generally accepted ground rules in existence. Some of the best, best-known and/or most active are not musicians. This is quite uncommon among producers in other types of music, but in jazz there is a fairly prevalent theory that it helps to be a nonmusician, since one thereby supposedly avoids the dangers of overdirecting, of (perhaps subconsciously) trying to get the musicians to play the material exactly the way the a&r man would if he were playing.

Today's jazz a&r men do include an increasing number of working musicians; it would appear that playing is no more of a barrier to a would-be producer than not playing. On the other hand, there are many who turned to producing from quite unrelated ways of making a living—I can readily think of a former publicity agent, a onetime movie director, an ex-editor. And merely being thoroughly steeped in the subject is not necessarily adequate training; I know of more than one retail record salesman who made the transition, but I also know of a celebrated jazz writer and a top-rated jazz disc jockey, both of whom readily admit that they flopped rather completely in a&r roles.

Fortunately or unfortunately, it's a skill that can only be learned on the job—which makes for expensive apprenticeships and usually means that a man must get his first assignment through some combination of luck, pull, or accident. It really isn't too surprising, then, that more than a few began by the simple process of starting their own record companies. This, however, does not necessarily mean that one is going to stay in business long enough to get the hang of it before the money runs out. It does serve to indicate, though, that the real common denominator is a deep love of jazz. Putting this the other way around, I'd say a man has to be insane to get involved in producing jazz records *unless* he loves the music deeply.

However, one man's love may, in someone else's view, look more like commerce. A great many of those most heavily concerned with recording the jazz of the '50s and '60s happened to be men who started out as devout traditionalists, what were once called "moldy figs." The list would include, in no particular order, men like Alfred Lion, John Hammond, George Avakian, Les Koenig, Bob Thiele, Nesuhi Ertegun, and myself. I would consider all of us sufficiently sensitive and flexible and alert to have managed a difficult changeover in fine style and with sincere motivation; yet I am sure that each of us was on at least one occasion vilified as an unprincipled, commercialized turncoat. (Undoubtedly the one lesson to be learned from this is the very broad one that you can't possibly please everyone all the time anyhow, which I consider a very valuable lesson for record producers to learn early in life.)

I have very probably given a rather exaggerated impression of the degree of chaos and individualism in the world of the jazz a&r man. To balance the picture, let me take you on an explanatory journey through the steps involved in the creation of what can at any rate be called a representative jazz album (even though it obviously can't be called a "typical" one, in view of my insistence that *nothing* in this area is typical):

To begin with, long before even approaching the recording studio, there is the original coming together of label and artist. In the case of an established star or a performer who has at least been around and making records for a while, the process is simple enough: you discover, or are informed, that he is available, and after negotiating terms, a contract is signed, usually one giving the company exclusive recording rights for a period of time. The customary exclusive contract makes basic sense to both parties: the company knows it will have the artist's new work in its catalog for the next couple of years, which can mean that just one best-seller can counterbalance the red ink of several LPs that are, either intentionally or unavoidably, merely artistic successes—or maybe no kind of success at all. Consequently, the company feels more able to give the artist that big-band date he wants, more able to concentrate its thinking and planning and promotion activities on him than if it were only going to have the benefit of an isolated one-shot album from him.

This same theory applies in the case of a new artist, but here the company's risk is much greater, for most newcomers don't attract appreciable public attention and record sales for several years— and many turn out to have been permanent wrong guesses, artistically or commercially, or both.

And it *is* a guess, for in the discovering of new talent the producer is certainly playing a game with no rules. He may hear someone in an obscure club or catch a newly arrived sideman in some star's band. He might even be impressed by the unknown musician with a demonstration record or tape nervously (or aggressively) tucked under his arm. More frequently than he might like to admit, the producer is steered in the right direction by the recommendation of an established musician. (Fellow performers, obviously, are likely to become aware of new talent most quickly. In order of alertness, musicians generally come first, followed by record companies and a few very attentive hip listeners. Then come the critics, with—as has been observed more than once—the general public last, if at all, and clubowners practically never.)

In my own experience, the recording careers of Bill Evans and Wes Montgomery began when and as they did because musicians tipped me off, when Bill was an obscure sideman and Wes was still self-confined to his home town of Indianapolis.

Anyway, assume contact has been made in one of these ways, a spark has been touched off, a decision has been reached. The a&r man will introduce the performer to the world.

At this point, a word about what I believe to be a fairly prevalent point of confusion. It is true, in a sense, that this young musician— and most older ones, too—will "pay for" his record date. But it is only true in a rather misleading and often meaningless way. The actual paying out of recording fees to the leader, the various sidemen involved, arrangers, etc., is done by the company. These costs are charged against the leader's royalty account—that is, he will receive additional royalty payments only when enough copies of his record have been sold to enable his earned royalties to "pay back" those company expenditures. If, as so often happens, the record never sells that much, the leader's negative royalty account "owes" a hypothetical and uncollectable balance; the real cash loss is the company's.

So much for high and low finance, which at this early stage undoubtedly concerns neither the artist nor the a&r man. They are probably busy figuring out the nature of the upcoming record date. Will it be a small group or something large, will there be formally scored arrangements, normal instrumentation, or something far out? Some of these points will be answered by decisions as to repertoire—whether for some reason it seems best to do a jazz album of Beatles hits with strings or whether (as is most often the case with a new artist) presenting the man in a program designed to showcase his strong points seems better than a gimmicked approach the first time around.

Even in the simpler cases, repertoire must be mulled. The a&r man has some material that to him sounds right for the artist, who in turn has some original tunes of his own (and a couple by a talented friend), and there is discussion for and against various old standards and recent pop hits and a Monk tune that hasn't been recorded in five years (and hasn't been recorded accurately in ten). The producer may be dictatorial, subtle or permissive, but eventually the selections are made.

Up to now the a&r man has functioned fairly directly in the areas of *a*rtist and *r*epertoire. At about this point he begins to be a producer in something of the Broadway-David Merrick sense.

There are musicians, and perhaps an arranger or so, to be hired. The featured artist's preferences will probably be respected to a substantial degree, but unless this is an album by a working group, the producer will very likely want to choose most of the sidemen from his own rather substantial roster of the tried-and-true—men who can be depended on to show up on time, sight-read swiftly if necessary, and in general take care of business. There are enough unavoidable imponderables in a record date; it's best to avoid what you can.

A mutually feasible time must be decided on for recording; a studio must be rented, and there is the sometimes agonizingly tricky business of getting the timetables of all to dovetail properly.

Finally, we can assume that everyone is in the recording studio at the appointed time, whereupon the basic role of the a&r man-producer shifts to something best described by such other terms as director and supervisor (*and* amateur psychologist).

As I described earlier, the hectic nature of the recording date makes it a place of tension. Well, perhaps the most important function of the producer-etc. at this point is to keep that tension from being generally felt. He is working within fairly rigid limits of time, circumstance, and practicality. The musicians' union measures the time on which the pay scale is based in three-hour units; it is most uneconomical not to shape a session around that fact. And within the given period, the proper recorded sound must be achieved (which involves the microphone-placing and dial-setting abilities of recording engineers, a class of men who are generally quite talented but on occasion temperamental), the music must get to be played right (on big-band dates, the general situation is that it has been physically impossible to have any rehearsal, which can make things rough), and it must—obviously—be performed with the proper jazz feeling. The key to all this, as I've noted, is to keep the feeling of tension and pressure from spilling over: be a clock-watcher if you must, but don't let anyone know you're watching it.

Above all, the featured performer must be kept in the best possible form. It is unfortunate, although certainly not surprising, that there are no over-all rules whatsoever for accomplishing this. Just about every jazz artist I can think of calls for a different approach. If you are lucky enough to be working with someone you have had experience with, you'll know whether he needs to be pep-talked or left alone (at that extreme end of the scale, there is the famous trumpet player who refused to allow the producer to leave the control room and enter the studio during an entire session), whether he is really as calm as he looks or a bundle of concealed nerve-ends, whether one more attempt to do a better job with that last tune will probably do the trick or make everyone blow sky-high. If you don't know your man, a producer is likely to find a record session largely a matter of fast verbal footwork and guesswork. And better luck next time.

Under any circumstances there will be much on-the-job adjustment. What do you do when the blues that you wanted to keep under three minutes (to get lots of air play) turns out to run twice as long, largely because everyone stretched his solo a bit—and they all played great? You might want to raise that tempo, get rid of that corny ending, eliminate that piano solo, or simply scream out loud at the one bad note that loused up the only decent ensemble chorus recorded on that tune all day. Well, you'll either speak up or not, you'll either ruin everybody's mood or come up a hero ("Why didn't *I* think of doing it that way?"), but it all has to be done according to your personal evaluation of the situation, your temperament, your a&r philosophy: are you a frustrated musician at heart, or do you subscribe to that baseball-manager theory?

Let me draw a curtain of silence over certain post-recording woes and glories. These would include both the number that never sounded right in the studio and is saved by a brilliant stroke of editing and the album that you love but can never get the promotion department to do anything for. They include the artist who thanks you for your help in his career and the one whose wife hates you because you didn't prevent the use of that awful picture on the album cover. And they most certainly include the reviewer who entirely misses what you were trying to do and puts the album down because he doesn't think the flute is really a jazz instrument anyhow.

I hope I have done something in this article to push aside at least some of the mystery and confusion surrounding this peculiar but honorable craft of which I am one of the practitioners. If I have, the reader will perhaps understand the full meaning of an old saying heard frequently at recording studios: "It's close enough for jazz." This sounds like a put-down but is actually quite the opposite. It refers to that optimum "take," when the ensemble may perhaps still be a little ragged but the solos sound just lovely and the over-all pace and feeling is *right.* It's a moment when you sense that further work might improve the precision but will certainly drag the high spots down from their present level and lessen the total impact. So you decide to stop right there and keep that as *the* performance of the number. Right or wrong, it is a good feeling, for it involves the realization that jazz is not concerned with perfection but with something much more desirable and more rare. To all of us to whom jazz really means something, it is a very reassuring phrase. It applies, of course, to more than just the recording scene; it is really a very valid sort of all-purpose tag line, referring to anything that is still a little rough and fouled-up around the edges but has its soul in shape.

Cannonball at the Jazz Workshop
1986

When the Cannonball Adderley band returned to San Francisco in the fall of '62, it was very much in the nature of a homecoming. Almost exactly three years earlier, a newly formed Adderley quintet had drawn capacity audiences and room-shaking enthusiasm in that city's celebrated Jazz Workshop, causing the leader to call on me to keep a promise. In 1958, when Cannonball had joined the young New York-based Riverside label, he was (along with John Coltrane and Bill Evans) part of the to-be-legendary Miles Davis Sextet, but planning to go out on his own again before long. So I had agreed then to show up whenever and wherever he considered his still-unformed next group ready to record. The following year Adderley called, I flew cross-country, and in the absence of any suitable studio, was forced into making an on-the-job recording that became the career-shaping blockbuster simply entitled *The Cannonball Adderley Quintet in San Francisco.*

That gigantic hit tended to overshadow some of the equally strong or even better albums that followed—but one tough, soulful, and hard-swinging effort that did enjoy comparable success was *Jazz Workshop Revisited,* recorded in exactly the same space three years later. In a sense this was a deliberate, defiant decision by both artist and producer to accept the challenge of our earlier hit, a point that is underlined by the album title.

We had some heavy weapons on our side in this internal battle. For one thing, the band was now a sextet: the huge and multi-talented reedman Yusef Lateef had joined the Adderley brothers on the bandstand, and after several months together they were meshing brilliantly in big-sounding ensembles and on vivid horn backgrounds for soloists. The piano spot had been the only changing element in the early years, Bobby Timmons giving way to Barry Harris and then Victor Feldman. But by 1962 Joe Zawinul (unquestionably the funkiest of all Austrians and later the driving force of Weather Report) had begun a full decade of soulful keyboard work with Cannonball.

I was also able to take advantage of Riverside's being (at least temporarily) in better fiscal shape than in '59. Instead of only two nights' work with a local engineer, I hired Wally Heider, deservedly one of the most highly regarded of location recording specialists, and scheduled the unheard-of luxury of *five* full shots at the music—Thursday through Sunday nights plus the then-customary Sunday matinee. My leisurely, unpressured approach almost wrecked the whole project! As I learned that week, tension can contribute a lot to the positive vibrations and immediacy of the best "live" recordings; the awareness that we had just about all the time in the world robbed the first nights' work of a small but significant edge. Despite powerful and unusual material from four band members and such distinguished friends as Quincy Jones and Donald Byrd, it really wasn't until well into Saturday evening (when my growing sense of panic undoubtedly communicated itself to the band) that performances strong enough for issuance began to emerge.

We were helped that night by some audience dramatics. The new Nat Adderley composition, a deliberately pseudo *bossa nova,* was to become something of a 45-rpm success. (One printing of the original album cover proclaimed that it "Contains the hit single 'Jive Samba.' ") I created that well-under-three-minute version of the band's full-length performance by the unique device of using only the final chorus; I was guided to this idea by some stimulating audience reaction that occurs midway through that chorus. That reaction, let me now confess, had nothing to do with the music: it was in response to a bouncer attempting to remove from a front table a fan who had come barreling into the club during the last set without stopping to pay the door charge!

The Bill Evans Sessions
1984

This collection brings together the output of the various recording sessions involved in the dozen Riverside Records projects under the leadership of Bill Evans that he and I worked on between 1956 and 1963. (Also included is the work of three sessions that led to a Cannonball Adderley album on which Bill was specifically in the position of a featured artist, and which therefore seems an appropriate element in a full-scale retrospective of the pianist's Riverside years.)

Some of these projects resulted (either intentionally or fortuitously) in more than one album; on the other hand, a few were left incomplete or were shelved because the artist and/or producer felt (generally incorrectly) that they were less than fully successful. The vast majority of the selections were initially issued on Riverside fairly promptly after being recorded; most of the originally unreleased material was brought out on the Milestone label during the '70s and early '80s. Several alternative versions are issued for the first time in this compilation, along with four previously unheard sides of unaccompanied piano performances recorded in January of 1963.

The individual sessions are remembered by me below.

Session 1
(September 11 and 27, 1956)
Bill Evans made his first appearance as a leader on these dates. He had been brought to Riverside's attention when his friend, guitarist

Mundell Lowe, had insisted that my partner, Bill Grauer, and I listen over the telephone to a demo tape. It is not a procedure I would normally recommend, but we were immediately impressed. Evans, however, was rather reluctant, providing my first taste of the self-deprecating attitude he usually displayed during the years we worked together. My notes for the album resulting from these initial sessions report that "it took some time for *us* to convince *him* that he was ready to record (which is decidedly the reverse of the usual situation)."

He was twenty-seven years old at the time, and a few discerning enthusiasts were aware of his work in a quartet led by clarinetist Tony Scott, which played mostly in obscure Greenwich Village clubs. (But they were really *very* few. Although some blame can surely be assigned to Riverside's being a young label and quite unadept at promotion, the fact remains that—despite strong reviews in *Down Beat* and *Metronome* and from such a major critic as Nat Hentoff—this debut album had no immediate impact on the jazz public. By the end of 1957, a full year after it was issued, total sales had barely reached 800 copies!)

In the studio, I tried to put Evans under as little pressure as possible. He selected the sidemen: Paul Motian was with him in the Scott group; Teddy Kotick was a very respected young bassist who had worked with Charlie Parker and Stan Getz. The repertoire, including the idea of three extremely brief unaccompanied pieces, was Bill's choice (and it was quite consistent with his status as a strongly talented but not yet fully individual bebop pianist). The studio was a relaxed place where Riverside went on to do most of its late-'50s work, and thus was to be the scene of Bill's next several sessions.

(Doing a full album in one day was the totally standard cost-conscious procedure for independent jazz labels in those days, although it certainly wasn't an easy task for an artist unaccustomed to recording. For many years it had been my clear recollection that this initial Evans project was handled in such a way; since it is the only one of his albums from which neither data sheets nor original tape boxes had survived, I had nothing but memory to rely on, and in preparing these notes for the 1984 Bill Evans *Complete Riverside Recordings* boxed set, I describe the making of this record as necessarily the result of a single trip to the studio. Some time later, I quite accidentally came across copies of *two* recording session contracts— the kind routinely filed with the local musicians' union—with Bill listed as leader of this trio. One was for the accepted September 27 date, but the other was for more than two weeks earlier. Obviously,

I had been even more considerate than I remembered; I had given him two separate days, and with breathing room between them! But I still have no better idea than before as to what pieces we recorded on which day—and under the circumstances I decline to alter the overall logistics of this memoir. I'll still refer to twenty Bill Evans Riverside sessions, not twenty-one.)

Session 2
(December 15, 1958)

More than two years separated the first two Evans albums, and in that interval a great deal had happened. At first, he simply remained unwilling to record again, claiming he "didn't have anything particularly different to say." But for most of the second year he was too busy: Miles Davis had discovered Bill and made him part of what was quickly recognized as one of the key groups in modern jazz—the Davis sextet that also included John Coltrane, Cannonball Adderley, Paul Chambers, and initially Philly Joe Jones (although during most of 1958 their drummer was Jimmy Cobb).

The experience brought about a number of changes in the pianist. Working regularly with three horns—and these were, of course, not just *any* three—seemed to make him a more vigorous and overtly swinging player than at any other time in his early career. The expressed approval of these impressive colleagues made it difficult for even this extremely self-critical artist not to gain confidence, and it also led a great many other musicians to start paying serious and respectful attention to him. When he agreed, shortly after an amicable parting from Miles, to record again, it was because he felt quite strong and self-assured. He turned to Philly Joe, with whom he was to work and record on several occasions in the years to come, knowing from recent experience that they made a good team. Sam Jones (no relation to Philly) was a less obvious choice, but they had played together on occasion. All three, for example, had formed the rhythm section on Cannonball's first Riverside album five months earlier, and it was clear that Sam (then working with Dizzy Gillespie and soon to become a longtime mainstay of Adderley's new quintet) could contribute the firm, full-bottomed "walking" bass Bill wanted for this occasion.

Part of the repertoire (a driving version of "Night and Day," and hard bop tunes like "Minority" and Sonny Rollins's "Oleo") accordingly does not sound like what might be expected from Evans. But there are a couple of typically relaxed ballads, and, above all—when we again arrive at unaccompanied numbers late in the session— there is the remarkable improvisation called "Peace Piece," possibly the best-known and most influential Evans work, and in some respects the *most* typical. The legend is true: he was working up an introduction for the Leonard Bernstein show tune "Some Other Time" and suddenly decided that he'd rather use what he'd invented as an independent entity. It is *not* based on the chords of the other tune, as jazz "originals" often are, but you can hear a suggestion of the Bernstein song at the start. And that version exists for easy comparison; apparently we stayed with previous planning and went on to tape "Some Other Time" before the end of the session, although it was omitted from the *Everybody Digs Bill Evans* album and remained unissued for many years. The final solo item was intended as a brief tag (hence the title "Epilogue"), and we whimsically decided to repeat the same recorded performance of it at the end of each side of the album.

Session 3
(January 19, 1959)
The existence of another session recorded barely a month later seems contrary to all expectations; the simple explanation is that it was entirely unplanned. Bill, Philly, and Paul Chambers were the rhythm section on a Chet Baker album that was being completed that evening; the three scheduled tunes went down quite smoothly and we were finished before eleven o'clock. Perhaps because everyone still seemed full of unused energy, and possibly because I was anxious to avoid another two-year hiatus between Evans dates, I spontaneously asked these three to remain in the studio and play more.

Bill cautiously insisted that I agree not to use the material if he didn't approve on later listening, and then this classic Miles Davis rhythm section started on its only session of trio work together. The repertoire reflects the lack of preparation, and certainly a large part of the interest here is the ease with which that was overcome by their well-established ability to interact. They began with "You and the Night and the Music," which had been performed just a couple of hours earlier (at a much slower tempo) as part of Chet's date; everybody knew "Woody'n You"; they agreed on a couple of familiar evergreens; and "Green Dolphin Street" was a standard item on Miles's play list. After that, short of a full album but beginning to feel worn down, we quit. When

Evans reviewed the material with me, he concluded that it was rhythmically quite interesting, but felt that not enough was happening on other levels. He invoked my promise, and the tapes just sat on the shelf for some fifteen years. Rather amazingly, they were neither actually lost nor "rediscovered" and issued during the years after Riverside went out of business, when ownership of its tapes passed through several hands. Finally, in the mid-'70s, when the tapes and Bill and I were coincidentally reunited at Fantasy/Prestige/Milestone, he and I listened again, with different results. Not only did he find the material to be better than remembered, but we agreed that it included some very fine examples of the work of Chambers, who had died in 1969. That combination of reactions led to a belated 1975 initial release, as part of a "twofer" package that also included the 1958 session.

Session 4
(December 28, 1959)
Evans began working almost exclusively as leader of his own trio early in 1959; over two decades, he was to make personnel changes only rarely. But it actually took him until late in that first year to settle on his first permanent lineup. Motian, of course, had been an early associate; Scott LaFaro, only twenty-three at this time, apparently worked his way into the trio by frequently sitting in while Bill was having trouble getting sidemen to stick with him through some unpleasant early club engagements. This was very much a transitional session for Evans, who still displays a lot of the more extroverted side that had emerged during the months with Miles, and only a few selections—most notably "Autumn Leaves" and "Blue in Green"—point with any clarity towards the concept of "simultaneous improvisation" that was to be such a major element in his association with the innovative but tragically short-lived LaFaro. Valuably, there are two available versions of both these numbers. In the case of "Blue in Green" (which Bill had written for the celebrated Miles Davis *Kind of Blue* album, although, to his outspoken dismay, his leader had received joint composer credit), it's simply that I have come across a previously unissued next-to-last take that the pianist and I had both almost approved. "Autumn Leaves" was originally issued in differing monaural and stereophonic versions for a reason peculiar to the technology of the times. In those days, two-track stereo was new and primitive and not yet part of the standard recording equipment at many studios. On this occasion, the

separate portable stereo machine had malfunctioned during the performance of what we adjudged the best take. Not wanting to be limited by stereo (which was still considered a dubious gimmick and accounted for perhaps 10 percent of record sales), we issued the preferred version in mono and a second-best on the stereo record.

Two continuing Bill Evans characteristics appear for the first time at this session. The readily apparent one was his penchant for reconstructing and revitalizing some very minor pop tunes, as well as some essentially strong ones that had grown stale with overuse. The second, known only to those who worked with him in the recording studio, was his unwillingness to keep plugging away at the same selection—as most jazz musicians do—until he was satisfied. Bill's alternative, which was more impatient, probably more creative, and often quite unsettling to his sidemen and producer, was to abandon a number if a couple of takes left him less than fully pleased, returning to it at some arbitrary point later in the session. Our present use of more than one version in two instances serves to illustrate this. The actual *recording* order for this material was: the second take of "Blue in Green," followed by an accepted "Come Rain or Come Shine" and then the monaural version of "Autumn Leaves," after which they returned to "Blue in Green" for the originally issued Take 3 and then went back to "Autumn Leaves" to play a satisfactory performance on which the stereo equipment was working properly! This date was originally released as the *Portrait in Jazz* album.

Session 6
(February 2, 1961)

This represents, to be extremely precise, our only departure from strict chronology. This session resulted in the *Explorations* album, the direct successor to his first working-trio record, but it did follow (by less than a week) the first of three trips to the studio in connection with a Cannonball Adderley album on which Evans was featured. Those sessions are appropriately considered as a unit just below.

The trio had now been together for more than a year, had spent much of that time on the road, and had made giant strides towards the goal of becoming a three-voice unit rather than a piano player and his accompanists. Inevitably—and properly—Bill remained the focal point, but his interweaving with Scotty and the freedom this truly unusual bassist was afforded were very much up front.

There had also been noticeable movement towards the more introspective style that is generally considered "typical" Bill Evans, and is certainly the most widely influential aspect of his work. Although this is really much more a matter of approach than of tempo, it is most readily apparent at the relaxed pace that predominated on this session.

Also much in evidence is that emphasis on the reworking of standard tunes: six of the nine selections are in that category. Of the others, "Nardis" is credited to Miles (although I have always wondered if perhaps an assist shouldn't also go to Bill, who took part in its first recording on Cannonball's 1958 Riverside debut album); "Israel" is an intriguing but neglected piece first heard on Davis's legendary *Birth of the Cool* set; and "Elsa" is one of several contributions made to Bill's repertoire over the years by his friend Earl Zindars. When we finished with more material than could comfortably fit on the album, Evans decided "The Boy Next Door" was most expendable, but it was eventually inserted into a '70s reissue package. I have included a previously unused first take of "Beautiful Love" as a prime example of his impatience with material. Early in the date, he had played the selection just once; I noted joint approval, and he moved on to something else. Two tape reels later, having worked briefly on seven other numbers, he returned to this for one more version, which he later preferred. I still impartially enjoy both.

My chief recollection of this session is as a classic case of personal factors influencing musical judgment. Evans was full of openly expressed negative feelings during the date, largely because of a running nonmusical argument with LaFaro. I felt equally negative, being annoyed with both of them and distressed by Bill's complaints about a presumably tension-induced headache. Although I kept insisting that the music sounded just fine, that was mostly pep talk; I actually shared his misgivings, and we were equally surprised when later listening proved my words to have been accurate. (In a 1976 interview, he went so far as to call this "one of my favorite albums.")

Sessions 5, 7, and 8
(January 27, February 21, and March 13, 1961)

These three sessions, overlapping the making of the Evans album just described, are his only nonleader performances warranting inclusion in this compilation. Actually, Cannonball's *Know What I Mean?* was largely constructed around Bill's presence.

It was Adderley's idea to use Percy Heath and Connie Kay, the long time bassist and drummer of the smooth-knit Modern Jazz Quartet, to help reach the desired goal—which was a point closer to Bill's lyricism than to the alto player's own hearty blues and bebop. My recollection is that it was also out of respect for the preference of his featured artist that Cannon agreed to the same studio and engineer as on the concurrent Evans album. Bill was not at all enthusiastic about the piano at Plaza Sound, which had recently become Riverside's regular recording room.

Because of difficulties in setting down some of these selections to the complete satisfaction of all concerned, three sessions proved necessary; considering that we had to maneuver around the schedules of three different working groups, we were probably lucky to set dates only three weeks apart. Things went smoothly for most of the first day, but the last item attempted was a real hang-up—the album's title tune, a modal piece set up by Bill at Cannonball's suggestion (and later named by me, using a frequent Adderley conversational mannerism). The number depended largely on getting the right flow and feeling in the solos, and it kept on just not *quite* happening. We got up to Take 12 (only two were complete) on the first day, tried another dozen starts (again just two played to completion) the next time, and issued the last of seven tries from the final session! (A longer take from the initial date attracted me on re-listening years later, and was included in a 1979 reissue). My personal favorite, their treatment of "Waltz for Debby," opened the March 13 activities.

Session 9
(June 25, 1961)

This is most accurately described as a single recording effort, even though it actually involves the work of five sets (two between 4:30 and about 6:30 in the afternoon, three beginning at 9:30 that night) in that famous New York cellar known as the Village Vanguard. This was, of course, the legendary "live" date taped on the last time the Evans-LaFaro-Motian trio ever played together, just ten days before Scott's tragic death in a highway accident.

I really don't recall with full certainty why Riverside was able to record this at all (although the trio's most recent album had been made almost five months before, that was far less than the usual interval between our Bill Evans sessions), or on the other hand why we waited until the very end of a two-week engagement. I must asssume that some pressure was exerted on Bill: the group was clearly in top form and should be recorded; I had been extremely enthusiastic about on-the-job taping since the vast success of *The Cannonball Adderley Quintet in San Francisco* a year earlier; and this type of session was a relatively painless way to extract an album from the usually foot-dragging pianist. The delay, while surely due in part to artist reluctance, also reflected the fact that our staff engineer, Ray Fowler, was not on hand, perhaps on vacation. (His replacement was Dave Jones, one of the best at "live" location recording in that two-track era; the sound of these selections remains as crisp and undated as the music.) The choice of the very last day is actually quite understandable; at the time, the Vanguard's schedule regularly included Sunday matinees, allowing for a really full amount of recording in one day. And of course we could not be aware of what a last-chance position we were in.

Accordingly, no one panicked at the brief power outage that ruined our taping of the first afternoon selection, "Gloria's Step." Whatever the cause, it never recurred; thereafter, all was technically—and also creatively—free of problems. The format of the compilation offers a unique opportunity to recreate *almost* totally the entire occasion in exactly the sequence of original performance.

(The re-creation of the day is only "almost" total because of two unavoidable omissions: the flawed opening number, and an unissued version of "My Man's Gone Now," which had been the only item left on one original reel apparently lost during the turmoil and travel the Riverside tape vaults went through in the years after 1964.)

Although we were only looking for one album, we felt there would be a better chance of capturing the spontaneous qualities of on-the-job recording in general—and of this trio in particular—by being able to make the eventual choice from a larger group of tunes rather than frequently repeating an exact pre-selected repertoire. Thirteen numbers were played in all, five only once, just two as many as three times. Evans was unusually pleased with the results and—perhaps also influenced by the realization that this now documented the end of an important period in his career— readily agreed to the release of two separate six-tune albums (*Sunday at the Village Vanguard*, followed by *Waltz for Debby*). The necessary choices were quite arbitrary; it is clear that nothing played this day was without considerable merit. "Porgy," originally omitted for reasons of overall time, was squeezed into an early-'70s reissue package, and seven "rediscovered" alternates filled a mid-1984 album.

Session 10
(April 4, 1962)
Bill was devastated by LaFaro's sudden death, and seemed reluctant to attempt the difficult task of finding not only another bassist but inevitably a somewhat different approach to trio playing. His very few club appearances over the next several months were unaccompanied. There *were* some Riverside sideman dates, including involvement in a sizable project of some importance—ten Tadd Dameron pieces, arranged and conducted by the composer. Evans was among the featured artists, with several solos; among other results, those February and March 1962 sessions might have lessened his earlier prejudice against the piano at Plaza Sound. Early in April he consented to begin a solo album there, but after four one-take performances (of widely varying length and intensity) we stopped. Considering that we were on the verge of the most active recording surge in Bill's lifetime, it's really not surprising that we both soon let this date slip out of our minds, and it remained forgotten and unissued until the late '70s.

Sessions 11, 12, and 13
(May 17, May 29, and June 5, 1962)
By the end of 1961 Bill had settled on a talented young bassist, Chuck Israels, who in my opinion also contributed the kind of aggressive approach needed to spur the pianist back into full-scale activity; they were to work together until 1966. By May of '62, following several weeks at both the Vanguard and Hickory House in New York, even the cautious Evans felt they were ready to record. But I had a special challenge for them: for some time I had wanted Bill to do a totally laid-back, all-ballads album, but feared that a steady dose of slower tempos might perhaps overrelax the group to the point of lethargy. My solution was to make a second, somewhat livelier album at the same time, literally alternating the two repertoires to provide enough variation to keep everyone alert.

The result was both the very pretty *Moonbeams* and the lyrical but more swinging *How My Heart Sings*. Bill's habit of leaving a tune and returning to it later—in this case, sometimes not until the next session—mixed the schedule even further; fully half the final takes are from the third date! The five new Evans compositions, Israels recalls, had obviously been well prepared by Bill, but were sprung on his sidemen without warning at recording time. This was his way, and they learned to cope with it and even benefit from it, but it wasn't easy. I must note that the the title of one of these originals: "Re: Person I Knew," is an anagram on my name, a rearrangement of all the letters in "Orrin Keepnews." It is something I will always treasure, a gesture from a uniquely talented artist and friend.

Sessions 14 and 15
(July 16 and 17, 1962)

In my notes accompanying a "twofer" package that combined the *Interplay* album (recorded at these sessions) with the results of two similar dates that followed, I discussed in detail Bill's personal problems at this time and their impact on his creativity and on our working relationship. [These notes are reprinted in Chapter 7, beginning on page 211.] There's no point in repeating, but some of the facts seem relevant here:

Between April and August 1962, the traditionally reluctant Evans entered three different studios on a total of eight occasions and recorded the equivalent of four and a half albums. One key factor in this spurt was undoubtedly his narcotics dependency and consequent financial needs. Riverside, although most willing to be helpful, was a relatively small company and had to at least justify all those advances by applying them against specific recording projects.

Accordingly, although I have never approved of the practice of "stockpiling" major-artist albums for future use, I found myself back in the studio long before we'd even thought about when to release the results of the May-June trio sessions. But it must be equally emphasized that this was a thoroughly valid, interesting, and unusual concept, definitely *not* some make-work job. It was the first larger-than-trio Evans album for the label; it involved a stellar cast of some of his personal favorites: Percy Heath, Jim Hall (with whom he had made a duet album for another label), and Philly Joe. Bill's first choice on trumpet, Art Farmer, was unavailable; I don't remember which of us suggested young Freddie Hubbard, then first beginning to attract attention with Art Blakey's Jazz Messengers, but he fitted in quite well. In some respects this is within the parameters of a normal early-'60s hard-bop quintet album, with tempos mostly *up* and the pianist displaying his less introspective side. But there are a number of elements that help make it distinctive—including the use of guitar as one "horn," the varied treatment of the ensemble choruses, and that remarkable Evans ability to reshape old standards. Hubbard turned out to be largely unfamiliar with these '30s tunes. For the most part, this was helpful; he had no pre-existing concepts to unlearn in dealing with Bill's versions.

Sessions 16 and 17
(August 21 and 22, 1962)

In many ways this is a companion piece to the preceding *Interplay,* but with additional difficulties that helped keep it from being issued for two decades. The idea hadn't even been presented to me until after the July dates, and I assumed that the total use of original tunes was probably to enable Bill to also draw advances from his music publisher. So I was beginning to feel a bit put-upon. In fairness, the new compositions were by *no* means simple potboilers; quite the contrary, some of them seemed too tough to be properly handled in the barely-rehearsed, limited-studio-time jazz recording format of that era. This despite again having a first-class supporting cast. There were two changes: Zoot Sims, because Bill felt tenor sax was best suited to the material; and the highly regarded young bassist Ron Carter (with whom he had played on the Tadd Dameron album), because Percy Heath was on tour with the Modern Jazz Quartet.

But tempers were shorter, there were sound-engineering problems, and some of the selections were indeed destroyers! When we had finished the second session, the feeling was that we had the makings of a good album, but that substantial editing was still needed. Circumstances, however, conspired against us. Knowing that there were other Evans records to be released before this one, we felt no sense of urgency. Bill and staff engineer Ray Fowler did work out a satisfactory version of the first number, "Loose Bloose," mostly using Take 3; they began on the next selection, but never finished. By year's end, Evans and Riverside had worked out an amicable solution to various pressures with a release from contract that enabled him to move over to Verve Records. By mid-1964, an unrelated set of problems forced Riverside out of business.

For many years, even after the Riverside master tapes and I had been reunited at Fantasy/Prestige/Milestone, I believed these session reels to be lost. Eventually they proved to have merely been misleadingly boxed and thus misfiled. With valuable assistance from Ed Michel, a very capable jazz producer who had been my assistant in the last years at Riverside, the long-deferred editing was finally accomplished. I learned that some of what I had remembered as performance difficulties really had not been that bad; nevertheless, there was a lot to be done. To me the real hero of the two days turns out to have been Philly Joe; his timekeeping had been incredibly consistent; otherwise, it would not have been possible for us to maneuver between takes and emerge with coherent performances.

Session 18
(January 10, 1963)

These seventeen unaccompanied solo performances, never previously released, remain in my mind as a single, unified whole: all of them were recorded with little pause during the same evening, and they express very much the same emotional attitude. I consider this unit to be a masterpiece; in many ways unlike anything else he ever recorded, it is—on its own terms—among his most moving work.

I also have no trouble in understanding why neither he nor I liked it very much at the time, and why it has not surfaced before.

Shortly before this time, Bill had left Riverside. The terms of his departure included provision for two final projects, to be recorded rather promptly. It seemed to me that a solo studio session (which I wanted to do in any case) and an in-performance trio set would present the fewest problems, and we began with this one. Feeling that such an album would progress most smoothly with the least possible intrusion from the control room, I recommended that Bill move from tune to tune without the customary pauses for on-tape identification and only occasional breaks for playback listening. But I did caution him to wait a few seconds past the end of each performance to allow the piano sound to completely die out before proceeding. He managed to ignore this caution a number of times, most spectacularly when the last note of the "*Spartacus* Love Theme" was identical with the first note of "Nardis." By now, this only necessitates a few lengthy "medley" tracks; back then, trying to obtain an album that met normal requirements, I found it highly aggravating. I was obviously annoyed at the circumstances that had ended our close and rewarding working relationship; his attitude is made clear by a repertoire that not only includes "What Kind of Fool Am I?" (the only number he played more than once that evening) and "Everything Happens to Me" but began with a version (not done well enough to warrant being released) of "Why Was I Born?"

His playing here is emotionally raw, probing, and revealing;

even technically it is quite unlike his other work of this period. "All the Things You Are" moves into unusual abstraction; "Ornithology" recalls in a sense the 1956 bebop pianist; "Nardis" is so full and personal—I find it the best of his several performances of the piece—as to support my feeling that it is at least partially his composition. I don't think either of us was prepared to accept this music when it was recorded; then it was just set aside and forgotten for years. I only came to reconsider it during the course of a fairly recent systematic examination of all unissued tapes by major Riverside artists. By that time it was too late to ask Bill to listen again. However, I had no hesitation in preparing this material for release; I think these performances honor his memory and very much belong in a full-scale retrospective of his Riverside years.

Sessions 19 and 20
(May 30 and 31, 1963)

These are the final Evans dates for Riverside, and the only ones of which I have no first-hand knowledge. In the hectic last year of the label, I was unable to go out to Los Angeles when it was suggested that the wind-up commitment be recorded there. But Shelly Manne's club seemed a likely setting, and there were friends on hand to cover for me. So we hired Wally Heider, one of the great location engineers, and asked Dick Bock, then head of World Pacific Records, to supervise the proceedings. The originally released single album—put out by those who briefly took over Riverside after bankruptcy—used the repertoire that Bock had listed on the musicians' union contracts filed for the sessions. Years later, during my comprehensive re-listening, I found several equally sound performances, notably the first trio usage of "Time Remembered," and these were all combined into a "twofer."

Chuck Israels, recalling some circumstances of recording, notes that—as had happened on his first session as part of the trio—some material was just thrust on them by Bill without warning. With an added year of Evans experience behind him, the bassist wasn't even very surprised. The drummer, Larry Bunker, had just joined them. A noted Los Angeles recording studio musician who had jumped at the chance to work with Evans, he presumably had the kind of background that kept him from being thrown off stride by such things. But it is also apparent that part of the repertoire had been on Bill's mind for some time: four of the selections had been played on the January solo date.

Producing McCoy Tyner
1981

One of the most satisfying aspects of my years of involvement with
the recording of jazz is the number of major artists with whom I
have been able to enjoy lengthy and productive working relationships. To be specifically relevant to *Keyboard,* the list includes
three of the most important jazz pianists of our time (make that of
any time): Thelonious Monk, Bill Evans, and McCoy Tyner.

Preparing this article led me to add up my statistics. Somewhat
to my surprise, I discovered that of the three it is the most recent—
Tyner—with whom I have worked for the longest period of time
and have produced by far the most recordings. My career just
about began with Monk in 1955; between then and 1960 there were
a dozen albums. Evans, who was sometimes a hard man to coax
into the recording studio, did his first session for the Riverside
label in 1956; when we parted company in 1963 we had—if you
include some material that remained unreleased for a long time,
and a much later (1974) live nightclub date—accomplished about
the same quantity. McCoy and I first went into the studio together
in January 1972. Our most recent project was a big-band album
completed in December 1980. Our product total comes to sixteen;
if you add in the set resulting from his 1978 cross-country "Milestone Jazzstars" tour with Sonny Rollins and Ron Carter, make it
seventeen. And since five of these are two-record sets, we could
easily claim a total of twenty-two.

Such quantity is rather staggering (at any rate it staggers *me*),
particularly in so constantly shifting a setting as the American
music scene. But quantity is of course far from the only measuring
stick. I also find it impressive that during this period there was
something like a seven-fold increase in sales of his records. But
what means the most are the standards of quality achieved and
maintained during this long collaboration—and to be able to say
that we have managed to come up with something substantially
different almost every time we've gone to work.

It has been during the past eight years, working with McCoy on
a consistent two-albums-a-year basis, that I've become most fully
aware of both the challenges and the rewards of long-term association. But it was back with Monk that I first had to deal with the
problem of deliberately striving for variety, and there clearly are
some parallels to be drawn between these two men. In the mid-
'50s, the general critical opinion was that Thelonious was an ex-

tremely limited, even monotonous performer; while no one is apt
to accuse Tyner of simply being technically deficient as a pianist
(which was what was said of Monk), he too has been put down for
seeming always to seek the same effects, for sounding "the same"
too often, for not varying tone, or volume, or intensity, or whatever. There are, in fact, similarities between them, largely because
McCoy is one of the many contemporary jazz artists who pay
Thelonious the compliment of being influenced to some degree by
his pioneering efforts. The percussive elements in McCoy's style,
the understanding that lyricism and beauty in music do not have to
be merely overtly "pretty"—such things are clearly related to
Monk. (I've always felt this to be the case, and you can hear it
quite strongly on those recorded occasions when Tyner accepted
my advice about playing Monk compositions such as "Ruby, My
Dear" and "Pannonica.")

With Monk, I was working from the start to refute the concept
that he was particularly limited; he was recorded in units of virtually every size from solo to big band; in studios, clubs, and concert
hall; with a very wide assortment of major supporting artists. By
and large, we achieved our goal. So when my work with McCoy
reached a point where change of pace became important, I felt well
prepared.

In the beginning, though, there was no hint that Tyner and I
would be doing very much together. We hardly knew each other,
and he had signed with Milestone, then a small New York jazz
label, with considerable reluctance. I had actually used him once as
a sideman on a 1960 record date, but don't recall having been
much impressed. Later, like many others, I drastically changed my
opinion mostly through hearing his work with John Coltrane; in
1971, learning that he was not under contract, I made an effort to
sign him. It wasn't that there was much competition: he was not yet
celebrated outside of strictly-jazz circles; and since the jazz "comeback" of the '70s still wasn't quite under way, not too many companies were in the market for fresh jazz talent. My problem was that
his last exclusive-contract experience had not been too happy; he
wanted to agree to only one album at a time, but I insisted on
something more nearly standard. We eventually settled on what
was supposed to be a two-year commitment and turned into much
more. (I later discovered he made his decision largely because two
old friends and associates of his—saxophonists Joe Henderson and
Gary Bartz, both of whom were then being recorded by me—had
recommended me as at least being worth taking a chance on.)

I was very much aware that McCoy was still making up his mind about me, and I also took very seriously my promise that he would have full artistic freedom. So on our first session together, early in 1972, I was basically content to stand back and let things happen. I had chosen the studio and engineer; McCoy was just using the piano available in that studio (in later years he has usually insisted on either the Yamaha grand at the Fantasy studios in Berkeley, purchased on his recommendation, or on a specific rented Steinway grand selected by him for use on New York-area sessions). The band was his working group at the time, and the first selection was simply played at length, much the way they would have performed it in a club. I was forced to make a few adjustments, such as shortening an introduction to keep that number down to a length that could be contained on a record: it turned out to run 23½ minutes and takes up all of side two of the album named for that composition, "Sahara."

From that beginning, Tyner and I have gone on to function under many different sets of circumstances, some simple and others complex, and we have made use of several different approaches, each of which has had its own virtues and its own problems. Flexibility is one of my major recording principles; the albums with McCoy are to me strong proof that the principle works. After a while we reached an almost instinctive level of operation, both in the pre-planning of a project and the decisions and last-minute changes that often must be made while recording. Sometimes the fine tuning between us has been too close for separation: a memorable example of this is in the format of the Jack DeJohnette composition "Bayou Fever," as recorded on the 1978 album *Together.* In this performance there are no solos as such; instead, the eight players are paired off for a series of four duets. It was my recollection that this had been Tyner's concept; then I read in a magazine interview with him that he credited me for it; and we finally agreed that we really didn't know whose idea it had been!

A more recent Tyner album, *Four Times Four,* is worth examining in detail as a good illustration of how we function. To begin with, it's another example of our interplay. It began with his suggesting a quartet album, since he hadn't worked in this format for several years. I pointed to the built-in danger for a pianist-leader of recording with a single horn: that other player inevitably handles most of the melody leads and can easily assume too dominant a position. So, how about a quartet album maintaining the same rhythm section and using a different fourth player on each tune? But McCoy felt that constant changing might make the album seem too cluttered, so we agreed on a six-tune album using three different fourth men for two selections apiece. Still later, in discussing exactly who to invite, we found ourselves with too many attractive candidates—which led me finally to come up with the concept of a double album with four guests. Each would play throughout one side, making this in effect a package containing four half-albums.

By rehearsing and recording each unit separately, and by selecting four significantly differing players, each side really became a self-contained entity to us, concentrating mainly (in choice of repertoire as well as performance) on the relationships between Tyner and each fourth man. What had begun as a fairly offhand thought about doing a quartet album finally emerged as a fully structured, unique concept that, among other things, emphasized his stylistic versatility.

The format also provided an opportunity for unusual flexibility while recording. Knowing that our goal on each session was to tape enough music for exactly one album side (which of course could vary by several minutes), we began each time prepared with three selections but quite willing to settle for two. This meant there was no need to worry about either stretching or condensing; we could simply let whatever length felt most comfortable to the performers be the "right" length. (Actually, there turned out to be three three-tune sessions and one with two.)

The repertoire on a Tyner album poses few problems for a producer, since the bulk of the material will almost always be McCoy's own compositions. I have achieved enough familiarity with what he has written over the years to make reasonably intelligent suggestions of older tunes that might suitably be re-worked for a new album; plus enough awareness of his taste to come up with a Monk melody or an old standard that's likely to strike a responsive chord.

The choice of the supporting cast had also been made in a highly unpressured way. The rhythm section consisted of Al Foster, who has been a favorite drummer since the 1978 Jazzstars tour, and Cecil McBee, who was chosen through almost opposite thinking. We had decided we wanted a first-rate acoustic bassist who had never previously recorded with McCoy; there really aren't very many, and Cecil clearly fit both parts of the description. As for the various "fourths," Freddie Hubbard and Bobby Hutcherson were both invited because they were old friends and it was easy to predict how well they would work into the concept. The other two were more adventurous choices, since neither had played with McCoy before—although when I mentioned Arthur Blythe to him, it turned out to be another example of instinctive teamwork: Tyner informed me that he'd recently been thinking he'd like to try playing with this young altoist. John Abercrombie was a different matter. McCoy wasn't really that familiar with his work, but I felt strongly that they would mesh well, and the fact that the guitarist is highly regarded by our mutual friend Jack DeJohnette carried more than a little weight. When Abercrombie and Tyner met for the first time at the pre-recording rehearsal, the blend I'd hoped for became an instant fact, relieving me of the anxiety I'll always feel when I go out on a limb like that.

In casually referring to rehearsals, I don't want to be misleading. For a variety of reasons (from budget restrictions to the mystique of jazz spontaneity) they are still far from automatic elements in jazz recording. But I've come to look on preparation as, rather paradoxically, an important aid to spontaneity and freshness. For an improvisation-minded player, it's essential that a tune be recorded in relatively few takes: if he has to attempt his solo too many times before the ensemble performance is precise enough to keep, he's very likely to get bored. McCoy happens to be an outstanding example of this; the fact that he understands the problem can be very helpful.

Tyner has actually displayed a constantly growing interest in the whole environment of recording, and in learning about the many aspects that can be altered and controlled in the best interests of creativity. It has been my experience that simply spending a lot of time in the studio doesn't necessarily create this attitude; many jazz musicians just don't want to know. McCoy, however, while remaining a totally acoustic player with a preference for the natural approach, has come to appreciate the importance of contemporary recording techniques. In person, it is often apparent that his full, forceful left hand can interfere with a listener's ability to follow the complexities of his right-hand runs. (The situation can be made even more difficult by his fondness for working with strong and aggressive drummers.) In the studio, the same problem existed, though to a lesser degree. Several recording engineers approached the problem in different ways over the years, with varying multi-microphone tactics. Eventually the solution came from McCoy's own expression of his priorities: he considers the right hand more important, and he prefers a bright overall piano sound. The two needs are entirely compatible—by brightening the total sound of the instrument, you can emphasize what the right hand is doing at the high end without any feeling of the piano being out of balance.

Tyner has also gradually come to accept the judicious use of overdubbing as a valuable tool. It is true that his most widely acclaimed album to date, *Fly with the Wind,* involved the considerable accomplishment of the entirely live, simultaneous recording of acoustic piano and bass, ten strings, two woodwinds, harp, *and* Billy Cobham's drums. That represented one kind of challenge, but the very next problem we took on dealt with displaying the multi-reed capabilities of his working group. On that album, *Focal Point,* a three-horn unit played the basic tracks; then the same three men added the rest of McCoy's arrangements (one composition having a total of nine horn parts). We have used procedures suited to our special needs, and possibly uniquely ours: on *Inner Voices,* four horns were recorded with the rhythm (which meant he could hear the full harmony of his arrangements while playing); other brass and reeds and some voices were then added to complete a full-scale project that was just too large and complex to be done any other way. On the other hand, our most recent band sessions, involving up to nine horns and two percussionists, were done virtually without overdub, the choice being to take advantage of the extreme separation at the Power Station studio in New York. But when a percussion expert we both wanted—Airto—was not available, we added his work on the West Coast two months later; not a purist approach, but a very helpful one.

The fundamental point here is that the artist has absorbed an important lesson: how to use whatever means make creative sense in reaching your goal, but always keeping technology from using you or leading you to alter any basic aspect of your music. Having made this point, I hasten to turn away from it, because I really don't want a discussion on recording with McCoy to end on any sort of impersonal or technical note. Some of the deepest satisfaction in my sixteen (or seventeen, or twenty-two) Tyner records has come from the almost tangible warmth and love and creativity that is generated. Several of these albums would quite literally have been impossible if McCoy weren't their cornerstone. Trio sessions in which an amazingly tight mesh was built up between the pianist and Ron Carter and Jack DeJohnette, or Ron and Tony Williams, or Jack and Eddie Gomez. Or an amazing five days late in 1978 in which, after breathtaking schedule-juggling, we assembled Stanley Clarke, Hubert Laws, Freddie Hubbard, Bobby Hutcherson, saxophonist Bennie Maupin, percussionist Bill Summers, and DeJohnette—and I watched some of the strongest players and best-established egos in jazz most willingly devote themselves to doing it McCoy's way. They were there because they considered it an honor to be working with him; they showed up at the studio on time (for the most part);

they rehearsed; they formed themselves into a *band* rather than a collection of guest stars.

I also don't want to leave the impression that Tyner is perfect, or an easy man to work with. He is as stubborn as I am, which is a lot. Despite his reluctance to do many takes, and his enjoyment of writing tough arrangements, he also likes to be as last-minute as possible in completing preparations. (I vividly recall one several-nights club recording situation in which, when we began, the band had never played two of the tunes—and in one case I still doubt that the composition had even been written before the second day.) But, with just a couple of dull exceptions, I've never worked with anyone who made it easy. So if it's going to be *that* challenging, it might as well be with an artist capable of making it *that* rewarding.

"Previously Unissued Performances..."
1983/84

In the three and a half decades since tape became the accepted way of recording music and the long-playing album the means of issuing it, a vast quantity of jazz has been set down on tape. In addition to all that has been released, a substantial amount has for one reason or another been set aside, unused. It should be understood that when a newly recorded album is being assembled, no one has the slightest interest in alternate takes or other future considerations. The task at hand is to select the "best" performances (sometimes a quite arbitrary decision) for immediate release. Often enough, the bypassed material deserves a better fate; the initial negative decisions may have involved bad judgement, confusion, economics— and above all the fact that artist and producer are almost always specifically involved in creating a single, two-sided 12-inch disc containing very close to forty minutes of music (much less is regarded as short-changing the purchaser; much more is technically unfeasible).

So a lot of valuable artistry and important documentation may never leave the shelf it is originally filed on. But, given enough time, other arbitrary factors can come to the rescue: things like curiosity, stubbornness, accident, or historical research. You might be motivated to search for additional values, for possibly important music that was underappreciated in the past. Or you might consider the phrase "previously unissued" a helpful added attraction in marketing old product. Or a little of both.

If the belated digging is done in the tape files of a label (like Riverside) that has passed through several hands and many miles since it ceased operations, you really should not expect too much. On the other hand, current techniques can often make it a relatively simple matter to improve sound qualities—and when you're resurrecting material after more than two decades of undeserved silence, a few rough moments in the performances don't really count for much.

(Adapted from the notes for two early-1980s
albums of previously unissued Thelonious Monk
material: *Evidence* and *Blues Five Spot*)

NYC Underground
1981

One of the most famous flights of stairs in the jazz world is the well-worn set that carries you down from the rather desolate Greenwich Village street level into the compact underground confines of the Village Vanguard. (If you've ever been there on a crowded night, you know the word "confines" is not being used loosely.) The Vanguard has been in existence far longer than you'd imagine possible for a jazz club. I know that I've been hanging out there ever since I was slightly under legal drinking age—which wasn't yesterday; and I've worked on many occasions to capture on tape the justly famous interaction between audience and performer that is generated down there—with Cannonball Adderley, Bill Evans, Bobby Timmons, Junior Mance, and Johnny Griffin.

The place exists, quite simply, because of Max Gordon, who is small, ageless, wiry, and obviously incredibly stubborn. He also understands and loves jazz and jazz musicians to a degree unmatched by any other club owner ever. And he is loved back, which helps. It used to be fashionable to refer to jazz clubs as "upholstered sewers." This is not true of the Vanguard, where there is no upholstery to be seen. Just the sight and sound of the music, with no frills and a not-too-cruel door charge.

(From notes to the Johnny Griffin album
NYC Underground)

7

Some of My Best Friends

All five of these essays were written to accompany examples of a particular form of album reissue called "twofers." The concept was thought up by Ralph Kaffel of Fantasy Records in the early 1970s and widely imitated by others (which is by no means a complaint on my part; it has meant the return to ready availability of a vast quantity of worthwhile jazz). Since these involved two records packaged together, there was always substantial room on the double interior surface for extensive annotation. And since this was *inside* space, not visible when the sealed unit was on display in stores, there was no incentive to have these notes do any sort of selling job. The result was often valuable and informative writing.

Being in the frequent role of handing out such writing assignments, I was able to reserve the opportunity to express myself about several Riverside colleagues who had been very important to me. At the times when these five pieces were written, however, there was a rather depressing ratio: three (Cannonball, Wes Montgomery, and Bill Evans) dead, and Johnny Griffin self-exiled to Europe for over a decade. It is somewhat helpful to note, as an update, that Nat Adderley remains a close friend, and that in 1978 Johnny Griffin began a series of regular return tours of this country, as one result of which we have been able to work together on five more albums. The 1983 Evans notes deal with a very specific portion of our association; although I had some internal reservations about their frankness, they surprised (and pleased) me by winning that year's Recording Academy Grammy award for Best Album Notes.

Wes Montgomery
1973

It has been more than two decades since I began making the switch from just plain jazz listener, fan, and record collector to a total (in bad moments I might call it an excessive) involvement with the music: first as a writer and, since the mid-1950s, primarily as a record producer. I have on the whole gained a lot from the move, but I have lost something, too. Most of all, I've lost a hobby—it has been a very long time since I could have that pleasantly voluntary degree of involvement that the fan has, listening to jazz only when you care to, listening only for enjoyment, having only a superficial or non-existent or gleaned-from-magazines knowledge of musicians as people. I know it doesn't affect everyone, but I happen to be one of those who has trouble enjoying a solo by a man I happen to know to be personally a son of a bitch.

But of course that personal level works both ways: I have been able to form some friendships that are among the most valuable things in my life. To be very specific (and without in any way minimizing certain other very important jazz-linked personal associations), if I had not gotten enmeshed in this music, I undoubtedly would not have come to know Wes Montgomery, and that would have been a very big loss to me.

Whether or not they realize it, almost everyone who ever heard Wes knew him to some extent—I can verify that the warmth and directness and spontaneity and love you seem to hear in his music was really there. What is on his records is actually that honest a projection of things that were in him. That is a pretty rare state of affairs. First of all, not many players make the kind of music that so directly reflects who and what they are. (To do so is not in itself necessarily "good" or "bad"; I'm simply stating a demonstrable fact.) Secondly, there are a great many more of the sons of bitches around. To put that in more formal terms, it is not at all uncommon for talent, genius, artistic superiority to be thoroughly intertwined with eccentricity, temperament, perversity of one sort or another, and a highly developed tendency on the part of the artist for both self-torture and the tormenting of those around him. (I think I understand as well as the next man why this is so often the case; at the moment, though, I'm not making any value judgments about society and creativity and such; I'm simply stating another demonstrable fact.) After a while, I must add, you come to think of the stresses and jolts involved in dealing with such men as an unavoidable part of the dues you have to pay, as perhaps the emotional entry fee into the world of creativity.

But Wes was obviously far more talented than most, as close to pure genius as any. Shortly after Wes died in 1968, Ralph Gleason wrote: "the two bosses of the jazz guitar were Charlie Christian and Wes Montgomery; he made that kind of a contribution", and the comment still holds up as truth, not eulogistic hype. Yet there was about him not a trace of any form of torturous or torturing egotism. Again, I am not making value judgments. Nor do I mean to imply that he was made out of spun sugar, or that you could faintly see a halo when he walked down the street without a hat. He was a man, with some routine traits and some faults and a few peculiarities and this one large touch of genius. He was also, as I'm trying to stress right here, a very rare and beautiful human being whose music sounded like his soul and who, as far as I know, never deliberately gave anybody a hard time.

In retrospect, though, he probably gave himself much more of a hard time than anyone realized. When I first met him, in his native Indianapolis in 1959, he was working evenings at a roadhouse called the Turf Bar and then moving on each night to the Missile Room, an after-hours club where he played until about six in the morning; he had only recently given up a variety of additional non-musical daytime jobs. The basic motivation for this extreme amount of activity was quite unmysterious: he was supporting a wife and six (later seven) children. This was also why he had not left town a few years earlier with his older brother Monk and younger brother Buddy when they had relocated in California and achieved some fame as half of a strong-selling pop/jazz group called The Mastersounds. The three brothers had grown up as a close personal and musical group (the Turf Bar engagement had been a family gig for years) and they remained tight-knit, although their relative (no pun intended) positions went through some flips that must have been rather confusing. Wes, who hadn't really turned to music until his late teens, played a bit with his brothers as a sort of added starter during the height of their Mastersounds success. When he began to gain some attention on records, the three realized their ambition to work together as The Montgomery Brothers—but that name didn't mean enough to bring many bookings and after a while they had to split up. When Wes really made it big they came back together, but with his name as the drawing card, for the last years of his life.

It is quite possible to look back over his career as a whole and find quite a bit of evidence of pressure and tension. There was his late start and lack of formal training (the story that he learned guitar from Charlie Christian records when he was 18 or older seems accurate). There was his even greater delay in coming out into the world as a musician—he had toured with Lionel Hampton's band between 1948 and '50, but not until 1960 (when he was already in his mid-thirties) did he begin to record and work regularly as a leader. Such things can certainly give a man a feeling that time is short and every minute counts, and I wondered almost from the start of my working years with him about the extent to which this might relate to certain physical and/or emotional hangups. He often spoke in a general way of suffering from "nerves," and more than once sought medical attention for spells of dizziness. He had a strong fear of flying: he took short trips if absolutely necessary, but they left him pretty shaken up. (The first time he was approached about a European tour he pointed out that he didn't much care for ocean voyages either, and finally claimed he'd go only if someone could figure out a way he could drive there.)

Particularly in the beginning, he was very outspoken about his feeling that he wasn't playing well, or had played much better at some time long before I had ever heard him. I used to get very impatient with him about such remarks—being extremely aware of the melodramatic thunderclap nature of my initial encounter with Wes. (I have the feeling that *this* story has already passed into legend or folklore; but, briefly, it is quite true that Cannonball Adderley burst into my office at Riverside one day, having just returned from hearing Wes at the Missile Room after a concert in Indianapolis; his enthusiasm was so convincing that a few days later I flew there to hear for myself; it took about thirty seconds to make a believer out of me; and Wes had signed a Riverside recording contract before dawn broke at the after-hours club.)

On the whole, though, I always felt that his doubts about his playing were just slightly excessive outcroppings of a kind of perfectionist self-criticism I've come across in quite a few major artists (Sonny Rollins and Bill Evans are two who come readily to mind as being about as negative as Montgomery). At times he actually was a bit less than perfect, but not very much so; and it is of far more consequence to note how quickly other musicians warmed to him and accepted him when he first showed up on the New York scene. I recall one incident that seems to wrap up these several points— how good he was, though not flawless; and how people felt about him from the start, as though by instinct. During either his first or second recording trip to New York, he sat in with Horace Silver's group at the Village Gate one night. The tune was "Nica's

Dream", I think; anyway, it was a Silver composition and Wes really tore up the crowd with his solo. After the set, Horace told him: "You know, you weren't in the same key as we were, but you sounded so good I didn't want to stop to tell you."

The initial attitude towards Montgomery could easily have been the opposite. When a man shows up in the big city preceded by all sorts of stories about his legendary accomplishments back home, the natural tendency is for the New York musicians to gang up on him and try cutting him down to size. This never happened to Wes: for one thing, it was immediately obvious that he was as good as the legends said; but, even more important, it was equally obvious that he was a totally non-arrogant, no-nonsense person whom it was just about impossible to dislike. From the start, no one had to coax players of the caliber of Percy Heath or Tommy Flanagan or Hank Jones to record with Wes, and I still remember his early sessions as among the most enjoyable I've ever been involved in—despite the fact that Percy could run Wes a close second in the fine art of complaining about the imperfection of his own performance. Other musicians were incredibly eager to play with Wes; in addition to co-star and guest-star recording with Cannonball, Milt Jackson, and George Shearing, there were many plans and requests from name performers that just never did get to happen—and, sadly, there wasn't even amateur recording equipment on hand during those few weeks in the early '60s, mostly at the Jazz Workshop in San Francisco, when he worked as part of John Coltrane's band. I never heard them and must wonder about how well they fitted together then (Wes expressed some reservations; and McCoy Tyner, who was in the group, says it was sometimes remarkably interesting and sometimes not). But I am most intrigued by the fact that they came together at Trane's urging.

Such enthusiasm from those around him, plus quick approval from virtually all jazz writers (it should be noted that men like Gleason and John Wilson and Nat Hentoff showed no signs of standard critics' caution about a new artist: they jumped in with those daring, even though entirely accurate, Charlie Christian comparisons) did begin to improve Wes's self-confidence. Large-scale public approval, however, did not come so swiftly. He did become a poll-winner almost overnight, but as many a jazz musician has learned to his sorrow, you cannot live by the applause of *Down Beat* readers alone. Wes was understandably unhappy about the incongruity of being hailed as the world's greatest jazz guitarist and still being unable to make money thereby. I explained to him, with tongue only somewhat in cheek, that he had to have more patience: "Only a year or so ago you were an unknown. You were a bum and broke; now you're a star and broke; that's real progress."

Actually, significant financial success did not arrive until after the end of his Riverside period. And mention of that brings me up against an admittedly very prejudiced personal evaluation: "early" as opposed to "late" Wes Montgomery. Bluntly, I considered the small-group, strictly-jazz settings of almost all the Montgomery albums I produced to have been the most fertile musical soil for him. I feel that those records, most of which present Wes with little more than first-class rhythm accompaniment—have far more validity and lasting importance than the albums he made later for others, the big-selling records with heavy backgrounds, pop-oriented repertoire, and hardly any room for improvisation.

Going against my position is the weight of the huge sales racked up by that other formula—but on my side is my own stubborn immodesty on the subject, the opinion of most musicians I know, and, I must feel, the opinion of Wes himself. Certainly he appreciated the fame and money that were beginning to come his way after the shutting-down of Riverside freed him to sign a recording contract with Verve. But I recall his complaining to me about how little he liked his first big success there, "Goin' Out of My Head." With vast illogic, I told him he couldn't do that: "As much as that number has done for you, you have to accept it. I can dislike it; you can't." Most seriously, though, and (I hope) without any aroma of sour grapes, I *can* dislike the fact that Wes was presented to a broad audience in a manner that I have to think of as falling far short of expressing his best qualities. That all those people fell in love with his music is a tribute to him, a triumph of artist over surroundings. Of course I would have preferred it if there could have been some middle ground, if he could have gone out to the mass market sounding rather more like the Wes I knew and worked with.

Anyway, the rest of the story is just that in 1968 Wes, with very little forewarning, had a heart attack and died while he was much too young. But I guess no matter *when* he died, he would have been too young for it. We were very closely attuned in several ways—for one, our birthdates are only four days apart (the sign is Pisces). Since we were no longer working together, we didn't see too much of each other during the last three years of his life. But the feeling of closeness remained for both of us—I'd have to say that there haven't been over half a dozen people in the world who have meant more to me.

Johnny Griffin
1973

Down at the lower level of the evolutionary process, there are species of animal life that on occasion eat their own young. Some primitive human tribes leave their useless elderly folk out in the wilderness to die. But as far as I know it is only the American public that, with terrible and monotonous regularity, deliberately destroys its own full-grown, youthful, and genuinely talented artists and entertainers.

Actually, it's not the *whole* American public that does this. After all, a very large proportion wouldn't even recognize an artist enough to say "hello" or "excuse me" if they ran into one on the street. And since I'm talking now about *deliberate* destruction, not just through ignorance, I'm not referring to that great silent majority (to coin a phrase). I am instead talking about *us,* the sensitive minority—listeners, fans, club-goers, and record-buyers like you (and, I guess, writers and record producers like me). What we manage to do is set our sights so supercritically high that we will not settle for anything much less than superstars. Anyone getting a grade below A-minus flunks our course.

This is not a passionate defense of the rights of the incompetent. The really awful painters, musicians, singers, and jugglers usually and quite properly fail (except for those that are so bad that they sometimes join the real geniuses in the ranks of the commercially successful). I'm not even campaigning for more work for mediocrities. What I am specifically bitching about is our refusal to give house room to the works of those who are merely good or very good, without being superb or trailblazers or true giants.

Obviously, these remarks are closely related to the fact that these are notes for a Johnny Griffin reissue package. Johnny is, unfortunately for him, a superb example—almost a prototype—of what I'm complaining about. The fact is that Johnny Griffin is no John Coltrane, no Sonny Rollins, no Coleman Hawkins or Lester Young or Ben Webster. But he is certainly the equal of, and more likely than not superior to, pretty nearly any other tenor player you might mention. Don't go running names in rebuttal: I have my favorites, and you have yours; and the fact that Johnny Griffin was a friend of mine is undoubtedly one of the reasons I'm prejudiced in his favor. And of course it's the fact that you, or I, might easily substitute many another name for Griffin's without tampering with the logic of what I'm claiming that makes me so vehement on this subject.

The point, then, is that Johnny Griffin is certainly a high B-plus tenorman, and that for about a decade he has lived and worked in Europe—primarily because that was preferable to the two other alternatives: to keep on scuffling for gigs in the cultural center of the universe, or to give up music. When I say that he "was" a friend of mine, therefore, I'm not referring to any overt break between us, but simply to the fact that between 1958 and 1963 we worked together a lot, saw a good deal of each other, enjoyed each other's company—and haven't laid eyes on each other for the past decade.

The time in which I knew Johnny best was, of course, a relatively happy time for jazz. There was a reasonable amount of club work, and there were lots of independent record companies (very much including Riverside) willing to take a fairly inexpensive few chances on recording a batch of B-plus musicians. Of course some of those had already (to stick to tenor saxophone examples) turned into Sonny Rollins or were about to turn into Coltrane. But most of them just stayed themselves: capable of specific bursts, or full evenings, or even entire albums, of notable creativity and joy; but never finishing first in a poll, or causing lines to form outside clubs, or having best-selling records.

And, failing to scale those heights, all such artists get to be adjudged failures (or at least non-successes) in our society. But who was it that decreed that art is a win-or-lose proposition? Who? Why, it was *us,* the same folks who can tolerate, but just barely, a baseball team that finishes second for a couple of years, but then are most likely to stop going to the ball park. You don't really have to be on the top end of the charts to be tolerable to a jazz record company. The economics of our specialized music world, particularly back in the late 1950s, enabled us to recoup our investment from an album that only sold a few thousand copies. Even a more ambitious project or two didn't hurt too much if they more or less bombed. And most jazz record companies of that era were owned and operated by fairly freaky, jazz-fan kinds of people; and we got very stubborn about continuing to record musicians we dug, and whose capabilities we enjoyed and believed in. (And when once in a while a young guitarist turned out to be Wes Montgomery and got straight-A grades, or an always-A-plus giant like Thelonious Monk broke through to salable recognition, that made it fiscally and emotionally possible for us to keep on being stubborn.)

But it was still a rather precarious life. A musician who doesn't sell enough records to earn additional royalties gets to feel pretty frustrated. He also doesn't get to work all that much in clubs or concerts, and when jazz begins to slide down the popularity scale, as it began to do in the early '60s, he is the first to feel the pinch. And when jazz really falls off a cliff, as it did in the mid-'60s, he either keeps on scuffling for gigs, or gives up music, or maybe leaves for Europe. (And after a while probably finds that Europe is part of our culture-laggard society, too, and maybe is being asked to absorb too many escapee musicians.)

Nobody starts out in any art form ever thinking about being B-plus or lower. Every member of every symphony orchestra violin section in the world believed as a child (or at least accepted Mama's belief) that he would be a famous concert artist. Nobody comes to his first big-band jazz job, or his first record date, doubting that the world will open up wide for him before long. To that extent, the artist usually begins as one of us, as a member of our victory-oriented culture, wanting to be the "best" tenor player in town. But most of them quickly come to understand that, within the society of the "good" players, there is no need for any permanent, definitive "best." (In the legendary cutting contests of an earlier jazz era, not even Coleman Hawkins or Louis Armstrong or Art Tatum was expected to be a winner every night.)

One important aspect of the jazz musician's realization that creative art should not be a win-or-lose proposition can be the growth of a sense of real comradeship. Quite possibly the fact that the public usually thought of them as competitors helped to build their own quite opposite attitudes, at least during the late-'50s/early-'60s "relatively happy time" I was referring to. To return specifically to Griffin, I first heard of him in 1956 when Thelonious Monk, returning from a job in Chicago, sounded off about the local tenor player he had worked with there. Blue Note Records had grabbed him before we had a chance to act, but for a year or so Johnny worked his way into the large, shifting group I sometimes think of as the Riverside stock company. Then and later he was a sideman on albums featuring Monk, Wes Montgomery, Nat Adderley, Blue Mitchell, Clark Terry, Philly Joe Jones, Chet Baker. By 1958 he had become established in New York, had reached the ripe old age of thirty, had served that almost inevitable apprenticeship as one of Art Blakey's Jazz Messengers (practically every trumpet and tenor worth his salt in the hard-bop idiom of the '50s seems to have done a valuable stretch with that band), and had succeeded Coltrane as the horn in Monk's Five Spot quartet.

By 1958 he was also newly signed to Riverside, and on his first albums as leader for us was able in turn to recruit comrades as sidemen: Philly Joe, Wilbur Ware, Donald Byrd, Pepper Adams,

Blue Mitchell, Wynton Kelly. Looking at my liner notes for his first albums, I am able to recall that he began his career in Lionel Hampton's big band, that his middle name is Arnold, that he was born and raised in Chicago, and that in high school he was primarily an alto player. Looking into my memory, I recall other facts—that this mild-looking, slight young man could execute brilliantly on his horn at killingly fast tempos (not an un-valuable quality when working in front of Blakey), but that he came to be very annoyed at being described as things like "the fastest gun in the West."

There were many reasons other than speed for singling Johnny out from his contemporaries. He had a richly deep sound, and he had a lovely awareness of roots—he knew blues and gospel and, to quote myself, he was "not one of those modernists who think that a reference to an old-time jazzman probably means Charlie Parker."

I also found it unusual and valuable that Griffin almost always thought of his albums as related wholes, not just a string of tunes united only by having the same personnel. Today, the "concept" album is not only commonplace, it is just about a necessity; in the more loose-jointed period in which Johnny recorded for Riverside, it was pretty daring. It was also pretty daring for a musician to suggest to one of us less-than-wealthy labels that we try anything larger than a sextet date. Griff dared both: he wanted to do a date tied together by being entirely in a funky, "church blues" bag, and he wanted at least a moderately big-band sound behind him. He kept on wanting, and not getting, for quite a while. Then we struck a good lick: Cannonball Adderley's new band recorded an album in 1959 for Riverside that featured Bobby Timmons' church-y tune, "This Here"; it did a lot for Cannon and the label and for something that the world (or at least the record business) decided to call "soul music."

That music happened to be very close to what Johnny had been talking about, so we found it hard to keep resisting the idea. Whereupon, Griffin and a goodly number of his and our friends went into the studio and generated an album that made some little noise in its own time (including the fact that another arranger lifted the scoring of "Wade in the Water" and created a hit for another artist—but that's life, isn't it?). It also is an album that I find still makes a lot of sense today, which is no small tribute for a 1960 recording featuring a non-famous player. Its sense of blues-and-spirituals roots remains valid, and the full-flavored "preaching" tenor sound carries a very timeless emotional pull.

The following year Johnny had another idea for a concept

album—it was again something that was quite fresh when he thought of it, but that others have made stale through overuse in the years since then. An instrumental tribute to Billie Holliday was a fine and offbeat idea back in 1961; Lady had died in the summer of 1959, and nobody had gotten around to eulogizing and canonizing her (it would of course be more than a decade before a movie biography, with Billie being imitated by a Motown star, would be a good commercial idea). Riverside had grown somewhat more affluent and self-assured in the period between the two albums; this time I even went for the luxurious touch of a few dark-sounding strings along with a sizable brass ensemble. All of which helped create an effectively mournful, soulful setting in which Griffin— without trying to imitate or even parallel Billie, but just being a musician who had known her and loved and understood her music—could do a remarkably fitting and creative job of "singing" some of her songs. (This is the sort of thing your B-plus musician can do, where an A type would possibly feel it was beneath him.)

These two albums are also pretty good working examples of that comradeship I was referring to: names like Nat Adderley and Clark Terry and Barry Harris and Ron Carter and Bob Cranshaw turn up here as they do on many Riverside sessions. (I recall Harry Lookofsky, one of the busiest studio violinists of that period, volunteering to round up the viola and cello players needed for the first day of the Holiday album, and then turning up himself to take one viola chair—just because, he said, the session sounded like fun and he wanted to be in on it.)

Neither these albums nor the many others that Griffin made in those years broke any sales records, but they were a very interesting lot: some straight-ahead, some experimental (like the one with two bassists and French horn Julius Watkins), and of course the series of *Tough Tenor* swingers made during the period when he was working side by side with Eddie "Lockjaw" Davis. Then came the leaner years and the departure for Europe, where he worked with pretty good regularity (including a long stretch with the formidable Kenny Clarke-Francy Boland big band), although, as I have noted, the European market has also become a declining one for expatriate American jazzmen.

My main point continues to be that it is a damn shame that the U.S. jazz scene has been unable to support and sustain, or in any way to directly or indirectly subsidize its Johnny Griffins. The only counterbalancing feature, in his specific case, is that the way things worked out in the very late '50s and very early '60s, it was possible for one of my favorite non-great musicians to set down some very strong examples of his very strong work.

Cannonball Adderley
1975

Julian Adderley was my friend. He was among the handful of people to whom I felt most closely connected during the almost two decades that I knew him. He was also a musician with whom I worked closely during two specific periods—the very important (to him and to me) six years between 1958 and 1964 that he spent at Riverside Records, and again on two 1975 projects during what turned out to be the last months of his life.

These facts are not in themselves exactly unique. I have other friends, including musicians with whom I have spent uncountable quantities of time in the recording studio. More than a few of the musicians I find myself working with now are men I knew and worked with more than a few years ago. Other friends have died, including vastly talented musicians with whom I felt deep ties, like Wes Montgomery and Wynton Kelly.

No, the facts are not unique. But the man was.

I first met Cannonball some time in 1957. I still remember with reasonable clarity the circumstances of that first meeting. As a matter of fact many of my memories of Cannon are in terms of specifically recalled scenes and incidents. And since—like me and like most of the people I've known in the jazz world—his life seemed in one way or another to be about 90 percent concerned with his music, those recollections and some of the thoughts and comments they stir up can very suitably be presented here.

To start with that first meeting: I know it was '57, and I figure it for spring or summer—the circumstantial evidence being that I was introduced to Cannon and his brother Nat by Clark Terry (whose own first Riverside album was recorded in April of that year), and that we were all standing around in front of a rather celebrated Greenwich Village jazz club called the Cafe Bohemia. That would seem to indicate a New York night too warm for either musicians or really hip customers to be inside the club between sets; therefore, possibly any time between May and September. Or being outside may just have been a safety measure. The Bohemia, in addition to being celebrated as the place where top bands like

Miles Davis's and the Modern Jazz Quartet played when in New York, and as the scene of Cannonball's legendary evening of sitting in with an Oscar Pettiford group when he first hit the big city in 1955, was also well known for a tough owner who shoved customers and musicians around when they clogged up the narrow bar area.

Anyway, there were Cannon and Nat and a midway point in a chain reaction that has always fascinated me (through Alfred Lion of Blue Note Records I first met Thelonious Monk, through whom I met Clark Terry, and thus Cannonball—who was the first man to turn me on to Wes Montgomery, and so on and on). I liked the men, and it seemed pretty mutual; and I liked their music, but not nearly enough other people did, because by late '57 the first Cannonball Adderley Quintet had disbanded. It was not at all a bad band (the brothers' rhythm section was Junior Mance, Sam Jones, and Jimmy Cobb), but the time wasn't right yet, or something, and they drew such slim audiences that, according to Julian's deadpan account, their best weeks were the ones they didn't work—"At least then we broke even."

The breaking up of that quintet turned out to be far from disastrous. Just consider the after-effects. For one thing, Cannon decided to put in some time collecting a salary without leadership headaches, and so he accepted Miles's job offer, a key step in the formation of probably the most significant and influential band in modern jazz: the sextet with Adderley, Coltrane, Evans, Chambers, and Philly Joe. Secondly, the Adderley brothers blamed their record company to some extent for their band's failure and Cannon began to take steps to terminate what proved to be a somewhat ambiguous contract with Mercury. By this time he was getting lots of moral encouragement from me, and Riverside (which had Monk, Bill Evans, and a couple of Sonny Rollins albums) was looking like an increasingly interesting label, and in June 1958 he signed a recording contract with us.

What I remember above all from the meeting at which the signing took place was that Cannonball was accompanied by his personal manager. I don't think I had ever before dealt with a musician who had a real honest-to-God professional manager. Hell, Julian was only a sideman at that time, and the contract involved the lowest imaginable advance payments, and we even used the standard printed form contract that the musicians' union provided. But there was a manager (John Levy, eventually one of the busiest and best, and associated with Adderley forever after) and there was one special condition. Mercury, it seems, had only recorded

Cannon's working group once (and hadn't issued that album until after the group broke up). So I promised that, as soon as Julian re-formed a band, and just as soon as he felt it was ready to record—whenever and wherever that might be—I would go there and record them. An interesting verbal commitment: a non-existent band would be promptly recorded someplace on the road by a still very shoestring company that had never sent its staff producer, me, to work any further than a subway ride away from home. But it turned out to be one of the neatest examples of the good results of bread-cast-upon-the-waters since the Bible.

Cannonball began by recording some strong albums for us (the first two involved men like Milt Jackson, Bill Evans, Art Blakey, Wynton Kelly—both because of Cannon's taste in picking sidemen and because of good players' desire to associate with him). Then by mid-1959, he was ready to make his move, to leave Miles and reshape his own band. Inevitably that meant Nat; and just about inevitably their longtime Florida buddy, Sam Jones, on bass. In those days, when there were a great many regularly working groups out there, it was hard to put together an experienced unit without raiding other bands. Julian wasn't happy about this, but he knew what drummer he had to have, and so he rather reluctantly forced himself to steal Lou Hayes away from Horace Silver.

He was a bit more indecisive about the piano slot: for a while he favored Phineas Newborn, and I remember going with Julian to Birdland one night to hear him. Newborn, always an impressive technician, was pretty overwhelming that night, and he was offered the job. But, Cannon informed me, Newborn had one impossible demand: he wanted featured billing. The trouble was, Nat was already guaranteed that—and how could you have a leader's name and two featured artists in what was only a five-man group without the other two feeling an awful draft. He just couldn't do that to Sam and Louis, Cannon said. So he turned to his almost-first choice and enticed Bobby Timmons away from Art Blakey's Jazz Messengers. And everyone concerned was very soon damn glad he did, for the cocky young pianist/composer, whose "Moanin' " had been a 1958 winner for the Blakey band, immediately came up with another one.

After breaking in their act for two weeks in Philadelphia, the quintet went to San Francisco for three weeks at the Jazz Work-shop. But even before they left for the West I had been put on notice that the "whenever and wherever" I had promised was go-ing to be then and there. The band was together; the first audience reactions to Timmons's new tune, "This Here," had convinced

Adderley that he had a hit; and what was I waiting for? If I'd had the sense and experience to know what to worry about, I'd have recognized plenty to wait for: among other things, San Francisco at that time had not a single recording studio; there were very few engineers anywhere with a command of the fledgling art of recording "live" in a club; and in any event I didn't know a single engineer in that area. But a promise is a promise, right? So I asked Dick Bock, head of the Los Angeles-based Pacific Jazz label, for advice, and he recommended a young man who, he informed me, had recently done a live recording for him in the very same club. (Dick neglected to tell me he had decided the session hadn't come out well enough to be issued.) Not to prolong the suspense: I found my way to San Francisco (incidentally beginning my still-heavy love affair with that city); I heard "This Here" for the first time (and was informed by the late Ralph Gleason that the audience reaction was *that* hectic every night), we recorded for a couple of nights and came up with a lovely album. Those nights were my first opportunity to really study Cannon as a bandleader, and thereby to discover the remarkable secret of his appeal.

The way I saw it, Julian was one of the most completely alive human beings I had ever encountered. Seeing and hearing him on the bandstand, you realized the several things that went to make up that aliveness: he was both figuratively and literally larger than life-sized; he was a multifaceted man and it seemed as if all those facets were constantly in evidence, churning away in front of you; and each aspect of him was consistent with every other part—so that you were automatically convinced that it was totally real and sincere, and you were instantly and permanently charmed.

That last paragraph is the emotional way of saying it; if I try real hard I can be more factual and objective. He was a big man and a joyous man. He was a player and a composer and a leader, and when someone else was soloing he was snapping his fingers and showing his enjoyment, and before and after the band's numbers he talked to the audience. (Not talking *at* them or just making announcements, but really talking *to* them and saying things about the music—some serious, some very witty.) So all that whirlwind of varied activity was always going on when he was on the stand, and it all fitted together, and you never even considered the possibility that it could be an act. Of course it wasn't; it was (to use today's cliché) just Cannon doing his thing; and part of his thing was wanting you to enjoy yourself, and you did.

His talking to the audience was then (and remained) pretty unique; in assembling that first Jazz Workshop album I somehow got the daring idea of not only including some talk but giving it the same position on record that it had in the club. So that album opened with almost a minute and a half of Julian conversing about "This Here" before you heard a note of music, and apparently it was a good idea, or at least it didn't hurt, since the album turned into a huge hit. It established Cannon and the band and the adventurous label that had gone cross-country to make the record. (And it and its imitators led, for better or worse, to a whole flood of "soul" jazz.) We stayed with the formula a lot—the band made four other "live" albums on Riverside—and years later, when he had an even bigger hit for Capitol with "Mercy, Mercy, Mercy" he explained it to me as "I finally talked Capitol into recording me the right way; the way *you and I* used to do it." In this ego-heavy music business, how can you *not* love a man like that?

Well, some people could manage to not do so, I guess. There were the usual put-downs by the critics (success really doesn't automatically mean you're not playing as well as before, but . . .); and there were similar put-downs by less successful musicians. Those had the power to hurt his feelings at times, but not always; for example, what could we do but laugh at the jazz giant who said that "This Here" was nothing more than rock and roll and then quickly added that anyway it was stolen from one of his compositions.

On the whole, however, there was a lot of approval and those were good times. Riverside in the Cannonball years was a very happy place; there was an unprecedented team spirit among the musicians working for the label, and Julian was very much a leading part of that. He was, as has often been recounted, responsible for our "discovery" of Wes Montgomery: he had heard Wes in Indianapolis one night, and as soon as he got back to New York came bursting into my office insisting that "we've got to have that guy on the label." Allow me to tell you that there are hardly any performers around at any time who are going to refer to the company they are under contract to as "we." He was the kind of star who volunteered his services as a sideman (at union scale) for the record dates of men he liked and respected: Jimmy Heath, Kenny Dorham, Philly Joe Jones. He came up with the idea of his producing albums that would present either unknown newcomers or underappreciated veterans; he felt that his name might help their careers (Chuck Mangione first recorded as a Cannonball Adderley "presentation").

He was an intensely loyal man, and he inspired loyalty. In the sixteen years between the re-forming of his quintet and his death, he had only two drummers (Lou Hayes eventually being suc-

ceeded by Roy McCurdy—who had been the drummer on the
first Cannonball-produced Mangione album), and not very many
more bass players. There were a few more piano players: Timmons left to return to Blakey and then go out on his own; a
couple of others didn't quite work out; Cannon was never able to
persuade one of his major personal favorites, Wynton Kelly, to
work in the band; but Joe Zawinul, who joined him in the very
early '60s, stayed around for a long time. My own strongest recollections of his loyalty relate, not too surprisingly, to when his
contracts with Riverside were running out. The first time, in
1961, he was a very hot artist and we were pretty resigned to his
being seduced away by major-league money. We made our best
gesture—and he took it, even though it turned out to be much
less than at least one major label had offered. The reason he
gave, that he felt comfortable and at home among friends with
Riverside, was just corny enough to be obviously true. Even
more impressive was the way he behaved in the spring of '64. The
label was then almost on the rocks: after the unexpected death of
my partner it became clear that Riverside's financial picture was
much more precarious than anyone had realized. I was fighting
for survival, and losing. So Julian volunteered that, regardless of
what any other companies might come up with, he'd simply ex-
tend his contract with us for another year. It could be announced
as a re-signing, and obviously the news that we were retaining our
top-selling artist would be a big help. I wrestled with the idea: the
main trouble was that Riverside was mortgaged up to slightly
above eye-level. We were at the mercy of financial types whose
shifting attitudes made it quite likely that the label was simply
beyond being saved even by Cannon's ploy. It was a very strange
situation: he kept offering and I kept hedging, and eventually one
day I called him and said, in effect: "This is final; we're not going
to be able to make it, so don't stay with us. Even if I call you
tomorrow with a different story, don't pay any attention. This is
the final true word: go away." Even then he was reluctant; and
how many major artists can you think of that a record company
would have to practically chase away with a club. (I was right,
incidentally; about ten days after his contract was allowed to run
out, Riverside closed its doors.)

For about eight years thereafter, we succeeded in the very tricky
art of being former co-workers who remained friends. Sometimes
we didn't see each other for long periods of time; on other occasions we got around to talking at great length on both musical and
non-musical subjects. Most musicians I have known are (under-

standably enough) so wrapped up in themselves and their art that the rest of the world just doesn't hold their interest. (The polite way to describe this is by saying that artists are non-political beings.) But Cannon happened to be vitally interested in all of life; he enmeshed himself in a wide variety of activities. He was also one of the few people I have ever come across who could consistently talk as much as I do. I'd say that his old friend Pete Long and I were only partly joking when we claimed that some day we were going to run him for senator.

Cannon and I also came up with some intriguing musical ideas that we never did anything about. My favorite remains our plan to collaborate on a musical comedy based on the life of Dinah Washington. It is still easy for me to hear his vivid description of one potential scene, backstage at the Apollo Theater, with Dinah's dressing room filled with a procession of stolen-goods salesmen ("everything from hot fur coats to hot Kotex").

Eventually, fate moved our professional lives back together. I joined the Fantasy organization. Cannonball signed with Fantasy, and the company also acquired the Riverside catalog. After a while we got back to working together. He and Nat and I began by co-producing a package that was a real natural for us—new reworkings of the best material from the good old days (as far back as "This Here" and "Work Song" and "Jive Samba"). Working together again felt comfortable and good; I gave the album a title intended to reflect the comparative immortality of a man who had been a jazz star for all those years and was still going strong. But *Phenix*—the reference is to the legendary bird that is reborn every few hundred years out of the ashes of a self-consuming fire—turned out to have more irony than prophecy to it. Only a few months after its completion, and while his next album remained unfinished, Julian had a stroke and, at the devastatingly young age of forty-six, was gone.

Cannon was certainly not a man without faults, but none of them were petty and the ones I was aware of were strictly self-injuring and directly connected with his huge love of life. He ate a lot (often his own food—he was a great cook) and drank a lot, and that's not really a good idea if you also happen to have high blood pressure and a touch of diabetes and a definite tendency to overweight. But there was no way in the world that he was going to scale himself down and be practical and cautious about his health. It would have been nice if he could have done so; most probably we'd still have him around now; but I'm afraid it just wasn't in his nature to play it that way.

And considering how much joy and warmth and creativity specifically came from that nature, how can any of us who knew and
loved him complain *too* hard at the way it worked out. We can and
do deeply mourn the unfair, untimely loss; but we also have the
still-vital memory of him. And we have his music—and one very
good thing about this music is how accurate a picture of the man it
has always given. That means the music will help keep Cannonball
extremely alive for us; and that's not bad at all.

Nat Adderley
1978

Nat Adderley is without doubt one of the better musicians and one
of the best human beings I have had the opportunity to work, talk,
eat, drink, and hang out with in the more than a few years I've
been involved in jazz. He was born just three years after his
brother, and their musical and personal lives stayed closely inter-
laced most of the time right up until Cannonball's death in 1975, so
it would be pretty silly to claim that Nat wasn't greatly influenced
by Julian in many ways. But it would be even more ridiculous to
claim that Nat became some kind of carbon copy.

Actually, I think one of the strangest things about their relationship was that it was so close—and close in an exceedingly honest,
no-bullshit way. In my opinion, the best thing that a couple of
brothers can do for each other in the vast majority of cases is to
stay far out of each other's way: love each other, but get together
for Christmas and maybe Mother's Day and otherwise forget it.
Particularly brothers who happen to be in the same line of work.
But the Adderley brothers really had a partnership going, and it
was strictly their own idea, and each had something very valuable
to contribute to the partnership, and it worked for a long time. If
Cannon hadn't gotten onto that terribly long list of jazz musicians
who died way before their time, it would still be working.

I first met Nat and Cannon (at the same time) by being introduced to them by Clark Terry in front of a fairly crummy Greenwich Village jazz point called the Cafe Bohemia where just about
every post-bop group of the era—it was the middle-to-late '50s—
played from time to time. The whole story of how that first meeting led to their both signing with the young, broke, but eager
record label I co-founded and produced for is a saga that has
already been written about as part of my reminiscences of Cannon.

But the story I have to tell here is something else, because it's basically about Nat.

Maybe my first reaction on meeting them was to take note of Julian, who was already the one jazz people were more aware of (in 1955 he had created a hell of a stir when, newly arrived from Florida, he had sat in with an Oscar Pettiford band at the Bohemia). But I very soon came to learn the other two key facts: they were a team, and Nat was very much his own person. Looking back at it, I think it was natural rather than deliberately planned for Cannonball to be the bandleader. He was older, more experienced (which meant something when they were both still in their twenties) and above all far more outspoken and flamboyant—a born master of ceremonies who became one of the first leaders of that period to talk to the audience rather than ignoring or snarling at them.

Not that Nat is or ever was the shy type. His sense of humor was as well-developed; it was just a lot more sly and sardonic—a lot like mine, which was one of the very first bonds we discovered between us. And as the pattern of the Adderley band developed, it was Nat who became the straw boss, the paymaster, the disciplinarian (all of these being things every successful jazz group needs to have, even if most of them didn't have them in those days.) After all, it was Nat who blew his cool and chased their piano player down the street one night when that otherwise excellent performer (who is going to remain anonymous in this telling of the story) let his playing get a little too obviously sarcastically corny in protest against having to repeat the band's super-funky big hit every set.

The Adderley team was a very voluntary association. (In later years they got into some formal partnerships; earlier they just split whatever usually small amount of income came in.) From the end of '57 to the middle of '59 they were apart; failure to draw paying customers had forced them to disband their first group. Cannon spent that time featured with Miles Davis; Nat had no trouble finding gigs with leaders like Woody Herman and J. J. Johnson; but as soon as they felt ready to try again, they went back together. I specifically recall that Horace Silver, looking for a trumpet player, approached Nat late in 1958; but Nat felt that the Adderley reunion was too likely to happen pretty soon, so instead he recommended their old Florida buddy Blue Mitchell, who got the job and kept it for about seven years.

What Cannon and Nat gave each other as much as anything else was a sense of stability that was (and is) incredibly rare in the jazz world. Since it happened that they honestly liked each other and worked smoothly together and that their musical styles and thoughts were quite compatible, right away they had a quintet— always to be billed as "The Cannonball Adderley Quintet featuring Nat Adderley"—that needed only to worry about assembling a rhythm section.

Nat also provided a consistently high level of composing talent in the earthy, bluesy, gospelish vein that made "soul" the most commercially viable (comparatively speaking) jazz idiom of the late '50s and early '60s. Tunes like "Sermonette," "Jive Samba," and, above all, "Work Song," which rang up a lot of unlikely cover recordings, my favorite candidate for farthest-out always having been the Tennessee Ernie Ford version.

I should point out that there was nothing automatic about signing both Adderleys to Riverside Records in 1958. It was not a package deal, but simply a recognition that *both* of these men— neither of whom had made it as yet—had a hell of a lot of potential. And there was a great deal of mutual enthusiasm in the air— Riverside was then in the early stages of building a team of frequently used sidemen, and the Adderleys liked that concept, fitted into it, and eventually helped us to add several regular members to that team. Nat, even more than Cannon, became a valuable part of the pattern. Not to make any mystery of it, this simply meant that in those days there was little or no time or money for rehearsal, it was necessary to make an album in as few hours of studio time as possible, to be able to buy formal arrangements was a rare luxury, and to pay any player more than minimum musicians' union scale was even rarer. The reason for this was simply that an independent jazz record company like Riverside or Prestige or Blue Note in the East, Contemporary or Pacific Jazz in California, was operating on a shoestring and issued mostly marginal-selling albums (with maybe an occasional semi-hit in the nick of time to keep the wolf from breaking down the door).

So a producer like me had to rely on combinations that started a date with some ease and familiarity about playing with each other, on arrangers like Benny Golson and Jimmy Heath who could provide inexpensive "sketches" as arrangements, on getting super-cooperation and attention in the studio, and on being charged minimum prices even by men who had graduated to being able to get bigger fees from richer companies. It all happened that way because those musicians recognized that people like me and the others were as crazy as they were, as caught up in the necessity to create jazz whether or not it really made any economic sense to do so.

In that context, a Nat Adderley was a damn good man to have around. A totally helpful player—sounding somewhat like Miles and Clark Terry were sounding then, but also a great deal like his own fiery, ballsy, witty self. Always willing and able to fit swiftly into a two- or three-horn ensemble with a Johnny Griffin, Benny Golson, Jimmy Heath, Curtis Fuller, Julian Priester, or whoever. A prolific and interesting writer who always had a tune or two to contribute to somebody else's session. A friend who could be counted on to help find a quick solution to an unlooked-for musical or personality-conflict problem that had just sprung up in the middle of a session.

And when it came to his own albums, a strikingly interesting thinker who was always eager to try something different—something challenging and stimulating and guaranteed not to be dull. For one reason or another (public taste, not quite enough slickness on the part of musicians and/or producer, the chronic lack of effective promotion common to us all independent jazz labels, or whatever), we never did crack through with an honest-to-God hit record with Nat. But in the studio we always felt we had a chance, which is part of the fun; and we always liked and respected the music we were making, which is another big part; and with the *Work Song* album we felt so close we could almost taste it.

That album, with its unique—you can even say bizarre if you prefer without hurting our feelings—cornet/cello/guitar front line, is extremely typical of our 1960 working techniques. Note that it's cornet because Nat always has preferred that slightly-more-sour-sounding older version of the trumpet; cello because the Adderley band's old friend and bass player, Sam Jones, was experimenting with that instrument, but plucking it rather than dealing with classical bowing; and guitar because we had worked out a timetable to make Nat's concept go into the studio almost simultaneously with the recording of Wes Montgomery's second album.

That was one of my specialities; I didn't mind paying the carfare to bring Wes in from his home in Indianapolis, but damned if it was going to be just to do one job. So the recording sheets remind me that Nat's album was scheduled for a Monday and Wednesday; on Tuesday and Thursday we took care of making a rather celebrated album I brashly titled *The Incredible Jazz Guitar of Wes Montgomery*. I also note that we had a few internal problems: on Wednesday, Nat's "Fallout" had been given its title because pianist Bobby Timmons had fallen out, on account of a little drinking, following completion of recording of that tune. So we tried a couple of non-piano selections, which worked out fine, but didn't leave Nat with enough time, peace of mind, or chops to deal with two scheduled pretty ballads. So we doubled up a bit on Thursday—after Montgomery finished work with his rhythm section of Tommy Flanagan and Percy and Tootie Heath, they went home and Wes was joined by Nat and Sam for those two ballads.

That was all the recording for the week, so maybe I slept late on Friday. Or maybe I went into the office to catch up on paperwork. Like everybody says, us guys in the romantic record business have all the fun!

Probably one of the elements that kept the brothers functioning so well together was that they kept a pretty large degree of separateness in their recording careers. Most of Cannon's non-working-group albums did not include Nat; and only on special occasions was Julian allowed to take part in one of the younger Adderley's studio concoctions. When Nat and I got around to the idea of backing him up with just a full saxophone section, it would have been carrying things a bit too far to use someone else on lead alto. So Cannon was permitted to play, but it remained important not to let the record seem in any way to be leaning on big (and by now big-selling) brother. So you'll find exactly one alto solo on the album we called *That's Right*.

You'll also find lots of members of the "team." Yusef Lateef, although still a couple of years away from joining the Adderleys in their first sextet, had recently done his initial album as a leader for Riverside, and so had Jimmy Heath—whose own next album had both Julian and Nat among the sidemen. Charlie Rouse was then working with the man who had been the very first Riverside star, Thelonious Monk; Wynton Kelly was probably the best piano accompanist of this period and most probably played on more of our albums than any other musician; his close friend Jimmy Cobb had played alongside Sam Jones in that abortive first Adderley quintet. And so it went. I don't know if we made better albums with this system, or if we did more or less or just about the same amount of this kind of ganging together as the other jazz independents. But it is a reasonably important footnote to the history of fairly recent jazz recording, and I can't recall seeing it explained anywhere else.

I went on to do more work with Nat before Riverside fell apart in 1964, but I happen to consider those two albums to have been musically the best of the batch. (I don't seem in this commentary to have gotten around to much mention of the quality of the music, which is OK with me—it's always my personal preference to deal with the context of the music rather than lecture about its content.)

Thereafter I was able to maintain friendships with both brothers while our professional lives ran in different directions, and then we three got together long enough to jointly produce a couple of Cannonball albums for Fantasy before Julian's very untimely death.

Getting his sense of direction together after that has understandably been none too easy for Nat. He's had his own group; he's traveled successfully to Europe and to Japan; and most recently seems on the verge of sliding rather accidentally into a new career. In the spring of 1978, just before the writing of these notes, he told me about his providing the answer to a tricky problem facing the off-Broadway producers of a showcase production of a musical play more or less based on the life of Mahalia Jackson. In search of someone who could play trumpet, sing a bit, and hopefully act (the part is that of a friend of Mahalia's more or less based on Louis Armstrong), they asked Nat to try it. New York reviewers praised his performance, describing him as a "natural" as an actor. I don't know whether this is really going to be the beginning of a new career. But it certainly is an unexpected turn of events. And when you figure that the man who did a cornet/cello/guitar album and a cornet-backed-by-five-saxes album is still doing the unexpected, it sounds as if everything is still as cool as ever with Nat Adderley. Which is the way it should be.

Bill Evans—"The Interplay Sessions"
1983

The late Bill Evans was one of the most innovative and influential piano stylists of his day. Since that "day" ended only a relatively short time ago, with his death in September 1980, it remains impossible to judge how far-reaching and long-lasting his influence will be. But if the depth and the extent of his impact on jazz performers of the past two decades is a reliable clue, we will be hearing partial and complete would-be Bill Evans clones for quite some time to come.

In one way, this is certainly not to be regretted: provided that enough future followers display much the same degree of taste and talent as has been shown by such artists as (just to pick two random examples) Herbie Hancock and Keith Jarrett, jazz listeners and the future libraries of recorded music can only gain. But looking at it another way, to be such a thorough influence both on your contemporaries and on succeeding generations poses certain dangers to the artistic status of the innovator. After a while, the original works may no longer seem as fresh and adventurous when we return to them—simply because we have heard so much music in approximately the same vein. Even worse, listening to various self-appointed disciples who actually only grasp (and consequentially exaggerate) one aspect of the master's style almost inevitably tends to leave a lopsided and diluted memory of what the original artist was really trying to say.

Louis Armstrong, who was the first to do so many things in jazz, may well have been the first to suffer from this. Certainly the legends and legacies of pioneers like Charlie Parker and John Coltrane have at times been at least momentarily tarnished by the work of decidedly lesser performers who claimed to be following in the path of the master. Evans, even during his lifetime, was similarly somewhat victimized by more than a few pallid pianists capable of playing old pop ballads at slow tempos with a few modal quirks thrown in, presumably sounding "just like Bill Evans" but actually very much missing the point.

One way of appreciating how far off the mark such players are—and of recognizing as well the shortsightedness of listeners and critics who stereotype Bill as a Debussy-ridden specialist in languid mood music—is to pay attention to the several examples of other aspects of his playing, to the non-introspective and occasionally even non-trio Evans.

It is of course true that ever since December 1958, when he ended an eight-month stay with the Miles Davis Sextet, Bill appeared in public almost exclusively as the leader of his own trio. There's certainly no question about that being his preferred and most comfortable setting, and there's also no doubt that if a running statistical count had been kept for two decades it would have shown many more *down* tunes than *up*.

But there were times when those trio sets swung like mad—and that more often than not corresponded to the several different periods when Philly Joe Jones was his drummer. Their association had begun when Bill joined Miles in the spring of '58, and even though it was very shortly thereafter that Joe left the band (or was fired, or both—his relationship with Davis having always been a rather temperamental one), their influence on each other remained substantial.

A Miles Davis album that prominently includes Evans, the ground-breaking *Kind of Blue,* is an excellent place to begin paying particular attention to the more forceful and aggressive elements in his playing. The *swinging* involved doesn't really have too much to do with tempo, because what I'm referring to is much more a matter of what gets called playing "hard" or (even on a slow ballad) "with fire" than of playing fast. The drummer on *Kind of Blues* is not Jones, but his successor, Jimmy Cobb. So what is heard are two of the three elements that I feel fueled Bill's performances of that period: the fact of working with three horns and the added confidence and adrenalin that came from being thoroughly accepted as belonging in such company.

For recorded examples of the third element—being propelled by Philly Joe—you have to look elsewhere, but not very far. The Milestone reissue package called *"Peace Piece" and Other Pieces* happens to be titled in honor of a most celebrated example of "normal" Evans—a moody, even Debussy-ish solo improvisation. But it is largely devoted to trio sides recorded immediately after Bill had quite amicably departed from Miles's band to permanently become his own leader. Several numbers include the longtime Davis bassist, Paul Chambers, and the drummer throughout is Philly.

The Davis and Evans sessions noted would seem to represent the culmination of Bill's early period. They take the shy and self-deprecating young bebop pianist I had first met and recorded for Riverside in 1956 to a point some two years later where he briefly admitted liking his own work, had contributed very substantially to the new modal music of Miles and Trane, and had gained the praise and respect of major black jazz artists (a rare accomplishment in those years for a fledgling white musician).

The very next phase in his career took him in quite another direction. Not only did he choose to lock himself exclusively into a trio format, but he concentrated heavily on the possibilities opened up by a remarkable young bassist he had hired after a brief amount of on-the-job auditioning. Scott LaFaro's unique approach to his instrument, plus the always adventurous work of drummer Paul Motian, led to a two-and-a-half-year period in which there was much emphasis on collective improvisation and a constantly growing rapport that, at its most successful, simply reached levels of performance interaction that no other trio has ever equaled. They were often close to their best on what turned out to be their final day's work together. By fortunate coincidence, it was fully taped; two albums (*Sunday at the Village Vanguard* and *Waltz for Debby*) resulted from their matinee and evening sets of June 21, 1961.

The unique achievements of that trio were primarily a matter of the tremendous musical empathy between Evans and LaFaro. So, when Scott was killed in an auto accident ten days later, there could be no direct successor and no valid follow-ups. What had been created were some marvelous moments, and a suggested path (which no one as yet has really retraced and extended), but unfortunately not a tradition. Actually, for quite some time there was room for doubt as to whether Bill Evans as a creative force would entirely survive. He took the loss very hard; for a while he declined to work at all, and then only accepted a couple of brief solo engagements. In all, it took the better part of a year before he found a bassist he felt he could relate to on a regular basis. That was Chuck Israels, who then remained with the trio from the spring of '62 until replaced by Eddie Gomez a full four years later.

Bill had already begun to get back into the studio: he appears on a mostly big-band Tadd Dameron LP recorded early in the spring, and in April had started on a never-completed solo piano project. The latter was abandoned largely because of a quite uncharacteristic spurt of recording activity that began when Evans surprised me by announcing that he was ready to record with his new trio. Eventually it meant that he was in three different studios on a total of eight separate occasions between April and August 1962, creating four and a half albums' worth of solo, trio, and quintet selections.

I don't know how impressive that sounds to anyone else; to me, who was on hand for all of it, it is still overwhelming. It must be understood that I had for years been frustrated by Bill's overly cautious approach to recording: more than two years had elapsed between his first and second albums (mostly because he felt he didn't have anything new to say!); and although there were four albums by the trio with LaFaro, two of these resulted from that one-day, last-chance taping at the Vanguard. Only rarely had he mixed with other players on the active New York recording scene: in the mid-'50s he had participated in some memorable experimental George Russell dates, but since then his only important non-trio moments had been on *Kind of Blue,* on Cannonball's 1958 Riverside debut album, and on a duet recording with Jim Hall made for another label in, I believe, 1959.

By early June of '62 we had two completed trio albums, only one of which was scheduled for quick release. So it was more than a little startling when Evans—that chronic under-recorder—came to me very shortly thereafter with the idea for a quintet album with trumpet and guitar. But it was a valid concept, and it was the sort of interplay with other major musicians that I had been hoping for. (Yes, the blues called "Interplay," which provided the album with its original title, was named by me.) In addition, it was an unfortunately practical idea. I am revealing nothing new when I note that Bill at this time and for some years before had been burdened with what often is described in public as "personal problems" and in real life as a severe dependency on narcotics.

I do not propose to discuss the physical, emotional, or sociological aspects of junk, or to make moral value judgments. I *am* specifically revealing some conflicting drives that I know to have been at work then, because I feel some awareness of the facts is helpful in appreciating the music and its setting. Evans, like certain others, was usually able to adjust externally to the problem; and I do not feel that his internal emotional reactions (whatever they might have been) detracted from his music. In other words, he could play. But this dependency uses up a lot of cash; the most feasible way for a musician who had not been working much in the past year to get money was from his record company. Bill's record company at that time was Riverside; I signed checks at Riverside. It was not easy in those days to be his friend and producer and record company all at the same time. Other jazz labels of that period stockpiled albums quite regularly; I have never liked the idea of recording a man's music with no intention of issuing it until two or three years later—when he might by then have drastically altered his musical concepts. Nevertheless, recording ahead—so that advances could legitimately be paid to Bill—seemed the only way to deal with both the artist's and the company's cash-flow problems in this situation. Rather ironically, it turned out that I was to delay the initial release of his second quintet album for not two or three but a full twenty years.

I have no reason to believe these two albums would have been recorded when they were if not for Evans's problem at that time. Actually, knowing his personality and recording attitudes, I'm not at all sure they would *ever* have been proposed under other circumstances. However, I also consider them to be fascinating and valuable pieces of work: quite different from each other, but both well conceived and well thought-out, and diligently (sometimes brilliantly) executed. Bill made some demands on me that summer; we struck a bargain; and he totally delivered as promised—as he always did.

The first album was quickly assembled: Philly Joe was an obvious choice, and Percy Heath (deeply involved in the Modern Jazz Quartet but still accepting occasional outside record dates) was a strong favorite with both of us. Evans decided that a guitar would give more lightness and flexibility than a second horn; besides, he welcomed a chance to work with Jim Hall. On trumpet, his first thought had been Art Farmer, who was unavailable; choosing young Freddie Hubbard, then only beginning to attract attention as an Art Blakey sideman, was a bit of a gamble, but it worked out just fine. Bill's repertoire choices were mainly standards from the '30s, and Freddie was somewhat too young to know them. Instead of presenting a problem, that turned out to be an asset: it was easy enough for him to learn the tunes, and he didn't have any previous concepts to *unlearn*. In most cases here the Evans approach runs against the grain of the usual interpretation of the song. (Lyrics are good clues to how a pop tune is normally treated, but even if you don't happen to know the words, it's soon clear that these versions are not trying to retain the emotions that led to titles like "I'll Never Smile Again" or "You and the Night and the Music.") Tempos and spirits are mostly bright.

The story of the previously unreleased August 1962 quintet sessions is rather more complex. First of all, I wasn't even asked to do this one until after the July dates, making me feel a bit overloaded. Second, Bill informed me that he intended to record no less than seven original compositions. My suspicion was that the publisher he was dealing with was willing to give him advances on new tunes only when they were scheduled to be recorded. This did not mean that he was shoving any substandard compositions at me. Quite the contrary, they were almost all strong, and some were possibly too tough for the usual circumstances of early-'60s jazz recording— which meant little or no rehearsal and very limited studio time, because that was all the label could afford. (Long after the fact, I was able to figure out that a couple more originals in July and a couple of standards this time would have lightened the load on everyone, but hindsight has never been of much value.)

Such factors contributed to making me feel pretty edgy going into the studio, which surely didn't help. There were two personnel changes: the shift to tenor saxophone was deliberate and based on Bill's feelings about how the music should be handled; Ron Carter was the bassist because Percy Heath was on the road. It was one of Ron's earlier record dates, but he was already highly regarded and was no less than second choice; certainly he doesn't seem to have had much difficulty fitting in. Both Sims and Hall appear to have jumped on some of the material and to have had trouble with other numbers. In my mental reconstruction of the long-ago scene, no one was entirely comfortable, but it is also true that on working with the tapes in 1982 I learned that my recollection of Zoot's having had a hard time throughout was vastly exaggerated. However, there clearly were a lot of physical and emotional ups and downs over the two days. We spent a well-over-average total of four three-hour sessions and came away with Bill and I agreeing that we probably had an album, but would have to do a lot of editing work to finalize things.

Over the next year, we were never able to get at it, obviously somewhat influenced by the knowledge that this material had to wait in line for release behind two or three other albums. By the middle of 1963, various pressures—including the fact that Creed Taylor was very anxious to have him come to Verve—led to a mutual decision to end Evans's Riverside period. Another year later, a whole lot of other, unrelated pressures had led to the bankruptcy of Riverside, and all of its master tapes passed out of my hands.

More than eight years after that, late in 1972, myself and the Riverside tapes, traveling separate and circuitous routes, both ended up in the Fantasy/Prestige/Milestone jazz record complex. But, although almost all sorts of recorded material appeared to have survived the travels, I could not find the unissued August 1962 Bill Evans reels. We did turn up an edited version of "Loose Bloose," which I remembered had been worked on by Riverside's staff engineer, Ray Fowler. It was included in the previously mentioned *Peace Piece* twofer, under the impression that it was the only surviving relic of the two days' work. Eventually, after a massive re-filing project had taken place in the Fantasy tape vaults, I did succeed in locating all the original reels from these sessions. Stored in poorly marked tape boxes (which looked a lot like some totally unrelated boxes and were therefore quite thoroughly misplaced), they had indeed been on hand but unrecognized all along.

Finally putting the material into shape, with the valuable assistance of Ed Michel (now a noted jazz producer, but once upon a time my assistant at Riverside), turned out to be a fascinating and instructive job. In the intervening years, we observed with interest, Evans had recorded only three of the tunes: "Time Remembered" (which became one of his most enduring ballads), "Funkallero," and "My Bells." And the last-named, whose maddeningly shifting tempo changes had made it the unquestioned primary strangler on our date, had been put into much simplified one-tempo form for its inclusion on a Verve "with Symphony Orchestra" album!

It was decided to program the material almost entirely in sequence as recorded, with only "Fudgesickle Built for Four" placed out of order to balance the length of the two sides. (The tricky title of that tricky tune surely calls for explanation. First of all, Bill dearly loved puns: the reference here, of course, is to "A Bicycle Built for

Two." Secondly, if fudgesickles aren't still around, be reminded that they were rather quick-melting ice-cream-on-a-stick concoctions; eating one that was specially constructed for four people would have been about as easy as recording this number.)

Three of the selections ("Time Remembered," "Funkallero," and "Fun Ride") had actually been recorded in relatively few takes. It was easy enough to decide on the preference in each case, and no editing was needed. The others did call for work, ranging from not much on up to the exasperating challenges of "My Bells," which had originally gone as far as Take 25 (although very few had been played to completion). I learned that Philly Joe, even though way back then his problems had been similar to Bill's, had managed to remain an unerring timekeeper—otherwise, the four necessary major splices we have made in that piece would not have been possible. I learned also that Zoot and Jim and Ron, who might at times have seemed a bit unhappy on those afternoons, had actually been models of patience. (I wasn't *too* bad at remaining cool myself, except perhaps for the moment late on the second day when a still-functioning journalist—who, therefore, I will not name—tried to continue an interview with Philly when I really wanted to get back to work. Some of my comments were preserved on the original tape; I decline to share them with you.)

But there was one lesson I didn't have to learn, or even relearn, because it has always been very easy for me to keep in mind: the vast talent, dedication to his art, and human warmth of my friend Bill Evans.

8

A Bad Idea,
Poorly Executed ...
1987

After all these years, I find myself unable to avoid an unhappy conclusion: jazz criticism is a bad idea, poorly executed.

Having opened with a sweeping generalization, it immediately becomes necessary to hedge somewhat. I do not think matters are really appreciably worse than when I entered the jazz world. I am well aware that right now, as has almost always been the case, there are at least a few admirable positive exceptions to my condemnation. And the fault by no means lies entirely with the individual writers. (It definitely is a two-step process: a great deal of the problem must be attributed to the critical concept itself.) But I cannot be dissuaded from a deep conviction that the general performance level among jazz writers is embarrassingly, dangerously low.

I have quite deliberately called this an *unhappy* conclusion: I would much prefer to feel otherwise. Nothing is likely to alter the fact that writing about the arts is a major American activity; as for jazz in particular, the number of words devoted to the subject annually may well exceed the quantity of record albums sold. This being the case, it would be comforting to hope that something valuable, or helpful to the cause of creativity, might come of it now or in the near future. However, since it seems to be a basic fact of jazz life that most new albums will be reviewed and most interviews conducted by young men not especially qualified to do so, there is no real reason to look for much improvement. I cannot be dissuaded from this negative attitude merely by being reminded of writers who may be considered suitably qualified. I am well aware of a number of them, very much including my son Peter Keepnews. More than a few can be capable of cogent analysis, among them (to give some wildly varied examples) Robert Palmer or Stanley Crouch or Gene Lees; the fact that I might disagree with them at least as often as not is certainly not to be held against them. There is a vastly knowledgeable historian like Dan Morgenstern—whom I would probably include as a finalist in any contest for Best of Breed. There is that superlative prose stylist, Whitney Balliett, whose command of the language can be so overwhelming that you might not get around to evaluating the content. Whitney, however, quite often tends to function in a straightforward journalistic fashion, as do such longtime hard workers as Ira Gitler and Leonard Feather. But one can only get into trouble with such indiscriminate and partial name-dropping. It should be clear that my omissions here carry no implications at all; I am not trying to be complete, but merely to indicate that I really am conscious of who is out there.

One problem may be that I have been around too long: the very first jazz writer I read with any consistency was the wonderful pioneer Charles Edward Smith (who, together with Frederic Ramsey, Jr., edited and partly wrote the ground-breaking 1939 book of essays, *Jazzmen*). Charlie Smith was an often turgid and badly organized writer—I edited several of his pieces in the early *Record Changer* days—but he combined encyclopedic knowledge with a passionate love and respect for the music and its creators that make most of his successors seem bloodless. Another problem definitely is that the competent writers (those I have named and as many more as you care to add) are vastly outnumbered by the hordes of shallow, opportunistic, and virtually unidentifiable magazine and newspaper hacks.

A sensible alternative might be merely to ignore what is being written; some of my friends seem able to do that, but I'm afraid it is beyond me. In a recent conversation, saxophonist Joe Henderson referred with a shrug to some negative mention: "You've got to do what you have to do, no matter what they say." It struck me as a slogan suitable for framing. Sonny Rollins quite seriously claims that he never reads any reviews of his work, and I think I believe him. I *know* I envy him. For I am not and never have been sufficiently level-headed, secure, self-protective, incurious—or whatever else might serve as a good enough reason—to ignore the exis-

tence of all those writers churning away out there, using their widely
varying degrees of competence and their often self-created positions
of authority to pass judgment on individual performances or entire
careers. Quite to the contrary, critical commentary has always held
a horrible fascination for me. I suppose it's something like the feelings of a rabbit for a snake, or the appeal Count Dracula had for his
full-blooded victims—I simply cannot turn away. Above all, I cannot resist reviews of records I am directly involved with. Since over
the years there have been hundreds of such albums, I must by now
have read several thousand conflicting opinions of my own work.
Rarely, if ever, have I gained anything thereby.

This is a subject on which I have usually forced myself to remain
uncharacteristically silent. Recognizing that I am highly partisan
and obviously prejudiced, I have felt that caustic letters to the editors or brilliant essays on the theory of jazz criticism, coming from
me, should probably be regarded with suspicion and ruled off-
limits. So, except for a couple of rare occasions when I found a
comment personally offensive or a fact seriously distorted, I have
avoided any form of response. That's how I looked at it for a long
time; I now feel I was wrong. Of course I am partisan, but I am also
deeply involved, concerned, knowledgeable, and (by nature, training, and experience) more readily articulate on paper than a good
many of my equally long-suffering friends and colleagues. A rare
opportunity now confronts me. Within this book I am, by definition,
primarily a writer and only inferentially a record producer—a position I haven't been in for many years. Having read this far, you have
come upon my opinions and comments over several decades on a
variety of related subjects. So you already know that I'm capable of
being as unkind as any currently active jazz writer, that I can turn
out a gratuitously nasty clever phrase with the best of them. This is
very possibly my only opportunity to open up on this subject; it
would take a much more generous and tolerant soul than mine to
pass up the chance.

I must initially establish a couple of personal ground rules. Most
people appear to use the terms "reviewer" and "critic" interchange-
ably, and even standard dictionaries don't clearly support my distinction, yet I have always believed that there's a vast difference. A
reviewer provides you with fairly brief and, one hopes, quite specific description and evaluation of a new play, movie, book, or
record. The intention is to pass summary judgment, perhaps to
condense everything into some arbitrary grading system (B-plus,
or two and a half stars); the presumable purpose is to provide
trustworthy evidence about whether or not to spend your time and

money on the product. A critic, on the other hand, is concerned with the larger and longer view. His territory embraces entire styles and careers; his time-span can be infinite; and if he does deal with specific commodities, it's unlikely to be less than half a dozen albums dissected in terms of some continuing major theme.

Admittedly, the lines of demarcation are not always entirely clear. Some writers routinely assume double duty, turning out their share of capsule reviews and writing a think-piece for the same issue. But the distinction does exist, and as a practical rule of thumb has a lot to do with the status (whether earned or self-proclaimed) of the individual. A critic may really have verifiable credentials or may simply have been around so long that he is accepted as a fact of life, a necessary evil. A reviewer might have a good deal of relevant background, or a little, or just a desire to make a name for himself or to acquire free albums; even after some forty years of reading, it is not always easy for me to figure out which category applies. At least in theory, a reviewer is presumed to be working swiftly and may be excused for being shallow as he strives to meet a deadline: for example, it remains an essential newspaper function to let its readers know the rating of a movie or play within twenty-four hours after it opens (although the significance of that consideration diminishes when various current jazz periodicals take almost a full year before getting around to publishing their definitive word on some "new" releases). It should be clear that my quarrel is largely—although by no means entirely—with reviewers and with the reviewing function as it is now conducted. A full-grown critic, particularly one with a lot of space made available to him in a reputable publication, can do major damage, but it's all those little mosquito bites that really eat you up alive. And by sheer force of numbers, it is the reviewers who turn out the bulk of the words and cumulatively reach the greatest number of readers.

(I recognize that these two subdivisions fall short of covering the full range of jazz writing. I am bypassing one segment of the critical community: writers of books which rarely if ever are concerned with the working-level activities that we in the art/business of jazz necessarily deal with on a daily basis, men I think of as basically "cultural historians." Again, there are people who have credentials in more than one category—Gunther Schuller comes to mind, or Stanley Dance—but I am *not* using the term simply to describe those who create entire books from scratch rather than just magazine or newspaper articles. My actual reference is to authors—for the most part, it would seem, inhabitants of universities—whose works advance theories, or offer either relatively straightforward

or boldly revisionist histories of the whole subject, and who therefore would appear to be most closely related to those scholars who
analyze and footnote other cultural phenomena. In a phrase, men
who view the music from an academic tower rather than at street
level. There is nothing intrinsically wrong with that position, but it
has nothing to do with jazz as I know and live it. Since I do not feel
that these people impinge on my reality, I will not be so rude as to
disturb theirs—except to point out here that I am deliberately, not
accidentally, excluding them from consideration.)

My other ground rule, equally arbitrary, concerns the actual
naming of names. I have no personal vendettas in progress at this
time, no embarrassing stories I'm anxious to tell. My quarrel is
with an entire concept far more than with individuals. Accordingly, my condemnations will remain non-specific or unidentified.
When I do use a name—as I have already demonstrated by strew-
ing a few of them around in an early paragraph—it will either be
for description or in praise.

Growing up in New York and paying attention to the popular arts
that surrounded me, I rather automatically came to accept and generally to respect the reviewing function as a part of life. Plays,
books, movies were analyzed and rated by a small group of usually
literate and experienced writers in the daily papers and various
magazines; if there were no reviews of jazz records except in obscure and highly specialized sheets, it was quite understandable.
Even then I knew that *our* music—which at that time was New
Orleans style and its offshoots as opposed to the much more widely
popular big-band swing—was a limited-market product. Besides,
recorded music was only available in the tiny three-minute units of
78-rpm singles; not until the late 1940s and the coming of the long-
play album was the form substantial enough to justify widespread
reviewing. (So it should be kept in mind that this whole genre is still
comparatively an infant industry, with no real history or tradition.)

But by 1948, and my first serious involvement with jazz at *The
Record Changer,* reviews were inevitably an important part of the
picture. There actually was still a substantial body of single records
around; some were new releases, but a great many were the controversial bootleg reissues of classics and legends owned (and ignored)
by the major labels. Forced to take an editorial stand, we elected to
publish reviews of the pirate records, on the dual basis of pragma-
tism (they *did* exist) and idealism (the initial and larger sin remained
the anti-cultural policy of RCA Victor and Columbia). We did keep
them away from our Number One reviewer, George Avakian, who
at the time was working at Columbia, where he eventually did push

through a magnificent reissue program. Which brings me quickly to a major point: the experience of working with the early *Changer* reviewing staff was a terribly misleading starting point; that was very possibly the most capable group of its kind ever assembled.

Avakian was thoroughly knowledgeable and experienced; he had been a student at Yale when the remarkable Professor Marshall Stearns (who later founded the Institute of Jazz Studies) was teaching English there, and had been professionally involved with the music since the late '30s as a producer, reissue advocate, and executive. He was joined by Bucklin Moon, a talented novelist, essayist, and editor who was a living encyclopedia of traditional jazz—and the one who had to take on all reviewing of bootlegs. Our initial "modern" specialist was the magazine's art director, Paul Bacon. Bill Grauer and I had met him on the evening we first encountered Thelonious Monk at the home of Alfred and Lorraine Lion of Blue Note. A good friend of the Lions, designer of Alfred's earliest album covers and then our first Riversides, and subsequently a book-jacket designer, Paul never really considered himself a critic. But he was an early and astute observer of the bebop scene, and I'm intrigued at how often his comments on Monk and other pioneers are still quoted. A psychology instructor at Columbia University named Robert Thompson, initially known to us as a traditionalist drummer and bandleader, was another early member of this staff, and by 1953 Martin Williams, then an aspiring young writer from Virginia, came on board. To my recollection, he began by taking on the tricky job of reviewing the very first Riverside albums; even though they were classic-jazz reissues (authorized ones, I must add), the possibilities of ethical and personal conflict were obviously huge.

I have given so detailed a picture of that working group because I have never before been in a position to acknowledge publicly this remarkably literate, concerned, uncruel reviewing team of my youth. Almost equally important is that the majority of them would surely have been disqualified from writing jazz record reviews today. Avakian worked for a major label and, whenever possible, produced reissue albums; Bacon had close ties to a leading independent jazz company; and Thompson was presumably too involved as a working musician to be impartial. But not only did they write a long series of informed and valid reviews, they also remained totally above suspicion. Rabid and fanatical as *Changer* readers could be, I cannot recall a single complaint about any of them. Buck Moon was at an opposite extreme: a dedicated and gifted man who earned his living entirely outside of music. (Jazz was very important to him, but he was a novelist and a book and magazine editor by trade. This surely makes him a great rarity among reviewers of any era—a highly skilled outsider, a non-professional who really knew what he was doing.) Only Williams fitted a standard pattern by being young and eager and quite determined to make his mark as a jazz critic; considering that he has been among the most active and respected in the field from then until now, it would seem to have been a good idea to give him his first assignments. He did, it should be noted, write very favorably about those earliest Riversides, but that basically just meant praising Louis Armstrong and Johnny Dodds and Ma Rainey—as well as my notes and Bacon's covers.

So it was not until after (and just possibly because of) the launching of Riverside Records that I began to develop negative feelings about reviewing. Obviously I am often heavily prejudiced in my reactions, but at least I like to think that I function on a somewhat higher level than "favorable reviews are *good*, negative ones *bad*." I'm actually aware of having produced some albums I now would not defend, and others that may have been overpraised. But down through the years my most frequent reaction has been frustration at having my records at the mercy of people who, for whatever reasons, seem unable to understand them. Being part of a record company means that you get to see a great many different reviews of each album, and I'd suggest that there are few more depressing experiences in life than the consecutive reading of multiple reviews. What you are exposed to could most charitably be described as diversity. More often, particularly when they are read in bulk, the effect is more like total chaos. To one writer a record swings like mad, but another feels that same rhythm section doesn't fit together—why couldn't we hear their obvious incompatability? One reviewer may praise the originality of your well-planned repertoire; the next clipping complains of trite and unthinking tune selection—the difference, of course, is entirely a matter of the writers' own listening backgrounds. What one man hears as too strictly arranged, another finds sloppy; entire albums are rejected or overpraised because of blatant bias against (or in favor of) electric pianos, or female vocalists, or the resurgence of bebop.

My negative conclusions have for the most part been reached gradually, as a result of having been repeatedly hit over the head for a long time. But I think I can actually trace the start of my mistrust back to an oddly matched pair of reviews of the two earliest 12-inch Riverside jazz albums, both written by the same even then noted writer and appearing in successive issues of Down Beat some thirty years ago. The first was a very lukewarm reaction to our initial Monk project—his treatment of eight Duke Ellington compositions. The passage of time has long since validated the concept, which began the helpful process of slightly demystifying Thelonious. But this particular critic spoke of how uncomfortable the pianist seemed with much of this material, and accused us of having "instructed" Monk to deal with music "for which he has little empathy." It's hard to say which baffled and disappointed me more: his belief that my partner and I had been able to "force" Thelonious into an unwanted musical decision, or the failure to grasp the deep and strongly expressed musical affinity between Monk and Ellington.

Then this very same reviewer went on to give highest five-star honors to a Joe Sullivan album we had acquired. While I loved Sullivan—as the first piece in this book should make clear—I knew that this specific record was in no way of major stature. So I asked a direct question and, to that writer's credit, got a frank and somewhat embarrassed answer: he had put this album on his turntable at the end of a full afternoon of listening to West Coast cool; as a result, it had at least temporarily sounded like the hardest-swinging music imaginable!

From such early experiences I began to get a mental picture of an assembly line moving too fast to permit rational evaluations, and that image has stayed with me over the years. I have come upon many variations and permutations, and in time have developed a tendency to fit them into broad general categories. There is, for example, *The Critical Bandwagon:* when a performer becomes so thoroughly accepted, so deified, that at least for a while you don't have to worry. Everyone will give each of his albums the same top rating for as long as the ride lasts. Then for no discernible reason it becomes time to toss him off the wagon, perhaps simply because some writer decides to attract attention by playing iconoclast and going against the tide of adulation. I've watched this happen very dramatically with Monk, and even with artists who began their careers as critics' favorites and thus for a long time seemed invulnerable, like Wes Montgomery and Bill Evans—although death does tend to restore artistic stature. The quality of the specific record doesn't seem at all relevant to the bandwagon process—a fact that is often grotesquely demonstrated these days by glowing reviews welcoming back the reissue versions of albums that were originally trashed years ago. It's merely that a musician who used to be "out" has now achieved the status of a definitely "in" elder statesman.

There is also the *Prior Premise Review:* the writer begins with a personal conclusion and structures his view of the album to fit. Recently, I have belatedly learned that it was foolish to have had the Kronos Quartet attempt arrangements of Monk and Evans material, because "everyone knows strings can't swing." Many years ago, I read in amazement a destruction of an album involving four-flute charts, by a reviewer who started by making it clear that he did not consider the flute a "legitimate" jazz instrument. The most common use of this category is in defense of the assumption that any commercially successful jazz artist has automatically become aesthetically deficient. (The contention may often be accurate, but it's hardly a routine matter of cause and effect.) I first directly encountered this form of cultural prejudice when I recorded the Cannonball Adderley Quintet in performance at a San Francisco club. Their buoyant and rhythmic repertoire, particularly pianist Bobby Timmons's funky tune, "This Here," struck all sorts of responsive audience chords and the resultant album became a 1960 jazz sales phenomenon. Adderley, a witty and erudite man with a natural affection for the blues, previously respected by critics while a member of the celebrated Miles Davis group that included John Coltrane and Bill Evans, was immediately savaged in print for selling out. *Down Beat* didn't get around to acknowledging the record for several months. When it did, the disparaging review began with a negative reference to its reported sales of close to 30,000 copies, and closed with the quite serious admonition: "If this is the road Cannonball is going to travel, he will only succeed in making money."

The *Assumed Fact Review* can place an undue strain on my temper. I have read that the producer must have "made" the musician play that commercial junk with those electrified sidemen because he wanted to make a lot of money; and on another occasion that the same dictator had "refused" to let an artist play his own compositions. My aggravation in such cases stems from the fact that the evil producer is me. One does just try to rise above it—and I do get beaten on less frequently than certain colleagues who are widely known as studio authoritarians. But there really is no extension of journalistic or critical license that can justify such pseudo-telepathic guesswork being passed on to readers as reality. The problem is of course partly a matter of shoddy ethics, but it is also a glaring example of a lack of any knowledge of what actually goes on in the recording process.

Even this, I suppose, is in some respects preferable to the *Immaculate Conception Review,* a sadly prevalent type in which there is no indication that a producer even exists. I don't think this is

entirely a matter of my own ego. While his functions and importance may vary greatly—depending on the artist, the nature of the
project, and (to a very great extent) the nature of the producer—
those functions *do* exist, and do have a bearing on how things turn
out. The basic fact is that the role of the producer and his working
relationship with the artist are among the more significant elements in the creation of a jazz record. A good deal of what you
have read in this book is of course concerned with precisely that.
Yet there has always been a vast (although in all probability, even I
must admit, unintentional) conspiracy of silence about us. Record
reviews, which often seek the praiseworthy goal of listing every
single performer, almost never list a producer; most discographies
follow the same rule. (In recent years, as my self-assurance has
grown and my never-very-large tolerance for anonymity has dimin-
ished, I have on occasion taken to describing my own role in the
liner notes, particularly if I'm presenting a new artist or if the
album concept is one that I've devised. For the most part, however, reviewers still react as if I were invisible.) I have never understood this apparent lack of basic curiosity: if "producer" is a credit
that appears on virtually every album liner, shouldn't more reviewers wonder about the degree of credit or blame that might properly
be assigned to that person?

Such thoughts inevitably lead me to wonder about the human
being behind each review. There is a byline on virtually every one,
but who really is the individual bearing that name and why is he
(or, very rarely, she) writing as he does? I feel that *identity* is a
crucial aspect of criticism. Examine other areas in which new material is automatically examined in print. There are very few new
plays in New York in a year, and not many people regularly writing
about them. Movies are reviewed in virtually every local newspaper, but there aren't more than a couple of writers handling this
job in any given city, and probably only one reviewer in each of the
national magazines you read regularly. So as a constant reader you
get a pretty good handle on these people; whether or not you fully
realize it, you come to know at least something about their tastes,
and how their views relate to your own. If eventually you become
aware of soft spots and prejudices as well as strengths, you've
become better prepared to extract the information that can enable
you to draw reasonably sound *personal* conclusions about the subject at hand.

This, however, is not fully comparable to the record-review situation, which is actually much closer in format to book reviewing.
While there may be only one regular on the subject in the daily

paper, there are dozens of reports in (for example) each issue of the *New York Times Book Review,* just as there are (also just for example) in *Jazz Times.* Each item does carry a byline, but with the jazz reviews how can we be expected to identify all those largely unknown and basically unknowable individuals? All too often they blur into each other, so that hardly anyone is disturbed when all that's remembered or quoted is that an album was given three stars "by *Down Beat.*" Which of course is an anthropomorphic impossibility: the publication itself does no such thing. It was in fact a conclusion reached by one of their all-but-anonymous writers, and how does one go about learning what *that* particular person means by "three stars" or whatever other abstruse rating system is used? Book review sections, on the other hand, traditionally display a certain sense of responsibility: in virtually every such Sunday supplement there's at least an identifying sentence for each writer. We are told whether this is a professor or a lawyer or a published novelist; if there is some special reason, some area of expertise that has led to his being assigned to this evaluation, we are given a clue. Some of us may not think it a particularly good idea to have novels reviewed by novelists, or to turn a work on Freud over to a leading anti-Freudian—but at least we do have that identification to bear in mind while reading the critique.

I have yet to see a jazz publication use this valuable device. Occasionally the reviewer is so well known as a critic or for some other reasons that there is no mystery (on occasion in the past, musicians *have* written record reviews; I recall that both Rex Stewart and Kenny Dorham displayed remarkably good chops in *Down Beat*). But much more often the name means nothing. Perhaps we are not told precisely because there isn't anything to be told: it may be that many of them have no discernible credentials, just a strong desire to write about jazz and a willingness to do so at the very low prevailing rate of pay. Being a fan is really not sufficient, and having been a music student or a disc jockey on college radio is not much better; but if that's all there is so say about a published reviewer, surely we should be told *that.* I am worried by a kind of chicken-or-egg question that is raised by my unfortunately wide range of review-reading. Quite a few of the names found in the national magazines also turn up in the record-review columns of small city newspapers. Which came first? Was writing for his home-town weekly the credential that led to assignments from *Jazziz,* or was the paper awed by the signed reviews in *Down Beat?* And does it really matter? Of course everyone must, by definition, begin someplace, but must they begin at—quite literally—our expense?

For in a performance art like jazz, which in our society has always been forced to exist in the marketplace, critics and reviewers have a special responsibility. They are not merely delivering abstract artistic commentaries; they are messing with a man's ability to make a living. This is not an argument in favor of praising bad merchandise because there's a wife and children to be fed; but it is in opposition to judgments with real economic consequences being arbitrarily disbursed by people who are not qualified to do so. Above all, I suppose, it is a passionate outcry against the smartly turned phrase that is used solely for the benefit of the phrase-turner. I'm afraid I have observed the pattern far too many times to have any tolerance for it: the young writer gets his first chance; being suitably ambitious, he wants to be noticed more than all those other young reviewers. Negatives, he decides, are most likely to turn the trick; brilliant figures of speech in support of something won't register nearly as strongly as the devastating image; being memorably nasty is surely the quickest way to stand out from the crowd. In the long run he may come to realize that venom all by itself doesn't really accomplish that much. For the most part, his predecessors had figured that out; those with sufficient talent or doggedness to continue usually do calm down and mellow out, but there are enough hit-and-run drivers in each generation to create a noticeable amount of destruction.

To some extent my specific attitude about jazz writers has been shaped by the more general feelings I have developed about the role of criticism in relation to any creative art form, and about the particular problems involved in analyzing one medium of expression in terms of another. The second part of that sentence is probably the easier to explain: I have come to believe that language can readily be applied to the explication of a book, a film, a play— anything that is itself directly a product of language—but that *writing* about paintings or dance or music is a much trickier matter. It is in effect a form of translation, and therefore calls for a more than minimal grasp of *both* vocabularies. To write effectively about jazz requires, therefore, some actual facility with English prose in addition to some real understanding of jazz. Neither brisk technical discussion of the music, on the one hand, nor mystical flights-of-fancy verbiage, on the other, is really good enough. True sensitivity helps, and so does experience; but both commodities are usually in short supply, and most writers who have a substantial amount of them to offer—like a Morgenstern or a Gary Giddins— have long since stopped being available for entry-level activities.

As for my major reservations about criticism: to put it most bluntly, I consider it to be with rare exceptions an inhibiting force, simply because it invariably tends to take measurements and give ratings and pass judgment. This may take the form of comparison between particular works or specific artists, leading to the assertion that one is "better" than another. Or it can be more coldly objective, making evaluations in accordance with pre-existing standards. None of this actually has anything at all to do with creativity.

It may be acceptable at the lowest pragmatic level: I admit that I find it hard to read a writer who has trouble handling basic English grammar, and I am uncomfortable when a musician plays wrong notes or fakes the melody line of a standard tune. But there are obviously severe limitations to this approach: it's not very helpful in evaluating a painting by Rousseau or Grandma Moses; and it was of real disservice to many of us when we were first exposed to Ornette Coleman. (I once got around to telling Ornette about my reaction the first time I had heard him play some straight-ahead blues: I had regretted not knowing sooner than he *could* play "normal" changes, that his avoidance of them was entirely voluntary. I do hope I made it clear to him that the knowledge would only have been to *my* advantage. After all, he had always known his own truth; my ignorance, or anyone else's, was quite irrelevant.)

I feel that rules and standards have no valid connection with artistic expression, just as grammar has no specific impact on literary creativity. Actually, I do pay a lot of attention to the "grammar" of various art forms, and find it to be quite important—but only on its own level. Such things have a great deal to do with whether or not you find a work technically competent or properly "professional," which can be very meaningful when writers or musicians are talking to each other (or, perhaps, when I am criticizing a reviewer). But to consider such things to be in any way binding on the artist is decidedly improper.

It seems to me that by now I have done quite enough complaining, and it might be a good idea at this point to become a bit more practical. I do realize that I am not singlehandedly going to abolish jazz criticism. Since it is going to continue to be done, how might it be done better? Let me switch, even if only briefly, to a somewhat more constructive approach by attempting to codify some of my personal standards, to indicate some elements that I consider essentials.

To begin with, as a onetime editor who greatly respects the leadership potential of a magazine editor, I have to admit the inequity of dumping exclusively on the reviewers. If I find young jazz writers inexperienced, immature, and indistinguishable, at least some of the blame must be allocated to those who hire them, give them assignments, and presumably read and edit what they turn in for publication. A couple of decades ago, when *Down Beat* was just about the only game in town, I often disagreed with its various editors, but it was certainly true that men like Gene Lees, Don DeMicheal, and later Dan Morgenstern were well-defined personalities, who could readily be perceived as giving instruction and a sense of direction to newcomers. I'm not in a position to condemn the current crop of magazine editors, because I just don't know what efforts of that kind they might be making, but the empirical evidence is not reassuring. There are some strong veterans out there now who established their own standards and patterns a long time ago; a Stanley Dance or a Douglas Ramsey is not particularly receptive to—or in need of—guidance. But where are their replacements going to come from—writers whom even crusty insiders like me can at least sometimes read with respect or even agreement? Without some editorial leadership, how can the publications ever begin to tap the vast knowledgeable pool of jazz professionals—the same sort of non-impartial potential reviewers that the book sections always utilize, or that *The Record Changer* relied on almost four decades ago?

Of course I'm aware that musicians have occasionally been spotlighted as writers over the years, usually very recognizable names, often under special circumstances as an attention-getting journalistic ploy. That's not what I'm talking about. I mean regular use of informed, involved, working-level musicians, sidemen and session players, young and old. What about a producer or two, or something as far-out as a jazz-oriented promotion man who might have an intriguing point of view on quality levels in overtly commercial forms of music? What I'm also saying is: where is the editorial courage to take a few chances? Even some really bad choices couldn't hurt that much, and would at least offer an occasional change of pace. And without a little daring, how can we ever hope to break the disgraceful mold that keeps jazz criticism virtually a white male enclave—after all these years, still no women to speak of and so few blacks that an Albert Murray and a Stanley Crouch remain tokens, and a vibrant gadfly like Amiri Baraka is rarely heard from.

I am scarcely making new suggestions. As far back as 1960, the late Bobby Timmons, then a brash young pianist and composer, angrily asked a *Down Beat* interviewer why the roster of critics didn't include "some of the older musicians who know every stage of development young musicians go through." He went on to complain of the "incompatibility" of critics being "predominantly" white: "They don't really know this music. They're interpreting what [we] say and play, and they don't really understand what's happening." There might have seemed an element of irony in the fact that he was talking to Barbara Gardner, a black woman who was then a frequent *Down Beat* contributor and staff record reviewer—but the real irony is that, a quarter-century later, Gardner turns out to have been unique. As for Timmons's remarks, the question of their relative or absolute accuracy seems vastly less important than the undeniable truth that they represent a long-standing and still widespread attitude among musicians. There is something seriously out of alignment when so many who create the music are consistently unable to trust or respect critics as a class.

As for that "constructive" summary of personal criteria, I offer a short list of elements that I hold to be necessary but generally missing in current criticism.

Above all, there is an attitude that I would label *respect for creativity*—which involves the basic realization that the artist is more significant than his critic and which, accordingly, calls for not overvaluing the critical function. In a recent article by Martin Williams, I find this cogent comment: "It's the business of writers like me to say what we think, but I don't like the idea of giving advice to musicians." These are words all critics should strive to live by, for all too often what is called "advice" is merely an attempt to superimpose the writer's values over the musician's. As a major example, there are the years of critical complaints about Sonny Rollins's refusal to return to the way he played in the late '50s. To my direct knowledge, he has not done so simply because he has no interest in retreating to his musical past—in imitating himself. But the answer is actually beside the point; the question should never have been raised. A writer who professes to admire and respect an artist must accept that artist's ability to make a "correct" creative decision for himself. He may not agree with that decision, but he must recognize its primacy. There is a truly immense difference between saying "I prefer" (which is proper critical language) and "he should" (which is not). It is far more difficult for the critic to give the same leeway to a young player—it may be almost impossible to stifle the urge to be a star-shaper, to offer paternalistic words of wisdom—but it is even more important. Rollins, after all, will pay no attention; someone less experienced and less confident may even be swayed.

An essential aspect of this "respect" is the realization that it is not the artist's duty to please a particular writer, and he should not be attacked for failing to do so. Critical evaluation that cannot rise above the level of "I do not like it; therefore it is bad art" is danger-ously invalid. This is not a denial of the critic's right to express personal views and reactions, but it is a protest against the kind of pontificating that seeks to present those views as absolute truth. Jazz, as we all like to proclaim, is a long-lived music; accordingly, its history is full of examples of negative reviews being drastically re-vised and reversed by the passage of time. Once again, an awareness of Monk can be valuable. I would recommend to all beginners the study of early critical comment on his music; it should lead to an appropriate mixture of perspective, humility, and caution.

Secondly, there is *knowledge of the process*—which very much includes some understanding of the realities of recording. There is a great difference between the requirements of club or concert activity and the steps that lead to the creation of a record; failure to appreciate this distinction literally makes it impossible to evaluate a recorded performance. I see no way to state the point at all equivocally; this *is* an absolute truth—and I remain constantly astonished at how rarely any critic has ever sought information on what goes on at a studio session or has asked to visit one. I don't believe they are deliberately avoiding knowledge, or even that they are lacking in curiosity; but I do suspect that, for the most part, they aren't even aware that there is anything unique to be curious about. There isn't time or space enough here to go into the details of what is special, but I assure you that there are a great many quite important distinctions and conventions. Effective re-corded sound is quite unlike what you hear in person; the approach to achieving an ultimately satisfactory performance is quite differ-ent; and there are of course many occasions that necessitate, for a variety of reasons, editing or combining, or the adding or substitut-ing of overdubbed supplements.

I realize that everyone more or less knows this—or, to be more accurate, knows *about* such things. But a general awareness is not the same as an understanding of the effect that various engineering facts and circumstances have on the art of recording. We who work in the studios are fully aware that only the finished product will be available for the world to judge (and we are frequently very pleased that no one who wasn't there will know just how much sweat and tension and repetition may have gone into it). But we also take for granted the essential fact that our job is to create what is best described as "realism"—the impression and effect of being real—which may be very different from plain unadorned reality. Ignorance of this distinction is surely not helpful to those who choose to pass judgment on the music. I have treasured for years the memory of a review that complained of our stupidity in having used a percussionist: the writer could hear quite clearly how those added rhythms were crowding and disturbing the drummer and throwing him off-stride; why hadn't the leader and I realized this? The only trouble with that criticism was (and there had been no attempt to hide the fact in the album-liner credits) that the "bothersome" percussionist had been added to the tape weeks later and in another studio; he and the drummer had indeed met each other, but not in connection with this project. It is not only to avoid such potential for embarrassment that I recommend knowledge of the process—would a film critic want to avoid all awareness of camera angles and directorial technique?—and I remain willing at any time to conduct a basic course in Studio Realities.

As a close corollary, there is certainly a need for an *understanding of history*. In an earlier period, those with an awareness of the past frequently used a scornful cliché: "When you talk about a jazz pioneer, he thinks you mean Charlie Parker." With the passage of time, Parker actually *is* recognizable as a pioneer; to update the remark you'd probably need to substitute Ornette Coleman or Cecil Taylor. But I suspect the revised version would remain widely applicable. I don't want to overstate the problem: there are many current writers with a strong sense of history; there is no shortage of historical and biographical literature—regardless of how one might evaluate such material, at least the *facts* of jazz are readily available. But I'm not so sure about how widely the lessons of history have been learned.

Having begun as a strict traditionalist, I have always had strong feelings about the continuity of the music. In the '50s, I became aware that contemporary musicians had for the most part very little awareness of the past (Monk, who as a youngster had listened appreciatively to James P. Johnson, was as always an exception). Efforts to bridge the gap had varying results: Randy Weston was fascinated by the incredible right-hand dexterity of Luckey Roberts; Cannonball Adderley began with more background knowledge than most, but was totally broken up by the primitive rhythm section on a Bix Beiderbecke record. It was actually the drastic differences in the rhythmic concepts of traditional jazz forms that presented the greatest problem; now, even though there have been vast changes since the early days of bebop, there is enough of a connective thread to make that forty-year-old tradition important to today's players. So many of them grasp the relevance of the past and feel a deep respect for who and what preceded them; it is in a sense a counterpart of the "second line" tradition in early New Orleans, and it is so strong an element in the mid-'80s jazz atmosphere that I'm sure most writers and many members of the public are aware of it.

But do they understand *what*—in addition to some stylistic mimicry and some pleasant repertoire—the young musicians have learned? One major lesson to be gained from history, for example, is how often time has altered, even reversed, critical judgments. I have already noted how often a reissue of a record that was originally poorly received is now greeted with cheers. I know that many musicians grasp the point that the music exists on its own merits, regardless of initial condemnation or praise, and that time has a way of straightening matters out. I hope that reviewers realize the significance for them of such reversals. They are certainly entitled to their own reactions, uninfluenced by past opinions (although I am sometimes disturbed by the thought that they may also be unaware of them). But do they at least appreciate the implied parallel? For the very same kind of revisionism may well be scheduled to take place when today's records are reconsidered in the future; the key point being demonstrated is that this long-lived music of ours, when it is young, is not necessarily in tune with the critical standards of the moment. Accordingly, it might be wise for the reviewer to try to be a little tender towards something that may strike him as too advanced (or too old-fashioned), to be careful not to choke it off in its infancy with gratuitous harshness.

As a footnote to the subject of understanding history, let me admit that discographers now seem to be an improving breed. I have been aware since my earliest reissue days of the great gaps in this area that will never be filled because paperwork is missing or players have died. I have also long realized that it is both unfair and risky to rely on a performer's memory of one long-past session out of many, and I soon discovered that the most likely answer will be what the musician feels the questioner wants ("That's right, it certainly was Satchmo on that date in Chicago in 1925. . . ."). For such reasons I have for many years—although, unfortunately, not from the very start—tried to set down (and preserve) detailed recording-session logs. For a long time, though, compilers of discographies just didn't seem able to figure out the value of asking people like me. I have some favorite aggravations: notably the celebrated Danish researcher Jorgen Jepsen making blatantly incorrect assumptions in his 1968 volume on Monk. Like deciding that the trio selection which adds John Coltrane and Wilbur Ware to an otherwise solo Monk album, and the only three numbers ever recorded by the original Five Spot Quartet (consisting of those three men plus drummer Shadow Wilson), were all made at the same April 1957 session. It's a tidy thought, but the fact is that the quartet was taped a few months later. And the question is: why not ask the producer? Some sort of barrier seems to have been broken in the early '80s when Michael Cuscuna, preparing a total discography of Thelonious for the Mosaic Records reissue package of his entire Blue Note output, asked me for full, verified Riverside data. Thereafter, a horde of researchers—all of them European, I must note—have probed me for recording truths about Bill Evans, Blue Mitchell, Wynton Kelly, Chet Baker, Kenny Dorham, et al. It can get quite time-consuming, and painfully memory-stirring as well; but of course such specialized, dedicated, and usually entirely non-profit activities must be encouraged; the creation of an accurate body of information of this kind can be one of our most valuable basic historical tools.

Finally, I consider it essential for writers to have an *awareness of the context* in which the music exists and—to the greatest possible degree—a sense of involvement with jazz and its people. I know an opposite school of thought advocates that the critic keep a suitable distance from the objects of his work; I find that view terribly wrong. A journalist I greatly respect recently admitted, a little sadly, that with only a few unavoidable exceptions he took care to avoid all personal relationships with musicians, for fear of weakening his critical objectivity. I was distressed to hear this; he is a warm human being with a valuable sense of history, and he and a number of artists in his region could learn from each other. I really cannot understand such self-imposed restraint and coldness in as emotional an arena as jazz. Surely an occasional self-disqualification on the grounds of friendly prejudice, or a non-objective interview instead of a review, would take care of the problem.

For there is so much that writers can learn by steeping themselves in the environment of jazz as deeply and directly as possible, by seeking to know the real world that the working musician inhabits. There are many aspects of this world that simply cannot be grasped by detached analysis, that demand a hands-on approach. I have often complained about how seldom I come upon other producers in clubs. Obviously you do find writers in such places quite regularly, usually in the first-night line of duty. But I'd recommend a good deal more attendance at the last set later in the week, without pad and pencil, maybe even buying their own drinks. I am reminded of two very different comments about Ahmad Jamal, an artist who has provoked a wide range of reactions over the years. A particularly visual-minded reviewer (he *was* also the newspaper's art critic) described the pianist as a "pointillist." It sounded meaningful, but when I found in my dictionary that it referred to a method of painting that utilizes small strokes or dots, I understood that it was merely a superficial aren't-I-erudite way of categorizing his rather sparse style. By contrast, Cannonball Adderley, responding to an attempt to dismiss Jamal as merely facile, offered some quite practical advice. Catch him very late at night, and when he knows there are other musicians in the house, he told us; then you'll really hear him play. A very concrete example of why knowing—and caring—is much more valuable than rhetoric.

No one ever said jazz was easy to understand. I'm sure an "easy" music could not have held my attention for so long. You do have to work hard at it. Consider how many faces jazz presents, frequently contradictory ones and often many at the same time. It is high art, and folk art, and a commercial enterprise; heartfelt and a put-on; instinctive and learned. It is above all a matter of individual expression that depends just as heavily on teamwork and ensemble. It exists through the people who performed it in the past and those who play it now, and they are about as varied and hard to categorize a body of artists as the world has ever known—humble, arrogant, clannish, solitary.

Among the things I am most certain about is that jazz cannot properly be perceived in any abstract way. I suppose you can enjoy it by simply sitting there and letting it wash over you. But to have any chance at understanding it well enough to be qualified to comment on the music, you somehow have to make the effort to get inside. No one can draw you a map, and I don't believe you can achieve it by taking courses. Jazz insists on belief, but just being an adoring fan isn't enough. Experience alone doesn't do it; I'm afraid that in my opinion there are writers who have been at it (and making a living thereby) almost forever without actually understanding at all.

It may even be true that—in approximately the words of Louis Armstrong, or Fats Waller, or whoever is supposed to have said it—if you have to ask, you'll never know. It should be obvious from my comments here that in my view damn few of those who have elected to pass judgment on the music-makers can be considered to know *enough*. Despite my strong misgivings about the concept of jazz criticism, I will grant that the music can use informed, intelligent, articulate, and impassioned commentary; and I'm sure it can survive the other kind. It always has survived, up to now, and so I'll continue to have faith. And now that I've discovered how gratifying it can be to complain and scold, I may even continue to do that.